FIVE
CHINESE
COMMUNIST
PLAYS

FIVE CHINESE COMMUNIST PLAYS

Edited by
**Martin
Ebon**

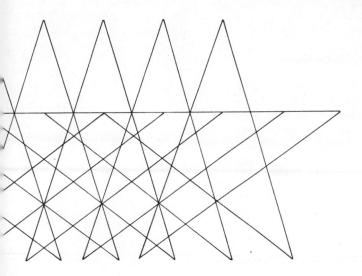

The John Day Company | NEW YORK

Library of Congress Cataloging in Publication Data
Main entry under title:

Five Chinese Communist plays.

    1. Operas—Librettos. 2. Opera, Chinese—History
and criticism. I. Ebon, Martin.
ML48.F36 1975   782.1'2   74-9366
ISBN 0-381-98281-5

10 9 8 7 6 5 4 3 2 1

Contents

Introduction:
The Brightest Sun, the Darkest Shadow

During more than a quarter century China has been much mis-
understood. Ignorance and prejudice have been partly responsible
for this lamentable condition, but so have Chinese secretiveness
and the exposure of mere fragments of China's scene to the outside world. Did Peking prefer to be isolated, at least on its own
terms? Was there too wide a political and cultural gap between
modern China and the West, notably the United States, to permit
a well-informed and open-minded appraisal? These questions still
have not been answered fully, although a thaw in relations between the U.S. and China in 1972 opened the way to China's ad-
mission to the United Nations; since then, selected visitors have
had the opportunity to travel in China.

Even the best informed China experts often have been severely
mistaken in the past. As one of the best qualified specialists, Rod-
erick MacFarquhar, puts it in *The Origins of the Cultural Revolution* (1974), "In the spring of 1966 China seemed a stable, disciplined and united nation," and no one suspected that it was on
the eve of a major internal upheaval, the recasting of Chinese
society which became known as the Cultural Revolution. Two
major figures were involved in this conflict: Communist Party
Secretary Liu Shao-chi; and head of the army and eventual deputy to Mao Tse-tung, Lin Piao. Lin and others denounced Liu as
"traveling the capitalist road." But even while Lin Piao made
speeches attacking the party secretary with euphemisms, Liu
Shao-chi remained technically prominent; he still shared the spotlight on Peking's T'ien an Men Square on August 17, although his
star was clearly descending.

Throughout this book, Liu Shao-chi and his supporters are pictured, in quotations from Chinese publications, as determined to influence art and literature, and particularly stage productions, in a manner opposed to the efforts of Chairman Mao's wife, Chiang Ching. Over and over again—and our selections are far from representative in extent and repetition—Liu is denounced either by name or as commander of the "bourgeois headquarters" within the party. In contrast, Mrs. Mao is constantly praised as the savior of Chinese opera, ballet, drama, and music. Those associated with the two main antagonists are at times named but more often anonymous groups.

By 1967, Liu's supporters had been nearly eliminated from the party apparatus, and he was being attacked by name, while Lin's influence rose. The army, under his command, gained control of so-called Revolutionary Committees that were replacing Communist Party control all over the country. The struggle for ultimate supremacy continued through 1968 and is reflected in the ideological conflict that spilled over into the production of operas, ballets, and plays. This upheaval, which had the full official label of "Great Proletarian Cultural Revolution," intimately linked the political with the cultural. The mobilization of literature and art was more than symbolic. The use of words such as "fortress" and "headquarters" for cultural institutions indicated that they were not only means of political expression but embattled vantage points in their own right.

In the midst of all this, "Chairman Mao's Five Militant Documents on Literature and Art" were republished, as if they were newly discovered items of lofty insight. The first of these documents was a letter, dated January 9, 1944, which Mao had sent to the Yenan Peking Opera Theatre after seeing a play dealing with mountain warfare. In it he thanked the cast and noted that although history was being made at that time, "the old opera (and all the old literature and art, which are divorced from the people) presents the people as if they were dirt, and the stage is dominated by lords and ladies and their pampered sons and daughters." He asked for more plays, for a "revolutionalization of the old opera."

The second Mao letter, dated May 20, 1951, was a critique of the film *The Life of Wu Hsun*. He expressed chagrin that the film had been made at all, and particularly at "the praise lavished on Wu Hsun and the film." Mao wrote: "Living in the era of the Chinese people's great struggle against foreign aggressors and the domestic reactionary feudal rulers toward the end of the Ching dynasty, people like Wu Hsun did not lift a finger to disturb the tiniest fragment of the feudal economic base or its superstructure."

The second document was a letter dated October 16, 1954, addressed by Mao to the Political Bureau of the Central Committee of the Chinese Community Party. It concerned criticisms by two young men of the novel *The Dream of the Red Chamber*, by Yu Ping-Po. Mao complained that the young critics had been ignored, and that "bourgeois idealism" concerning this and other Chinese classics had been poisoning young people for decades. He recalled that the film *The Life of Wu Hsun* had been criticized—certainly by Mao himself, three years earlier—but that "no lessons have been drawn."

Finally, two instructions concerning literature and art were republished. The first, written by Mao on December 12, 1963, is worth citing in full; this is the text:

"Problems abound in all forms of art such as the drama, ballads, music, the fine arts, the dance, the cinema, poetry and literature; the people engaged in them are numerous; and in many departments very little has been achieved so far in socialist transformation. The 'dead' still dominate in many departments. What has been achieved in the cinema, new poetry, folk songs, the fine arts and the novel should not be underestimated, but there, too, there are quite a few problems. As for such departments as the drama, the problems are even more serious. The social and economic base has changed, but the arts as part of the superstructure, which serve this base, still remain a serious problem. Hence we should proceed with investigation and study and attend to this matter in earnest. Isn't it absurd that many Communists are enthusiastic about promoting feudal and capitalist art, but not socialist art?"

Mao's second instructions, dated June 27, 1964, were reprinted in mid-1967 without any clarification as to his references. He spoke of "associations," which presumably were literary or other cultural groups under the guidance of the Communist Party. He also mentioned "the Hungarian Petöfi Club." This was a reference to the literary clubs in Hungary, named after the lyric poet Alexander Petöfi (1823-1849), which during the Hungarian uprising in 1956 had acted as centers of resistance. Mao's instructions read as follows:

"In the last 15 years these associations and most of their publications (it is said that a few are good) and by and large the people in them (that is, not everybody) have not carried out the policies of the Party. They have acted as high and mighty bureaucrats, have not gone to the workers, peasants and soldiers and have not reflected the socialist revolution and socialist construction. In recent years, they have slid right down to the brink of revisionism. Unless they remould themselves in real earnest, at some future date they are bound to become groups like the Hungarian Petöfi Club."

The four Mao documents were widely publicized in mid-1967, together with a letter addressed by Lin Piao to the Standing Committee of the Military Commission of the Communist Party's Central Committee—a letter which, dated March 22, 1966, was more than one year old. It was, in effect, a transmittal letter that accompanied a report on the Forum on the Work in Literature and Art in the Armed Forces which Chiang Ching, Mao's wife, had convened in Shanghai from February 2 to 20, 1966. The document which Lin thus forwarded, entitled *Summary of the Forum on the Work in Literature and Art in the Armed Forces with which Comrade Lin Piao Entrusted Comrade Chiang Ching*, is reprinted in full in this volume. What was striking even then was the emphasis that it was Lin who had "entrusted" Mao's wife with this task; that she, in fact, needed his approval and clearance to hold such a meeting.

Lin's letter of transmittal noted that Mao himself had "personally examined and revised" the *Summary* three times. Lin asked the Committee to "let me know your opinions" on the report "before it is submitted to the Central Committee for examination and approval." The delay in transmission, together with the request for the Committee's opinions, suggests a reluctance on Lin's part to permit Chiang Ching's role as a sort of Commissar of Culture to gain too much strength within the armed forces.

Elsewhere on the cultural front, Mrs. Mao's activities may have encountered more direct opposition—at least, if one credits information published later. One prominent and influential victim of the cultural revolution was Peng Cheng, the Mayor of Peking. In an article in the party monthly *Hung Chi* (No. 7, 1967) which dealt with the five Mao documents, Peng was described as "ringleader of the counter-revolutionary revisionists of the former Peking Municipal Committee of the Chinese Communist Party." The periodical accused Peng and five others of carrying out "activities in drama, cinema, fiction and theory on literature and art which were all aimed at creating public opinion for the overthrow of the dictatorship of the proletariat." The article summarized the Mao letters and linked Peng Chen to "the top Party person in authority taking the capitalist road," namely, Liu Shao-chi.

Joan Robinson, in her book *The Cultural Revolution in China* (1969), said that Peng Chen had opposed one new opera, *The Lakeside Village,* so vigorously that he "dispersed the company so that it could not play in other parts of the country." However, Chiang Ching went down to Shanghai to arrange some productions there. Meanwhile, Peng "encouraged performances of old operas to be kept going and prevented public performances of the new." Allegedly, Peng criticized certain plays with such remarks as, "This is neither fish nor fowl," and "It tastes like tepid water." Referring to the Communist soldier who in *Taking Tiger Mountain by Strategy* infiltrates an enemy stronghold, Peng Chen is supposed to have objected to his lack of disguise and other unrealistic aspects of the production.

Such tidbits are trivial against the background of the very real power struggle that took place in the upper echelons of the Chinese Communist Party. The way in which it spilled over onto the theatrical scene is illustrated by the play *Hai Jui Dismissed from Office*, by Wu Hsan, who was Peng Chen's deputy. The play was apparently an historical allegory, set during the Ming period of Chinese history but regarded as a clear allusion to Mao's dismissal of Peng Teh-huai as chief of the army. He was replaced by Lin Piao in 1959. Joan Robinson states that Mao's wife could not get articles critical of this play published in Peking and had to get the support of Shanghai officials. An article critical of the play, according to Robinson, was written in secret; she added: "But somehow Peng Chen came to hear of it and demanded to see it. His next dodge was to accept the article, provided the fourth paragraph was deleted. This paragraph contained the whole point of the argument—that Wu Hsan was covertly attacking Chairman Mao. Chiang Ching refused to allow it to be cut. Peng Chen would not allow the article to be published in Peking." It eventually appeared in Shanghai, and it was the opening gun of the Cultural Revolution.

Over and over again, Chairman Mao's observations are used in articles, pamphlets, and talks to bolster specific theatrical and other cultural changes. In many cases, these are taken from Mao Tse-tung's *Talks at the Yenan Forum on Literature and Art*. In 1967 these were widely publicized on the occasion of their twenty-fifth anniversary. Comments from Chinese actors and overseas visitors were also published. For example, Tan Yuan-shou, prominent in the No. 1 Peking Opera Company in Peking, issued a statement which said that "throughout the past seventeen years, the revisionist line in literature and art has been opposing Chairman Mao's proletarian line in literature and art. It prevented Peking opera from serving the workers, peasants and soldiers. At the critical moment in the struggle between the two lines, Comrade Chiang Ching came to our opera company." The actor then related how Mao's wife defied Peng Chen and Liu Shao-chi, referring to them in the established euphemistic but unmistakable way.

Two writers from the Congo (Brazzaville), Lounda and Aba, were quoted in the *Peking Review* of January 1, 1967, as making the following comments: "Several years ago we saw Peking opera in Paris. Frankly speaking, we didn't like them because we wanted to acquaint ourselves with life in New China through the media of Chinese works of art. But those Peking operas presented the life of the past which we could not accept. So revolutionaries didn't like them. The French bourgeoisie enjoyed them. This time when we saw Peking opera reflecting present-day life and struggles, we Africans could follow without interpreters the content and tell friend from foe among the characters on the stage."

By doing away with the subtleties and traditions of Peking opera, Chinese dramas and ballets have certainly become more easily understood in terms of heroism and villainy, in the propaganda polarization of Good and Evil. This had been done quite consciously, although with obvious reluctance on the part of major figures in political and cultural affairs. Chiang Ching told an American visitor, Roxane Witke, in August 1972 that her own contributions to China's cultural world might ease the way for future generations of women. Speaking to a *Christian Science Monitor* correspondent, Miss Witke said that Mao's wife conveyed the impression that she had been a powerful influence on her husband's political and other judgments during her long years by his side. She referred to Mao simply as "the Chairman," and, although they share a common residence outside Peking, Chiang Ching left no doubt that she leads an independent life and career.

Unavoidably, Chiang Ching's drive and determination on the

Chinese cultural scene have caused speculation about her conscious and unconscious motivation. Miss Witke's interviewer, Frederic A. Moritz, noted that Mao's wife had been a "little known, previously married, Shanghai stage-and-screen actress using the name Lan Ping before Mao divorced his second wife to wed her." Moritz observed: "One version has it that Mao's new wife was a moral and political embarrassment for other leaders of the Communist guerrillas then encamped in Yenan after the Long March from South China." This interpretation suggests Chairman Mao "was forced to keep his new wife in the background for years."

He goes on to say that Mrs. Mao "was said to have wanted to 'settle accounts' with her old enemies when she rose to great influence and led the attack on 'revisionism' in art and literature during the Cultural Revolution." Chiang Ching, twenty years younger than Mao, "grew up with low standing as a daughter in a poor family." Her subsequent career would appear to have more than adequately compensated for her humble origin and early life.

While allowing for the obvious limitations of such interpretations, certain trends in Peking plays should be noted. Under Chiang Ching's influence, the prominence of women heros in such plays has notably increased. In the most recent play printed in this volume, *Azalea Mountain*, a Communist woman leader is pitted against a treacherous deputy commander who bears a certain resemblance to Lin Piao. There can be little doubt that Lin sought to restrict and restrain Chiang Ching's influence during the Cultural Revolution, particularly in the army. At the same time, Lin Piao originated the little red book, *Quotations from Chairman Mao*. As Lin's influence lifted Mao to a pedestal, single hero worship could also be noted in the stage plays. After Lin's own disgrace and death in an airplane crash in 1971, this theme subsided, but that of the woman hero emerged more strongly.

Following Mao's takeover in 1949, the cultural scene was at first neglected, or at least left to its own devices. Older Peking operas were screened and certain plays dropped from the repertoire of the opera companies, but there was an effort to retain and adapt as much of the country's cultural heritage as possible. Although later attacks on Chiang Ching's opponents prominently mention the deputy director of the Communist Party's Propaganda Department, Chou Yang, it should not be assumed that he took a position hostile to adaptation. He was quoted on September 25, 1959, as saying: "Peking Opera should continue to leap forward in its portrayal of modern life. Our task of rearranging and revising the excellent plays of the past should continue also to leap forward. From now on, we should encourage the creation of new plays to depict modern life. However, we should not expect too much. In the meantime, we should carry on our work in selecting, revising and rearranging the best numbers from the traditional repertoire."

Among the abandoned traditions of Peking opera were several that would certainly have struck Western observers as archaic. Among these was the presence of orchestral instruments on the stage and the movement of stagehands in full view of the audience, as they were rearranging a setting. So-called lotus feet disappeared; these were low wooden stilts symbolizing the bound and thus distorted feet of women. Kneeling, kow-towing and spanking were also eliminated.

The last of the great female impersonators of the Peking opera, Mei Lan-fang (who died in 1961, having previously become a Communist Party member), addressed a meeting organized in 1954 by the Ministry of Culture. Mei, who later became director of the Chinese Academy of the Peking Opera, told the conference that some traditional features should be abandoned, others changed, and still others retained. He did not favor stage settings for opera, but thought them "more suitable to new plays." In his view, the actor on an empty stage changes the nature of the space around him: "The stage setting is wrapped around the actor himself, and nothing else is needed. Then, when he swings a whip, it suggests riding a horse; when he moves an oar, it suggests a ride in a boat; when he walks around the stage for a few steps, it suggests the traveling of several blocks or a distance of several miles."

This art of the mime has, in fact, been retained in such current stage productions as *Taking the Bandits' Stronghold* (*Taking Tiger Mountain by Strategy*), which has a mass skiing scene, as well as the hero's riding dance, following the Peking opera tradition of symbolic acting out. Stage settings have been introduced which suggest a wider scene with relatively few props. On the other hand, special effects—such as snowstorms, sounds of fighting, thunder and lightning—are being used generously. The use of Western instruments has tended to replace the traditional sound of Chinese string instruments with a kind of symphonic grandeur which foreign critics have compared to "film music" and such compositions as the "Grand Canyon Suite." Mao's wife expressed great interest in receiving a fresh print of the Hollywood movie *The Sound of Music*, which Miss Witke obtained for her in return for a print of the Chinese motion picture *The White-Haired Girl*.

Efforts to bring actual Peking stage productions to the United States have been unsuccessful, although the motion picture version of *The Red Detachment of Women* has been shown on American television and an acrobatic troupe visited in 1973. Norman Singer, executive director of New York's City Center wrote to Chiang Ching in November 1969 and again in April 1971, suggesting that a Peking opera company visit the United States. Although Mao's wife did not answer personally, an air mail letter dated May 7, 1971, and signed by Liu Hsing, said: "Our model dramas are specially prepared for the appreciation of our working people, not for our enemy and money-scented capitalists like you by whom a criticism and attack on the Opera after seeing it may be repeated." The letter, written before the rapprochement worked out by Henry Kissinger for the United States and Chou En-lai for China, accused Mr. Singer of making his offer in order to "soften up the Chinese people's fighting will by inviting the Peking Opera performing in the United States." The letter added: "This is what we cannot tolerate. Imperialism and all reactionaries are all paper tigers. They must be broken through and over-thrown." The letter also asserted that "undoubtedly you want to utilize this opportunity to make big money, but our leader's think-ing is quite different from yours. All our performers are of work-ers, peasants and soldiers origin. We do not have to let them creep into the capitalist muddy pit, so as to make their thought de-teriorate."

Fear that the Peking performers might be ideologically weak-ened by exposure to the fleshpots of capitalism did not prevent the touring of ping-pong players and acrobats, and so Mr. Singer san-guinely assumed that the letter "probably means just the begin-ning of negotiations." However, subsequent letters went unan-swered; his office stated in May 1974 that it had received no further replies from Peking. The strongly worded turndown by Mrs. Mao's assistant was not entirely consistent with her aim to make Peking's stage productions a worldwide instrument of revo-lutionary thought. Presumably, the ideological appeal of Chinese operas, ballets, plays, and music could find a proletarian reso-nance within the appropriate "class" in the United States as else-where. Whether such a class would be representative of the "workers, peasants and soldiers," to whom these productions are addressed, is open to doubt. Instead of Detroit auto workers, Iowa farmers, or members of the U.S. armed forces, Peking opera pro-duction would most likely be received with appreciation by the urban audiences throughout the United States that have for years flocked to performances of the Bolshoi Ballet and of dance ensem-bles from the Ukraine, Poland, Hungary, and other Communist-governed countries.

That Americans might subject Peking opera performances to

"criticism and attack," as the letter to Mr. Singer suggested, would be true in the sense that an open society permits criticism in the arts and literature from a variety of viewpoints, rather than from the single direction of ideological purity and propagandistic effectiveness. No doubt, the technical skill of Peking dancers, acrobats, and certain aspects of stage direction would greatly appeal to Western audiences. In fact, the use of Western instruments have made contemporary Chinese operas and ballets more easily understood by westerners, although the mixture of Chinese and Western instruments may well have alienated segments of Chinese audiences.

Within China itself, the debate has been fierce and continuous. Chiang Ching attended a concert given by the Philadelphia Orchestra, directed by Eugene Ormandy, in Peking in September 1973. The Chinese pianist Yin Cheng-chung was a soloist with the orchestra, as it performed his "Yellow River Concerto." Apparently at the behest of Mao's wife, the orchestra played Beethoven's "Pastoral," although it did not have the music for this piece and had to borrow it from the Peking orchestra. Chiang Ching gave a party for the American orchestra, and *Jen-min Jih pao*, the Peking daily, wrote, "The success of the first performance by the artists of the two countries demonstrated the deep friendship of the Chinese and American people."

Harold C. Schonberg recalled in *The New York Times* (April 14, 1974) that, in the cordial atmosphere of the Philadelphia Orchestra's visit, various exchange visits were discussed, including a U.S. tour by Yin Cheng-chung: "Everybody thought at the time, innocents that we were, that a brand-new era was opening, certainly in cultural relationships. The Chinese would be sending us Yin and the marvelous little orchestra that specialized in old instruments, and perhaps an opera company. We would be sending them such natural resources as Van Cliburn, Duke Ellington and the Globetrotters."

But even before a new cultural thunderstorm crashed down on these plans, Yin tempered his hopes. *Hsin Hua*, the New China News Agency, reported from Peking on December 27, 1973, that the pianist had expressed second thoughts, quoting him as saying: "There has been a fierce struggle between the two classes and between the two lines around whether the piano, a foreign instrument in China, could serve the workers, peasants and soldiers and play a militant role in uniting and educating the people and attacking the enemy. I have been tempered in this struggle." If one notes the violent arguments that surrounded the use of the piano in *The Red Lantern* (see page 212, "The Battle of the Piano"), Yin's comments indicate that controversy concerning the use of Western instruments and compositions remains very much alive.

Yin was also quoted as saying that cultural "revisionists" had spoken of the piano as a "pearl in the diadem of musical art," which could not be appreciated by the masses. These revisionists, he said, had asked pianists to "play well to win honor for China in world contests, and that would be serving the workers, peasants and soldiers." In other words, the piano might be useful for export and a domestic Chinese élite of connoisseurs, but not for workers, peasants, and soldiers. Yin said that the revisionists had stated, "The piano shall not go to the villages and factories," as "it is useless there." In this way, they "aimed at luring the piano onto the revisionist path that would divorce them from the workers, peasants and soldiers," making the people eventually "completely Westernized." All these are phrases straight out of earlier confrontations within the Chinese Communist party leadership. Yin named Liu Shao-chi as the main figure behind a plot to "use piano music, which the bourgeoisie had dominated for hundreds of years, to serve as a capitalist comeback."

A few days after Yin's confession, *Jen-min Jih pao* attacked Western music on a wider front. On January 14, 1974, the paper called Beethoven a "German capitalist composer," described Schubert's "Unfinished Symphony" as an expression of gloom induced by the oppression the composer suffered as a member of the petty bourgoisie under Austrian feudalism, and said that Mozart's works could not stand comparison with the score of *The White-Haired Girl*. As the Philadelphia Orchestra had played Beethoven and Mozart, this criticism seemed designed to counteract any musico-cultural slippage from Mao's doctrine of utilizing foreign things for Chinese Communist purposes and any music-for-music's-sake detachment.

Simultaneously, an ideological attack was mounted, directed simultaneously against the memory of Lin Piao and the classical Chinese philosopher, Confucius. One example of this juxtaposition comes from an article by Cheh Chun of Peking University published in the *Peking Review* (April 12, 1974) and entitled "Confucius' Doctrine of the Mean Is a Philosophy Opposed to Social Change." The Confucian "mean," simply put, called for "neither excess nor deficiency." The Cheh Chun article stated that one of Confucius' central ideas was returning to the "rites of the Chou dynasty" without "the slightest breach and deviation." The atavistic critique of Confucius, and specifically the reference to the Chou dynasty was interpreted by some Pekingologists early in 1974 as a euphemistic attack on Chou En-lai, whose efforts at modification of excesses during and after the Cultural Revolution, as well as his many contacts with such westerners as Kissinger, could make him a target for some of the radical supporters of Chiang Ching, possibly Yao Wen-yuan. It was Yao who had written the first attacks on Peng Cheng, the Mayor of Peking, and on Chou Yang, the party's deputy propaganda director.

Political seesawing was reflected into 1975, when attacks on Confucian ideas were partly supplanted by new emphasis on "dictatorship of the proletariat" over "new bourgeois elements." Once again, the policy was put forward by Yao Wen-yuan ("On the Social Basis of the Lin Piao Anti-Party Clique," *Hung Chi*, No. 3, 1975). At the same time, Chou En-lai emerged newly strengthened from the first session of the Fourth National People's Congress (January 13 to 17).

Three major cultural events served to dramatize these developments. In the spring and summer of 1974, festivals held in Peking presented several dramas adapted for different linguistic regions of China. In February 1975, a third festival was held in the capital, increasing the number of adaptations of "model revolutionary theatrical works." Reporting on this festival, the *Peking Review* (February 21, 1975) noted that the performances, which lasted from the 11th to the 13th of the month, were designed to promote "the proletarian revolution in art and literature."

Whether one writes from New York, Paris, Hong Kong, or any other foreign center, it is well to view the Peking cultural scene with calm and sympathy. Westerners should avoid an air of patronizing forgiveness for the obvious zealotry and intolerance that has marked, and presumably still shapes, literature and the arts in contemporary China; we are not dealing with some primitive tribe that practices exotically charming rites, but with the heirs of a cultural tradition that is, or should be, part of mankind's total heritage. One cannot very well ignore the self-imposed ideological purities in Chinese stage productions today. In our age of global television transmissions, the curtain that goes up in Peking has a potential audience throughout the world. And while the propaganda images permit only the brightest sunlight, contrasted by the darkest shadows, the hidden, ongoing struggle for hues indicates China's essential humanity.

FIVE
CHINESE
COMMUNIST
PLAYS

On the Revolution of the Peking Opera

BY CHIANG CHING

Numerous commentaries credit Mao Tse-tung's wife, Chiang Ching, with revolutionary stage productions and films in contemporary China. Her own statements on this subject are rare. Reprinted below is Chiang Ching's address to the Forum of Theatrical Workers Participating in the Festival of Peking Opera on Contemporary Themes. Mrs. Mao used the occasion to restate her own views succinctly. As the Festival, which included a repertory of stage productions, took place in July 1964, allowance must be made for changes that have taken place in the interim (including the increase of China's population to an estimated total of more than 800 million). Chiang Ching's role was temporarily unclear during the Cultural Revolution that followed, but she later succeeded in continuing her drive for fundamental changes in "Peking opera" and other theatrical categories. Less than two years after the Peking Festival, the Shanghai Forum took place; a report on this event is published on pages 7-21 under the title, "The Shanghai Policy."

I offer you my congratulations on the festival, for which you have worked so hard. This is the first campaign in the revolution of Peking opera. It has achieved promising results and will have relatively far-reaching influence.

Peking opera on revolutionary contemporary themes has now been staged. But do we all look at it in the same way? I don't think we can say so just yet.

We must have unshakable confidence in the staging of Peking opera on revolutionary contemporary themes. It is inconceivable that, in our socialist country led by the Communist Party, the dominant position on the stage is not occupied by the workers, peasants and soldiers, who are the real creators of history and the true masters of our country. We should create literature and art which protect our socialist economic base. When we are not clear about our orientation, we should try our best to become so. Here I would like to give two groups of figures for your reference. These figures strike me as shocking.

Here is the first group: according to a rough estimate, there are 3,000 theatrical companies in the country (not including amateur troupes and unlicensed companies). Of these, around 90 are professional modern drama companies, 80 odd are cultural troupes, and the rest, over 2,800 are companies staging various kinds of operas and balladry. Our operatic stage is occupied by emperors, princes, generals, ministers, scholars and beauties, and, on top of these, ghosts and monsters. As for those 90 modern drama companies, they don't necessarily all depict the workers, peasants and soldiers either. They, too, lay stress on staging full-length plays, foreign plays and plays on ancient themes. So we can say that the modern drama stage is also occupied by ancient Chinese and foreign figures. Theaters are places in which to educate the people, but at present the stage is dominated by emperors, princes, generals, ministers, scholars and beauties—by feudal and bourgeois stuff. This state of affairs cannot serve to protect but will undermine our economic base.

And here is the second group of figures: there are well over 600 million workers, peasants and soldiers in our country, whereas there is only a handful of landlords, rich peasants, counter-revolutionaries, bad elements, Rightists and bourgeois elements. Shall we serve this handful, or the 600 million? This question calls for consideration not only by Communists but also by all those literary and art workers who love their country. The grain we eat is grown by the peasants, the clothes we wear and the houses we live in are all made by the workers, and the People's Liberation Army stands guard at the fronts of national defense for us and yet we do not portray them on the stage. May I ask which class stand you artists do take? And where is the artists' "conscience" you always talk about?

For Peking opera to present revolutionary contemporary themes will not be all plain sailing. There will be reverses, but if you consider carefully the two groups of figures I have mentioned above, there may be no reverses, or at least fewer of them. Even if there are reverses, it won't matter. History always goes forward on a zigzag course but its wheels can never be turned backwards. We stress operas on revolutionary contemporary themes which reflect real life in the fifteen years since the founding of the Chinese People's Republic and which create images of contemporary revolutionary heroes on our operatic stage. This is our foremost task. Not that we don't want historical operas. Revolutionary historical operas have formed no small proportion of the programme of the present festival. Historical operas portraying the life and struggles of the people before our Party came into being are also needed. Moreover, we need to foster some pace-setters, to produce some historical operas which are really written from the standpoint of historical materialism and which can make the past serve the present. Of course, we should take up historical operas only on the condition that the carrying out of the main task (that of portraying contemporary life and creating images of workers, peasants and soldiers) is not impeded. Not that we don't want any traditional operas either. Except for those about ghosts and those extolling capitulation and betrayal, all good traditional operas can be staged. But these traditional operas will have no audience worth mentioning unless they are carefully re-edited and revised. I have made systematic visits to theaters for more than two years and my observation of both actors and audiences led me to this conclusion. In future, the re-editing and revising of traditional operas is necessary, but this work must not replace our foremost task.

I will next discuss the question of where to make a start.

I think the key question is that you must have the plays. If you have only directors and actors and no plays there is nothing to be directed or acted. People say that plays form the basis of theatrical productions. I think that is quite true. Therefore attention must be devoted to creative writing.

In the last few years the writing of new plays has lagged far behind real life. This is even more true in the case of Peking opera. Playwrights are few and they lack experience of life. So it is only natural that no good plays are being created. The key to tackling the problem of creative writing is the formation of a three-way combination of the leadership, the playwrights and the masses. Recently, I studied the way in which the play *Great Wall Along the Southern Sea* was created and I found that they did it exactly like this. First the leadership set the theme. Then the playwrights went three times to acquire experience of life, even taking part in a military operation to round up enemy spies. When the play was written, many leading members of the Kwangchow military command took part in discussions on it, and after it had been rehearsed, opinions were widely canvassed and revisions made. In this way, as a result of constantly asking for opinions and constantly making revisions they succeeded in turning out in a fairly short time a good topical play reflecting a real life struggle.

In the case of the Shanghai Municipal Party Committee it was Comrade Ko Ching-shih himself who came to grips with the problem of creative writing. All localities must appoint competent cadres to handle this problem.

It will be difficult for some time yet to write plays specially for Peking opera. Nevertheless, people have to be appointed right now to do the job. They must first be given some special training and then go out to attain experience of life. They can begin by writing short plays and gradually work out full-length operas. It is also good to have short works, if well written.

In creative writing, new forces must be cultivated. Send them to work at the grass roots level and in three to five years they will blossom and bear fruit.

Another good way to get plays is by adaptation.

Theatrical items for adaptation must be carefully chosen. First, we must see whether or not they are good politically and secondly, whether or not they suit the conditions of the company concerned. Serious analysis of the original must be made when adapting it, its good points must be affirmed and kept intact, while its weak points must be remedied. In adapting for Peking opera attention must be paid to two aspects: on the one hand, the adaptations must be in keeping with the characteristics of Peking opera, having singing and acrobatics, and words must fit the melodies in Peking opera singing. The language used must be that of Peking opera. Otherwise the performers will not be able to sing. On the other hand, excessive compromises should not be made with the performers. An opera must have a clear-cut theme with a tightly knit structure and striking characters. In no case should the whole opera be allowed to become diffuse and flat in order to provide a few principal performers with star parts.

Peking opera uses artistic exaggeration. At the same time, it has always depicted ancient times and people belonging to those times. Therefore, it is comparatively easy for Peking opera to portray negative characters and this is what some people like about it so much. On the other hand, it is very difficult to create positive characters, and yet we must build up characters of advanced revolutionary heroes. In the original version of the opera *Taking the Bandits' Stronghold* produced by Shanghai the negative characters appeared to be overpowering, while the positive characters looked quite wizened. Since the leadership gave direct guidance, this opera has been positively improved. Now, the scene about the Taoist Ting Ho has been cut, whereas the part of Eagle—nickname of the bandit leader—has been only slightly altered (the actor who plays the part acts very well). But since the roles of the People's Liberation Army men Yang Tzu-jung and Shao Chien-po have been made more prominent, the images of those negative characters have paled by comparison. It has been said that there are different views on this opera. Debates can be held on this subject. You must consider which side you stand on. Should you stand on the side of the positive characters or on the side of the negative characters? It has been said that there are still people who oppose writing about positive characters. This is wrong. Good people are always the great majority. This is true not only in our socialist countries, but even in imperialist countries, where the overwhelming majority are laboring people. In revisionist countries, the revisionists are only a minority. We should place the emphasis on creating artistic images of advanced revolutionaries so as to educate and inspire the people and lead them forward. Our purpose in producing operas on revolutionary contemporary themes is mainly to exalt the positive characters. The opera *Little Heroic Sisters on the Grassland* performed by the Peking Opera Troupe of the Inner Mongolian Art Theater is very good. The playwrights wrote the script for this opera with their revolutionary feeling, inspired by the outstanding deeds of the two little heroines. The middle section of the opera is very moving. It was only because the playwrights still lacked experience of real life, worked in haste and had no time for careful polishing that the beginning and the end of the opera are not so good. As it is now, it looks like a fine painting placed in a crude old frame. In this opera there is one more point worth noticing: it is a Peking opera composed for our children. In short, this opera has a firm foundation and is good. I hope that the playwrights will go back to experience the life of the people more deeply and do their best to perfect their script. In my opinion, we should treasure the fruits of our labor, and should not scrap them lightly. Some comrades are unwilling to revise works they have done, but this prevents them from making bigger achievements. In this respect, Shanghai has set us a good example. Because the Shanghai artists have been willing to polish their scripts over and over again, they have succeeded in improving *Taking the Bandits' Stronghold* to what it is today. All the items in the repertory of the present festival should be given further polishing when you return home. The items which have already been set on their feet should not be let fall lightly.

Finally, I hope that you will spend some energy on learning from one another's presentations so that audiences throughout the country will be able to see this festival's achievements.

The Shanghai Policy

Below is the text of a policy statement on literature and art, which was issued under the title Summary of the Forum on the Work in Literature and Art in the Armed Forces with which Comrade Lin Piao Entrusted Comrade Chiang Ching. *It was issued at a time when Lin was strongly entrenched as Mao Tse-tung's deputy and chief of the armed forces. Therefore, even Mao's wife had to take orders, at least in theory, from Lin Piao. The full text of this document appeared in* Renmin Ribao *on May 29, 1967. It provides a narrative of the struggle, during the Cultural Revolution, between proponents of a relatively large variety of plays, operas, and other stage productions, with a certain amount of variety in plots and characterizations, and Chiang Ching's determination to achieve the strongest, simplest, propagandistic impact. Lin Piao's disappearance from the scene does not, in any way, outdate the validity of this document, as his approval appears to have been a mere hierarchical formality.*

I

Entrusted by Comrade Lin Piao with the task, Comrade Chiang Ching invited some comrades in the armed forces to a forum held in Shanghai from February 2 to 20, 1966, to discuss certain questions concerning the work in literature and art in the armed forces.

Before these comrades left for Shanghai, Comrade Lin Piao gave them the following instructions: "Comrade Chiang Ching talked with me yesterday. She is very sharp politically on questions of literature and art, and she is really knowledgeable about art. She has many valuable ideas. You should pay good attention to them and take measures to ensure that they are applied ideologically and organizationally. To

7

improve literary and art work in the armed forces, from now on the army's documents concerning literature and art should be sent to her, and you should get in touch with her when you have any useful information, to keep her well posted on the situation in literary and art work in the armed forces and seek her views. We should be content with neither the present ideological level nor the present artistic level of such work, both of which need further improvement."

At the beginning of the forum and in the course of the exchange of views, Comrade Chiang Ching said time and again that she had not studied Chairman Mao's works well enough and that her comprehension of Chairman Mao's thought was not profound, but that whatever points she had grasped she would act upon resolutely. She said that during the last four years she had largely concentrated on reading a number of literary works and had formed certain ideas, not all of which were necessarily correct. She said that we were all Party members and that for the cause of the Party we should discuss things together on an equal footing. This discussion should have been held last year but had been postponed because she had not been in good health. As her health had recently improved, she had invited the comrades to join in discussions according to Comrade Lin Piao's instructions.

Comrade Chiang Ching suggested that we read and see a number of items first and then study relevant documents and material before discussing them. She advised us to read Chariman Mao's relevant writings, had eight private discussions with comrades from the army and attended four group discussions, thirteen film shows and three theatrical performances together with us. She also exchanged opinions with us while watching the films and the theatrical performances. And she advised us to see twenty-one other films. During this period, Comrade Chiang Ching saw the rushes of the film *The Great Wall Along the South China Sea,* received the directors, cameramen and part of the cast and talked with them three times, which was a great education and inspiration to them. From our contacts with Comrade Chiang Ching we realize that her understanding of Chairman Mao's thought is quite profound and that she has made a prolonged and fairly full investigation and study of current problems in the field of literature and art and has gained rich practical experience through her personal exertions in carrying on experiments in this field. Taking up her work while she was still in poor health, she held discussions and saw films and theatrical performances together with us and was always modest, warm and sincere. All this has enlightened and helped us a great deal.

In the course of about twenty days, we read two of Chairman Mao's essays and other relevant material, listened to Comrade Chiang Ching's many highly important opinions and saw more than thirty films, including good and bad ones and others with shortcomings and mistakes of varying degrees. We also saw two comparatively successful Peking operas on contemporary revolutionary themes, namely, *Raid on the White Tiger Regiment* and *Taking the Bandits' Stronghold*. All this helped to deepen our comprehension of Chairman Mao's thought on literature and art and raise the level of our understanding of the socialist cultural revolution. Here are a number of ideas which we discussed and agreed upon at the forum:

1. The last sixteen years have witnessed sharp class struggles on the cultural front.

In both stages of our revolution, the new-democratic stage and the socialist stage, there has been a struggle between the two classes and the two lines on the cultural front, that is, the struggle between the proletariat and the bourgeoisie for leadership on this front. In the history of our Party, the struggle against both "Left" and Right opportunism has also included struggles between the two lines on the cultural front. Wang Ming's line represented bourgeois thinking which was once rampant within our Party. In the rectification movement which started in 1942, Chairman Mao made a thorough theoretical refutation first of Wang Ming's political, military and organizational lines and then, immediately afterwards, of the cultural lines he represented. Chairman Mao's "On New Democracy," "Talks at the Yenan Forum on Literature and Art," and "Letter to the Yenan Peking Opera Theatre After Seeing *Driven to Join the Liangshan Mountain Rebels*," are the most complete, comprehensive and systematic historical summaries of this struggle between the two lines on the cultural front. They carry on and develop the Marxist-Leninist world outlook and theory on literature and art. After our revolution entered the socialist stage, Chairman Mao's two writings, "On the Correct Handling of Contradictions Among the People" and "Speech at the Chinese Communist Party's National Conference on Propaganda Work," were published. They are the most recent summaries of the historical experience of the movements for a revolutionary ideology and a revolutionary literature and art in China and other countries. They represent a new development of the Marxist-Leninist world outlook and of the Marxist-Leninist theory on literature and art. These five writings by Chairman Mao meet the needs of the proletariat adequately and for a long time to come.

More than twenty years have elapsed since the publication of the first three of these five works by Chairman Mao and nearly ten years since the publication of the last two. However, since the founding of our People's Republic, the ideas in these works have basically not been carried out by literary and art circles. Instead, we have been under the dictatorship of a black anti-Party and anti-socialist line which is diametrically opposed to Chairman Mao's thought. This black line is a combination of bourgeois ideas on literature and art, modern revisionist ideas on literature and art and what is known as the literature and art of the 1930s (in the Kuomintang areas of China). Typical expressions of this line are such theories as those of "truthful writing,"[1] "the broad path of realism,"[2] "the deepening of realism,"[3] opposition to "subject matter as the decisive factor,"[4] "middle characters,"[5] opposition to "the smell of gunpowder"[6] and "the merging of various trends as the spirit of the age."[7] Most of these views were refuted long ago by Chairman Mao in his "Talks at the Yenan Forum on Literature and Art." In film circles there are people who advocate "discarding the classics and rebelling against orthodoxy," in other words, discarding the classics of Marxism-Leninism, of Mao Tse-tung's thought, and rebelling against the orthodoxy of people's revolutionary war. As a result of the influence or domination of this bourgeois and modern revisionist counter-current in literature and art, there have been few good or basically good works in the last decade or so (although there have been some) which truly praise worker, peasant and soldier heroes and which serve the workers, peasants and soldiers; many are mediocre, while some are anti-Party and anti-socialist poisonous weeds. In accordance with the instructions of the Central Committee of the Party, we must resolutely carry on a great socialist revolution on the cultural front and completely eliminate this black line. After this black line is destroyed, still others will appear. The struggle will have to go on. Therefore, our struggle is an arduous, complex and long-term struggle demanding decades or even centuries of effort. This is a cardinal issue which has a vital bearing on the future of the Chinese revolution and the world revolution.

A lesson to be drawn from the last decade or so is that we began to tackle the problem a little late. We have taken up only a few specific questions and have not dealt with the whole problem systematically and comprehensively. So long as we do not seize hold of the field of culture, we will inevitably forfeit many positions in this field to the black line, and this is a serious lesson. After the Tenth Plenary Session of the Central Committee in 1962 adopted a resolution on the unfolding of class struggle throughout the country, the struggle to foster proletarian ideology and liquidate bourgeois ideology in the cultural field has gradually developed.

2. The last three years have seen a new situation in the great socialist cultural revolution. The most outstanding example is the rise of Peking operas on contemporary revolutionary themes. Led by the Central Committee of the Party, headed by Chairman Mao, and armed with Marxism-Leninism, Mao Tse-tung's thought, literary and art workers engaged in revolutionizing Peking opera have launched a heroic and tenacious offensive against the literature and art of the feudal class, the bourgeoisie and the modern revisionists. Under the irresistible impact of this offensive, Peking opera, formerly the most stubborn of strongholds, has been radically revolutionized, both in ideology and in form, which has started a revolutionary change in literary and art circles. Peking operas with contemporary revolutionary themes like *The Red Lantern, Shachiapang, Taking the Bandits' Stronghold* and *Raid on the White Tiger Regiment,* the ballet *Red Detachment of Women,* the symphony *Shachiapang* and the group of clay sculptures *Rent Collection Courtyard* have been approved by the broad masses of workers, peasants and soldiers and acclaimed by Chinese and foreign audiences. They are pioneer efforts which will exert a profound and far-reaching influence on the socialist cultural revolution. They effectively prove that even that most stubborn of strongholds, Peking opera, can be taken by storm and revolutionized and that foreign classical art forms such as the ballet and symphonic music can also be remolded to serve our purpose. This should give us still greater confidence in revolutionizing other art forms. Some people say that Peking operas with contemporary revolutionary themes have discarded the traditions and basic skills of Peking opera. On the contrary, the fact is that Peking operas with contemporary revolutionary themes have inherited the Peking opera traditions in a critical way and have really weeded out the old to let the new emerge. The fact is not that the basic skills of Peking opera have been discarded but that they are no longer adequate. Those which cannot be used to reflect present-day life should and must be discarded. In order to reflect present-day life we urgently need to refine, create, and gradually develop and enrich the basic skills

of Peking opera through our experience of real life. At the same time, these successes deal a powerful blow at conservatives of various descriptions and such views as the "box-office earnings" theory, the "foreign exchange earnings" theory and the theory that "revolutionary works can't travel abroad."

Another outstanding feature of the socialist cultural revolution in the last three years is the widespread mass activity of workers, peasants and soldiers on the fronts of ideology, literature and art. Workers, peasants and soldiers are now producing many fine philosophical articles which splendidly express Mao Tse-tung's thought in terms of their own practice. They are also producing many fine works of literature and art in praise of the triumph of our socialist revolution, the big leap forward on all the fronts of socialist construction, our new heroes, and the brilliant leadership of our great Party and our great leader. In particular, both in content and in form the numerous poems by workers, peasants and soldiers appearing on wall-newspapers and blackboards herald an entirely new age.

Of course, these are merely the first fruits of our socialist cultural revolution, the first step in our long march of ten thousand *li*. In order to safeguard and extend these achievements and to carry the socialist cultural revolution through to the end, we must work hard for a long time.

3. The struggle between the two roads on the front of literature and art is bound to be reflected in the armed forces which do not exist in a vacuum and cannot possibly be an exception to the rule. The Chinese People's Liberation Army is the chief instrument of the dictatorship of the proletariat in China. It represents the mainstay and hope of the Chinese people and the revolutionary people of the world. Without a people's army, neither the victory of our revolution nor the dictatorship of the proletariat and socialism would have been possible and the people would have nothing. Therefore, the enemy will inevitably try to undermine it from all sides and will inevitably use literature and art as weapons in his attempt to corrupt it ideologically. However, after Chairman Mao pointed out that basically literary and art circles had not carried out the policies of the Party over the past fifteen years, certain persons still claimed that the problem of the orientation of literature and art in our armed forces had already been solved, and that the problem to be solved was mainly one of raising the artistic level. This point of view is wrong and is not based on concrete analysis. In point

of fact, some works of literature and art by our armed forces have a correct orientation and have reached a comparatively high artistic level; some have a correct orientation but their artistic level is low; others have serious defects or mistakes in both political orientation and artistic form, and still others are anti-Party and anti-socialist poisonous weeds. The August First Studio has produced as bad a film as the *Pressgang*. This shows that the work in literature and art in the armed forces has also come under the influence of the black line to a greater or lesser degree. Besides, we have as yet trained relatively few creative workers who are really up to the mark; the ideological problems in creative work are still numerous, and there are still some undesirable persons in our ranks. We must analyze and solve these problems properly.

4. The Liberation Army must play an important role in the socialist cultural revolution. Comrade Lin Piao has kept a firm hold on the work in literature and art and has given many correct instructions on this work since he has been in charge of the work of the Military Commission of the Central Committee of the Party. "The Resolution on Strengthening Political and Ideological Work in the Armed Forces" adopted at the enlarged session of the Military Commission clearly specified that the aim of the work in literature and art in the armed forces was "to serve the cause of fostering proletarian ideology and liquidating bourgeois ideology and consolidating and improving fighting capacity in close connection with the tasks of the armed forces and in the context of their ideological situation." There is already a nucleus of literary and art workers in the armed forces whom we have trained and who have been tempered in revolutionary war. A number of good works have been produced in the armed forces. Therefore the Liberation Army must play its due role in the socialist cultural revolution and must fight bravely and unswervingly to carry out the policy that literature and art should serve the workers, peasants and soldiers and serve socialism.

5. In the cultural revolution, there must be both destruction and construction. Leaders must take personal charge and see to it that good models are created. The bourgeoisie has its reactionary "monologue on creating the new." We, too, should create what is new and original, new in the sense that it is socialist and original in the sense that it is proletarian. The basic task of socialist literature and art is to work hard and create heroic models of workers, peasants and soldiers. Only when

we have such models and successful experience in creating them will we be able to convince people, to consolidate the positions we hold, and to knock the reactionaries' stick out of their hands.

On this question, we should have a sense of pride and not of inferiority.

We must destroy the blind faith in what is known as the literature and art of the 1930s (in the Kuomintang areas of China). At that time, the Left-wing movement in literature and art followed Wang Ming's "Left" opportunist line politically; organizationally it practised closed-doorism and sectarianism; and its ideas on literature and art were virtually those of Russian bourgeois literary critics such as Belinsky, Chernyshevsky and Dobrolyubov and of Stanislavsky in the theatrical field, all of whom were bourgeois democrats in tsarist Russia with bourgeois ideas and not Marxist ones. The bourgeois-democratic revolution is a revolution in which one exploiting class replaces another. It is only the proletarian socialist revolution that finally destroys all exploiting classes. Therefore, we must not take the ideas of any bourgeois revolutionary as guiding principles for our proletarian movement in ideology or in literature and art. There were of course good things in the 1930s too, namely, the militant Left-wing movement in literature and art led by Lu Hsun. Around the middle of the 1930s, some Left-wing leaders under the influence of Wang Ming's Right capitulationist line abandoned the Marxist-Leninist class standpoint and put forward the slogan of "a literature of national defense." This was a bourgeois slogan. It was Lu Hsun who put forward the proletarian slogan of "a mass literature for the national revolutionary war." Some Left-wing writers and artists, notably Lu Hsun, also raised the slogans that literature and art should serve the workers and peasants and that the workers and peasants should create their own literature and art. However, no systematic solution was found for the fundamental problem of the integration of literature and art with the workers, peasants and soldiers. The great majority of those Left-wing writers and artists were bourgeois nationalist-democrats, and a number failed to pass the test of the democratic revolution, while others have not given a good account of themselves under the test of socialism.

We must destroy blind faith in Chinese and foreign classical literature. Stalin was a great Marxist-Leninist. His criticism of the modernist literature and art of the bourgeoisie was very sharp. But he uncritically took over what are known as the classics of Russia and Europe and the consequences were bad. The classical literature and art of China and of

Europe (including Russia) and even American films have exercised a considerable influence on our literary and art circles, and some people have regarded them as holy writ and accepted them in their entirety. We should draw a lesson from Stalin's experience. Old and foreign works should be studied too, and refusal to study them would be wrong; but we must study them critically, making the past serve the present and foreign works serve China.

As for the relatively good Soviet revolutionary works of literature and art which appeared after the October Revolution, they too must be analyzed and not blindly worshipped or, still less, blindly imitated. Blind imitation can never become art. Literature and art can only spring from the life of the people which is their sole source. This is borne out by the whole history of literature and art, past and present, Chinese and foreign.

It has always been the case in the world that the rising forces defeat the forces of decay. Our People's Liberation Army was weak and small at the beginning, but it eventually became strong and defeated the U.S.–Chiang Kai-shek reactionaries. Confronted with the excellent revolutionary situation at home and abroad and our glorious tasks, we should be proud to be thoroughgoing revolutionaries. We must have the confidence and courage to do things never previously attempted, because ours is a revolution to eliminate all exploiting classes and systems of exploitation once and for all and to root out all exploiting-class ideologies, which poison the minds of the people. Under the leadership of the Central Committee of the Party and Chairman Mao and under the guidance of Marxism-Leninism, Mao Tse-tung's thought, we must create a new socialist revolutionary literature and art worthy of our great country, our great Party, our great people and our great army. This will be a most brilliant new literature and art opening up a new era in human history.

But it is no easy matter to create good models. Strategically we must take the difficulties in creative work lightly, but tactically we must take them seriously. To create a fine work is an arduous process, and the comrades in charge of creative work must never adopt a bureaucratic or casual attitude but must work really hard and share the writers' and artists' joys and hardships. It is essential to get first-hand material as far as possible, or when this is impossible at least to get the material at second hand. There should be no fear of failures or mistakes. Allowance should be made for them, and people must be permitted to correct their mistakes. It is necessary to rely on the masses, follow the line of "from the masses, to the masses," and repeatedly undergo the test of practice over a long period, so that a work may become better and better and achieve the unity of revolutionary political content and the best possible artistic form. In the course of practice it is necessary to sum up experience in good time and gradually grasp the laws of various forms of art. Otherwise, no good models can be created.

We should give the fullest attention to the themes of socialist revolution and socialist construction, and it would be entirely wrong to ignore them.

A serious effort should now be made to create works of literature and art about the three great military campaigns of Liaohsi-Shenyang, Huai-Hai and Peiping-Tientsin and other important campaigns while the comrades who led and directed them are still alive. There are many important revolutionary themes, historical and contemporary, on which work urgently needs to be done in a planned and systematic way. A success must be made of the film, *The Great Wall Along the South China Sea*. The film *The Long March* must be revised successfully. A nucleus of truly proletarian writers and artists should be trained in the process.

6. People engaged in the work of literature and art, whether they are leaders or writers and artists, must all practice the Party's democratic centralism. We favor "rule by the voice of the many" and oppose "rule by the voice of one man alone." We must follow the mass line. In the past, some people pressed the leadership to nod and applaud when they produced something. This is a very bad style of work. As for the cadres in charge of creative work in literature and art, they should always bear two points in mind: First, be good at listening to the opinions of the broad masses; second, be good at analyzing these opinions, accept the right ones and reject the wrong ones. Completely flawless works of literature and art are nonexistent, and as long as the keynote of a work is good, we should help improve it by pointing out its shortcomings and errors. Bad works should not be hidden away, but should be shown to the masses for their comment. We must not be afraid of the masses but should have firm trust in them, and they can give us much valuable advice. Besides, this will improve their powers of discrimination. It costs several hundred thousand or as much as a million yuan to produce a film. To hide a bad film away is wasteful. Why not show it to the public so as to give a lesson to writers and artists and the masses and at the same time make up for its cost to the state and thus turn it to good account ideologically and economically?

The film *Beleagured City* has been shown for a long time but it received no criticism. Shouldn't the *Jiefangjun Bao* (*Liberation Army Daily*) write an article criticizing it?

7. We must encourage revolutionary, militant mass criticism on literature and art and break the monopoly of literary and art criticism by a few so-called critics (those wrong in orientation or deficient in militancy). We must place the weapon of literary and art criticism in the hands of the masses of workers, peasants and soldiers and integrate professional critics with critics from among the masses. We must make this criticism more militant and oppose unprincipled vulgar praise. We must reform our style of writing, encourage the writing of short, popular articles, turn our literary and art criticism into daggers and hand grenades and learn to handle them effectively in close combat. Of course, we must at the same time write longer, systematic articles of theoretical depth. We oppose the use of terminology and jargon to frighten people. Only in this way can we disarm the self-styled literary and art critics. The *Jiefangjun Bao* and the *Jiefangjun Wenyi* (*Liberation Army Literature and Art*) should set up special columns, regular or occasional, for comment on literature and art. Warm support should be given to good or basically good works and their shortcomings pointed out in a helpful way. And principled criticism must be made of bad works. In the theoretical field, we must thoroughly and systematically criticize typical fallacies on literature and art and the many other fallacies spread by certain people who attempt to falsify history and to boost themselves in such books as the *History of the Development of the Chinese Film, A Collection of Historical Data on the Chinese Drama Movement in the Last Fifty Years* and *A Preliminary Study of the Repertory of Peking Opera*. We must not mind being accused of "brandishing the stick." When some people charge us with oversimplification and crudeness, we must analyze these charges. Some of our criticisms are basically correct but are not sufficiently convincing because our analysis and evidence adduced are inadequate. This state of affairs must be improved. With some people it is a matter of understanding; they start by accusing us of oversimplification and crudeness but eventually drop the charge. But when the enemy condemns our correct criticisms as oversimplified and crude, we must stand firm. Literary and art criticism should become one of our day-to-day tasks, an important method both in the struggle in the field of literature and art and in Party leadership in this field of work. Without correct literary and art criticism it is impossible for creative work to flourish.

8. In the struggle against foreign revisionism in the field of literature and art, we must not only catch small figures like Chukhrai. We should catch the big ones, catch Sholokhov and dare to tackle him. He is the father of revisionist literature and art. His *And Quiet Flows the Don, Virgin Soil Upturned* and *The Fate of a Man* have exercised a big influence on a number of Chinese writers and readers. Shouldn't the army organize people to study his works and write convincing critical articles containing well-documented analysis? This will have a profound influence in China and the rest of the world. The same thing should be done with similar works by Chinese writers.

9. As for method, we must combine revolutionary realism with revolutionary romanticism in our creative work, and must not adopt bourgeois critical realism or bourgeois romanticism.

The fine qualities of the worker, peasant and soldier heroes who have emerged under the guidance of the correct line of the Party are the concentrated expression of the class character of the proletariat. We must work with wholehearted enthusiasm and do everything possible to create heroic models of workers, peasants and soldiers. We should create typical characters. Chairman Mao has said: ". . . life as reflected in works of literature and art can and ought to be on a higher plane, more intense, more concentrated, more typical, nearer the ideal, and therefore more universal than actual everyday life." We should not confine ourselves to actual persons and events. Nor should we portray a hero only after he is dead. In fact, there are many more living heroes than dead ones. This means that our writers must concentrate and generalize experience from real life accumulated over a long period of time to create a variety of typical characters.

When we write about revolutionary wars, we must first be clear about their nature—ours is the side of justice and the enemy's is the side of injustice. Our works must show our arduous struggles and heroic sacrifices, but must also express revolutionary heroism and revolutionary optimism. While depicting the cruelty of war, we must not exaggerate or glorify its horrors. While depicting the arduousness of the revolutionary struggle, we must not exaggerate or glorify the sufferings involved. The cruelty of a revolutionary war and revolutionary heroism, the arduousness of the revolutionary struggle and revolutionary optimism constitute a unity of opposites, but we must be clear about which is the principal aspect of the contradiction; otherwise, if we make the wrong emphasis, a bourgeois pacifist trend will emerge. Moreover, while depicting our people's revolutionary war, whether in the stage in which guerrilla warfare was primary and mobile warfare supplementary, or in the stage in which mobile warfare was primary, we must correctly show the relationship between the regular forces, the guerrillas and the people's militia and between the armed masses and the unarmed masses under the leadership of the Party.

Regarding the selection of subject matter, only when we plunge into the thick of life and do a good job of investigation and study can we make the selection properly and correctly. Playwrights should unreservedly plunge into the heat of the struggle for a long period. Directors, actors and actresses, cameramen, painters and composers should also go into the thick of life and make serious investigations and studies. In the past, some works distorted the historical facts, concentrating on the portrayal of erroneous lines instead of the correct line; some described heroic characters who nevertheless invariably violate discipline, or created heroes only to have them die in a contrived tragic ending; other works do not present heroic characters but only "middle" characters who are actually backward people, or caricatures of workers, peasants or soldiers; in depicting the enemy, they fail to expose his class nature as an exploiter and oppressor of the people, and even glamorize him; still others are concerned only with love and romance, pandering to philistine tastes and claiming that love and death are the eternal themes. All such bourgeois and revisionist trash must be resolutely opposed.

10.   Re-educate the cadres in charge of the work of literature and art and reorganize the ranks of writers and artists. For historical reasons, before the whole country was liberated it was rather difficult for us proletarians to train our own workers in literature and art in the areas under enemy rule. Our cultural level was relatively low and our experience limited. Many of our workers in literature and art had received a bourgeois education. In the course of their revolutionary activities in literature and art, some failed to pass the test of enemy persecution and turned traitor, while others failed to resist the corrosive influence of bourgeois ideas and became rotten. In the base areas, we trained a considerable number of revolutionary workers in literature and art. Especially after the publication of the "Talk at the Yenan Forum on Literature and Art," they had the correct orientation, embarked on the path of integration with the workers, peasants and soldiers, and play a positive role in the revolution. The weakness was that, after the country was liberated and we entered the big cities, many comrades failed to resist the corrosion of bourgeois ideology in the

ranks of our writers and artists, with the result that some of them have fallen out in the course of advance. Ours is the literature and art of the proletariat, the literature and art of the Party. The principle of proletarian Party spirit is the outstanding feature distinguishing us from other classes. It must be understood that representatives of other classes also have their principle of party spirit, and that they are very stubborn too. We must firmly adhere to the principle of proletarian Party spirit and combat the corrosion of bourgeois ideology in creative thinking, in organizational line and in style of work. As for bourgeois ideology, we must draw a clear line of demarcation and must on no account enter into peaceful coexistence with it. A variety of problems now exist in literary and art circles which, for most people, are problems of ideological understanding and of raising such understanding through education. We must earnestly study Chairman Mao's works, creatively study and apply them, tie up what we learn from them with our own thinking and practice and study them with specific problems in mind. Only in this way can we really understand, grasp and master Chairman Mao's thought. We must plunge into the thick of life for a long period of time, integrate ourselves with the workers, peasants and soldiers to raise the level of our class consciousness, remold our ideology and wholeheartedly serve the people without any regard for personal fame or gain. It is necessary to teach our comrades to study Marxism-Leninism and Chairman Mao's works and to remain revolutionary all their lives, and pay special attention to the maintenance of proletarian integrity in later life, which is not at all easy.

III

By taking part in the forum, we have acquired a relatively clear understanding of all the questions mentioned above, and our opinions on them now correspond with the realities in the work in literature and art among the armed forces. As a result, the level of our political consciousness has been raised, and our determination to carry out the socialist cultural revolution and our sense of responsibility in this respect have likewise been strengthened. We will continue to study Chairman Mao's works conscientiously, make serious investigations and studies and do well in the carrying out of experiments and in the production of good models, so as to take the lead in the current struggle of the cultural revolution to foster proletarian ideology and liquidate bourgeois ideology.

NOTES

1 The theory of "truthful writing" was advocated by the revisionists. The counter-revolutionary Hu Feng was an exponent of it, and so was Feng Hsueh-feng. They had ulterior motives and under the cover of "truthful writing" tried to oppose the class character and tendency of socialist literature and art, as well as the use of the socialist spirit in literature and art to educate the people. They advocated "truthful writing" in order to seek out the "seamy side" of life in socialist society and the rotten things left over from history, so as to paint our splendid socialist society in dark colors.

2 The theory of "the broad path of realism" was advocated by some anti-Party and anti-socialist writers and artists who, opposing Chairman Mao's "Talks at the Yenan Forum on Literature and Art," argued that it was out of date and urged that a different and broader path should be found. This was the nature of "the broad path of realism" advocated by Chin Chao-yang and others. In their view, the correct, broad path of serving the workers, peasants and soldiers was too narrow, was "hard-boiled dogmatism" and "confined writers to an unalterable, narrow path." They argued that each author should write whatever he pleased according to his "different personal experience of life, education and temperament and artistic individuality." They wanted writers to abandon the worker-peasant-soldier orientation and explore "new fields which would give unlimited scope to their creativeness."

3 Shao Chuan-lin, formerly Vice-Chairman of the Chinese Writers' Union, advanced the theory of "the deepening of realism" while advocating "writing about middle characters." According to this theory, writers should depict "the old traits" in the people, summarize "the spiritual burdens of individual peasants through the centuries" and create complex "middle characters." They should write about "everyday" events to "reveal the greatness in trivial things" and attempt to show "the rich diversity of the world in a grain of rice." To Shao Chuan-lin, the only realist writing was that depicting "middle characters" riddled with inner contradictions, summarizing "the spiritual burdens of individual peasants through the centuries" and presenting the "painful stages" of the peasants' transition from an individual to a collective economy. This, he contended, was the only way to "deepen realism," whereas praising the revolutionary heroism of the people and describing the heroes among them was neither true nor realistic. This theory of "the deepening of realism," which was taken directly from bourgeois critical realism, is thoroughly reactionary.

4 The theory of opposition to "subject matter as the decisive factor," which was opposed to the socialist view of literature and art, found keen support from Tien Han, Hsia Yen and others. Proletarian writers must consider what subject matter is of value to the people before they start writing and a specific subject should be selected and written up in order to foster proletarian ideology and liquidate bourgeois ideology and encourage the masses to be firm in taking the socialist road. But to advocates of this theory, these correct views were restrictions and fetters which "must be thoroughly eliminated." Under the pretext of enlarging the scope of subject matter, they proposed discarding the classics of revolution and rebelling

against the orthodoxy of war. They argued that too many of our films dealt with the revolution and armed struggle and that unless a break was made, no really new films could be produced. Other advocates of this theory were in favor of writing works with "human interest," "love of mankind," "insignificant people" and "minor events." The aim of these proposals was actually to lead literature and art astray from the path of serving proletarian politics.

5 The chief exponent of the theory of "middle characters" was Shao Chuan-lin. He put forward this proposal time and again between the winter of 1960 and the summer of 1962. He slandered the vast majority of our poor and lower-middle peasants as people in an "intermediate state" vacillating between socialism and capitalism. He hoped that more writing about middle characters would undermine readers' faith in socialism and serve to curb or oppose the creation of heroes of the socialist age in works of literature and art.

6 Opposition to "the smell of gunpowder." Modern revisionist literature plays up the horrors of war and propagates the philosophy of survival and capitulationism to sap the people's fighting will and serve the needs of the imperialists. In recent years there were also some people in China who repeatedly clamored that our writing reeked of gunpowder and our stage bristled with guns, and that this was inartistic. They wanted writers to discard the classics of revolution and rebel against the orthodoxy of war. This theory was in essence a reflection of the revisionist trend in our literary and art circles.

7 "The merging of various trends as the spirit of the age" was an anti-Marxist-Leninist fallacy put forward by Chou Ku-cheng, who denied that the spirit of the age is the spirit which propels the age forward and that the representative of this spirit is the advanced class which propels the age forward. He argued that the spirit of the age was a "merging" of the "different ideologies of different classes," and that it included "pseudo-revolutionary, non-revolutionary and even counter-revolutionary ideas." This was a thoroughly reactionary theory aimed at class conciliation.

"The Fortress of Peking Opera"

The following editorial appeared in Hung Chi, Peking, issue No.
7, 1967. *Its publication in the authoritative monthly journal illustrated the relative importance which Communist Party and government officials attributed to the struggle for political dominance on the cultural scene. The editorial, entitled "Hail the Victory in the Revolution of Peking Opera," contains this rhetorical question: "Can there possibly be any other old fortress that cannot be taken, now that we have succeeded in taking the fortress of Peking opera, which was under the strictest control of the counter-revolutionary revisionists and where the old forces were most stubborn?" Although there is no reference by name to Liu Shao-chi, he is referred to obliquely as "the top capitalist roader in the Party." Among other personalities mentioned, Chou Yang is probably the most noteworthy; he had occupied the position of Deputy Director of the Communist Party's Propaganda Department under Liu.*

The revolution of Peking opera sounded a call to arms for China's great proletarian cultural revolution and marked an excellent beginning of it. It was a tremendous victory for Mao Tse-tung's thought and for Chairman Mao's *Talks at the Yenan Forum on Literature and Art!*

Drama and opera are important positions in the struggle between the two classes and between the two lines on the literary and art front. Our great leader Chairman Mao has always attached great importance to them. In 1944, he pointed out after seeing *Driven to Join the Liangshan Mountain Rebels* presented by the Yenan Peking Opera Theatre: "History is made by the people, yet the old opera (and all the old literature and art, which are divorced from the people) presents the people as though they were dirt, and the stage is dominated by lords and ladies and their pampered sons and daughters. Now you have reversed this reversal of history and restored historical truth, and thus a new life is opening up for the old opera. That is why this merits congratulations."

After liberation Chairman Mao further put forward the important policies of "letting a hundred flowers blossom and weeding through the old to bring forth the new" and "making the past serve the present and foreign things serve China." Chairman Mao's instructions, the supreme criteria for guiding the revolution of drama and opera, have solved a series of basic questions in this revolution.

Using Mao Tse-tung's thought, Comrade Chiang Ching discussed the great significance of the revolution of Peking opera and expounded its guiding principles, as formulated by Chairman Mao, in her July 1964 speech at the forum of theatrical workers participating in the festival of Peking opera on contemporary themes. This speech is an important document which uses Marxism-Leninism, Mao Tse-tung's thought, to solve the problems in the revolution of Peking opera.

For a long time, because of the domination of the counter-revolutionary revisionist line in the field of literature and art represented by Chou Yang, Chi Yen-ming, Hsia Yen and Lin Mo-han, Chairman Mao's revolutionary line could not be carried through in the field of Peking opera. Many bad operas glorifying emperors, princes, generals, ministers, scholars and beauties dominated the Peking opera stage. These bad operas played the reactionary role of disintegrating the socialist economic base to pave the way for the restoration of capitalism.

Abusing their usurped power and position, a handful of Party persons in authority taking the capitalist road and some reactionary "authorities" controlled Peking opera circles, and, by drawing deserters and traitors into their service and forming cliques in pursuit of their own selfish interests, turned these circles into an impenetrable independent kingdom of the feudal landlords and the bourgeoisie.

The top capitalist roader in the Party was the main pillar and support for bourgeois reactionary forces and all ghosts and monsters in Peking opera circles and the biggest obstacle to the revolution of Peking opera. For a long time he stubbornly opposed the revolution of Peking opera and spread the idea that "old operas have much educational value." He heaped praise upon *Fourth Son Visits His Mother*, an opera which disseminated a traitor's philosophy, the philosophy of survival. He said, "It doesn't matter much if this opera is staged. It has been performed for so many years; didn't New China emerge in spite of that?" He lauded *Fierce Tiger Village* which made every effort to prettify scoundrels like Huang Tien-pa, a lackey of the feudal land-lords, and described it as "an opera which has been well revised." He even recommended such an obscene Peking opera as *The Dragon Flirts with the Phoenix*. He worked closely with the top counter-revolutionary revisionists in the former Peking Municipal Party Committee and Chou Yang, Chi Yen-ming, Hsia Yen, Lin Mo-han, Tien Han, Chang Keng and company to use old Peking opera to serve a counter-revolutionary restoration of capitalism.

But the new-born forces eventually defeat all that is decadent. Illu-minated by the radiance of the great thought of Mao Tse-tung, guided by Comrade Chiang Ching and with the efforts of the great numbers of revolutionary comrades in Peking opera circles, new revolutionary Peking opera finally broke down stubborn resistance to fight its way out from the old fortress of emperors, princes, generals, ministers, scholars and beauties.

Rich results have already been achieved in the revolution of Peking opera. Such model Peking operas as *Taking the Bandits' Stronghold, On the Docks, The Red Lantern, Shachiapang* and *Raid on the White Tiger Regiment* represent most valuable achievements. They are fine models not only for Peking opera, but for proletarian literature and art as a whole. They also serve as fine examples for "struggle-criticism-transformation"* on all fronts of the great proletarian cultural revolu-tion. These splendid results of the revolution of Peking opera have shaken the entire field of the arts like a spring thunderstorm, indicat-ing that it is now time for the hundred flowers of the proletariat to bloom. This will have an immense impact and influence on the develop-ment of proletarian literature and art as a whole.

Only a short while ago, the handful of capitalist roaders in the Party sneered at the vanguards in the revolution of Peking opera, "So you people want to capture the stronghold?" Yes, we do want to capture the stronghold, to attack this most stubborn "fortress" in theatrical art and to capture for the proletariat this most closely guarded position of

---

* "Struggle-criticism-transformation" is the abbreviation of the statement in the Decision of the Central Committee of the Chinese Communist Party Concerning the Great Proletarian Cultural Revolution, which reads, "At present, our objective is to struggle against and overthrow those persons in authority who are taking the capitalist road, to criticize and repudiate the reactionary bourgeois academic 'authorities' and the ideology of the bourgeoisie and all other exploiting classes and to transform education, literature and art and all other parts of the superstruc-ture not in correspondence with the socialist economic base, so as to facilitate the consolidation and development of the social system."

the bourgeois reactionary forces. Today, Peking opera has broken through the bonds of counter-revolutionary revisionism. The great red banner of Mao Tse-tung's thought has now been hoisted high over the opera stage. The stage once occupied by emperors, princes, generals, ministers, scholars and beauties has been turned into a place where the workers, peasants and soldiers can fully display all their talents. The position for spreading feudalism and capitalism has been turned into one for the propagation of Mao Tse-tung's thought. This is a great victory for Chairman Mao's revolutionary line on literature and art, an earth-shaking transformation. It proves to the masses that the great thought of Mao Tse-tung is all-conquering. Can there possibly be any other old fortress that cannot be taken now that we have succeeded in taking the fortress of Peking opera which was under the strictest control of the counter-revolutionary revisionists and where the old forces were most stubborn?

The victory in the revolution of Peking opera has proclaimed the bankruptcy of the counter-revolutionary revisionist line on literature and art and ushered in a brand-new era for the development of new, proletarian literature and art.

The revolution of Peking opera is an important part of China's proletarian cultural revolution. We must make a high appraisal of the tremendous achievements in the revolution of Peking opera and lay great stress on its immense historical significance. A clear understanding of its achievements and significance will increase considerably our confidence in the proletarian cultural revolution. We are convinced that after this cultural revolution, a completely new situation never before seen in history, an encouraging prospect of a hundred flowers blooming luxuriantly, will appear in the field of culture and art in our country.

The White-Haired Girl

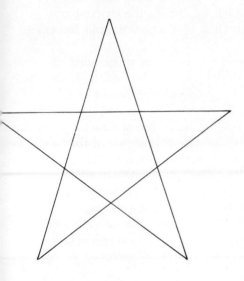

Ghost, Goddess, Revolutionary

One of the oldest fear-inspiring images in the history of mankind is that of the hungry ghost. Fear of such a predatory spirit dates back to prehistoric times and is shared by China with the ancient civilizations of Assyria and Babylonia. A hungry, restless ghost may be the spirit of a murdered man, or of some unfulfilled person such as a woman who died in childbirth. To ward off such an apparition, and to guard against its evil designs, rituals of appeasement were developed. To this day, overseas Chinese communities, as in Hong Kong, celebrate the annual festival of "feeding the hungry ghosts" with the presentation of food at shrines.

Out of this theme emerged the ballet The White-Haired Girl, *which, after going through many stages in China, was produced as a motion picture and shown in the United States on educational television. Even this final version contained a scene that showed the ghostlike, white-haired girl going to a mountain shrine for food. Its folkloric origin carried over into the ballet's earlier versions, but elements regarded as detracting from its political message were gradually eliminated. Yet, the overall theme of this traditional melodrama retains human elements that give the ballet universal appeal, and there can be no doubt of its widespread popularity in Chinese cities and countryside.*

The popular legend, or dramatized reality, underlying The White-Haired Girl *was summarized by one of its original writers, Ho Ching-chih (Peking, 1954). He recalled that stories about a "white-haired goddess" were making the rounds in the northwestern part of Hopei province in 1940, then under the control of the Communist Eighth Route Army. Villagers said that the white apparition howled at night, made its home in a temple just outside the*

*village, and had ordered the peasants to offer sacrifices twice a
month. Ho Ching-chih wrote: "For a long time her command was
obeyed and, strange to relate, the sacrifice set out one evening always disappeared by the following morning. When the villagers
neglected to place offerings there at the appointed time, a shrill,
strange voice sounded from the dark shrine: 'You who neglect
your goddess—beware!' "*

*Once, when the Communist party had organized a village meet-
ing, no one attended it. A villager explained, "Today there's a full
moon; they've all gone to sacrifice to the 'White-haired Goddess.' "
Eventually, a soldier hidden in the shrine surprised the white figure as it came to snatch the food sacrifice: "Startled, the apparition gave a wild shriek, then rushed at him. The cadre fired, and
it fell, only to struggle at once to its feet and make hastily off.
Two men pursued the white figure through the woods and up
the mountain, until, after passing several cliffs, they lost sight of
it. They were standing there irresolutely when they heard a child
crying in the distance, and peering through the darkness saw a
mysterious flicker of light at the end of the dark mountain gully."*

*The soldiers discovered the "white-haired goddess" in the dark
cave, huddled against the wall and holding a small child. They
threatened to shoot her; she dropped to her knees and poured out
her story. Nine years earlier, before the Japanese invasion, a landlord "who oppressed the peasants cruelly," had taken a fancy to
the seventeen-year-old daughter of one of his old tenants. He
drove the father to suicide, under the pretext of collecting rent,
then carried off the girl and raped her. When she became pregnant, the landlord planned to murder her and take a new wife.
But "his plot was discovered by a kindhearted maidservant, who
helped the girl to escape in the night."*

*Ho Ching-chih's account adds that the girl had the baby in a far-
off mountain cave: "Nursing her hatred and bitterness, she remained several years in the cave. Because she went cold and*

hungry, was seldom in the sun, and had no salt in her diet, her hair turned white. Villagers who saw her stealing offerings from the temple thought her a goddess, and sacrificed to her." The girl managed to keep herself and her child alive, but she lived a frightened, hermitlike existence and was totally isolated. Told that society had changed, she came "out of the dark cave into the bright sunlight." Ho's account notes that "this story was told and retold, amended and amplified and polished by the people. It was written out in stories, and songs, and reached [Communist headquarters in] Yenan in 1944."

Ho Ching-chih notes that "as with all stories handed down orally, there were many different versions, and ours is only one of many. However, the variants differ only in certain episodes: the central theme, chief characteristics and main episodes are common to all." The libretto which Ho, as coauthor with Ting Yi, prepared, retained these main characters and episodes; but, as he wrote, "to bring out the main theme clearly and forcefully and adapt it for effective stage representation, certain alterations were made to the original story." The crucial points, Ho recalled, were these:

"It took some time to understand and portray the main theme. To begin with, it was considered by some as a ghost story devoid of any social significance. Others felt it could be written up as a story to overcome superstition. Later, however, after careful study, we came to consider it not merely a ghost story or an attack upon superstition but grasped its more positive aspects—the portrayal of contrasts between the two types of society and the significance of the people's liberation."

The writing of the libretto and initial rehearsals took place from January to April 1945, when the opera was produced in Yenan. Revisions were made in 1947 and 1949, and the following text is that of the opera as it was performed shortly thereafter. It won the Stalin Peace Prize for Literature and Art in 1951. During the Cultural Revolution, further changes were made. These account for

differences between the text in this volume and such later produc-
tions as the motion picture version shown in the United States. In
the 1951 version, the girl's father commits suicide as the curtain
falls at the end of Scene III. In the later versions he is killed by
the landlord's bodyguard; the passive act of self-destruction is out
of keeping with the aggressive heroism now universal in the revo-
lutionary stage productions. Further, rape and pregnancy were
eliminated in later versions; sexual or simply romantic elements
are not permitted to detract from collective military and political
action. The heroine, Hsi-erh, emerges as a symbol of courageous
resistance, a leadership figure who fits herself into a group of
armed revolutionaries.

The road toward this ultimate version of The White-Haired Girl
covered numerous obstacles and detours. The revisions in the play
itself, as well as its adaptation into ballet form, reflected the
political-cultural tug-of-war between different factions within the
Communist Party of China. That the characterizations, the music,
and choreography of this modern legend should have been the
subject of violent disagreement and personality clashes illustrates
the role which the arts have played in the Peking power struggle.
Subsequent explanations assert that the group around former
Communist Party secretary Liu Shao-chi resisted revisions of the
play advocated by others, notably Mao's wife, Chiang Ching.
With Liu in disgrace, denounced as "China's Khrushchev" and
advocate of "the capitalist road," it is exceedingly difficult to trace
these disagreements objectively. If recent explanations given in
Peking are even partly valid, Liu preferred characterizations that
permitted artistic reflections of internal personality struggles,
opposed blatant propagandistic polarization in plot, and favored
subtlety in direction and acting.

Writing in Chinese Literature *(No. 4, 1969), members of the*
Shanghai School of Dance gave their version of the conflict. It is
worth quoting several paragraphs from this account, which is

clearly partisan but also quite revelatory of the overall political significance, the conflict of personalities, and the ideological disputes that preceded the revision of the ballet. It is significant that the final version was prepared in Shanghai, which has often been the center of politico-cultural ferment. The article, entitled "An Appreciation of the Ballet The White-Haired Girl," *stated in part:*

"The focal point was the question of political power. For a dozen or more years Liu Shao-chi had been constantly dreaming of restoring capitalism. Banding together with a gang of renegades and enemy agents, he clamped down a counter-revolutionary dictatorship on the proletarians in the cultural field, and attempted to prepare public opinion for a capitalist restoration. He inserted his henchmen into influential positions everywhere in the field of culture, including our Shanghai School of Dance. They obeyed him implicitly, and used literature and art in every way to impose a dictatorship against the proletariat, to oppose Chairman Mao's revolutionary line in literature and the arts, and to oppose the revolution in literature and art led by Comrade Chiang Ching.

"Liu Shao-chi, big renegade, traitor, and scab, persistently hated and opposed the proletarian revolution in literature and art. We can't compel a reflection of present day life, he babbled. Ballet and foreign-style opera are not really suitable for it. The master had only to give the word, and his slaves hurried to comply. In 1963 our school's capitalist roaders flagrantly opposed the call to write extensively about the post-liberation period put forward by Chairman Mao's good student, Comrade Ko Ching-shih, First Secretary of the East China Bureau of the Central Committee of the Chinese Communist Party. Instead, they put on a big production of* Swan Lake *and* Red Scarfs Dance *and turned our school into a hotbed of capitalist restoration.

"When, thanks to the personal attention Comrade Chiang Ching was giving us, we decided to create a revolutionary ballet* The White-Haired Girl, *the counter-revolutionary revisionist clique in* our school tried to switch us into producing a sickly story of frustrated love among aristocrats in days gone by. When proletarian headquarters urged us to study the ballet Red Detachment of Women *put on in Peking, the clique flatly refused to let us go. But they sent us to Hangchow to learn a foreign dance,* Pas de Quatre *[a choreographic sequence involving four dancers], then being performed there."*

This account speaks of "the savage ambition of these counter-revolutionaries" as having been "beyond belief" and states that "the capitalist roaders in the propaganda department of the former Shanghai municipal Party committee and their cronies" in the local dance school "tried to get our ballet The White-Haired Girl to tout Liu Shao-chi's infamous dictum: 'class struggle has ended.'" This account also notes that several supporters of Liu proposed a finale which would have emphasized "the joy of re-union and the peasants pitching into production at the expense of the ballet's powerful revolutionary spirit." They are also accused of trying "everything to change the lyrics of a song in praise of Chairman Mao," because "those scoundrels dreaded the thought of Mao Tse-tung like an owl fears the sun." They are quoted as arguing, "What's the point of singing 'the sun is Mao Tse-tung, the sun is the Communist Party'? Everyone knows that." When it was proposed that when Hung, the despotic landlord, is killed at the end of the ballet, the crowd cheers "Long live Chairman Mao!" as "an expression of revolutionary gratitude," the critics maintained, "There's no connection between the two. It spoils the effect." They lost the argument, and the viewpoint of Chiang Ching won out. Thus the fate of the girl's father, Yang, was changed from suicide in disgrace to a fight with the landlord and his bodyguard. The Shanghai Dance School account notes that Yang "furiously resists" and "with one blow of his carrying pole [the shoulder pole used widely for carrying loads] he knocks the landlord to the ground," while his daughter "refuses to swallow insults" and "indignantly fights the landlord when he tries to trifle with her"—very different from the opening scene of Act III in the earlier version, printed on the following pages. Hsi-erh's pregnancy becomes evident, she is to be sold to a procurer, still believing that the landlord would marry her, whereas he gives orders to have her strangled.

The Shanghai appraisal concludes that the final version of the ballet "trenchantly depicts the essence of the centuries-long struggle to the death between China's laboring masses and the landlord class, between the proletariat and the bourgeosie" and "demonstrates in a concentrated form Chairman Mao's wise concept of people's war," and proves that "political power grows out of the barrel of a gun." It adds that "this revolutionary modern ballet is an artistic pearl glistening with the brilliance of Mao Tse-tung's thought" and "teaches us" to "remember always class bitterness and his saying, 'never forget class struggle.'" This analysis of the ballet alerts us to the symbolism of certain details. For example, during the period of the girl's bondage in the landlord's household, she picks up an incense burner, symbolic of such Chinese traditions as ancestor worship; later, when Hsi-erh has joined the Red Army, she appears in uniform and, as the Shanghai analysis puts it, "shoulders a red-tasseled spear and marches down the revolutionary road" with the Eighth Route Army, thus progressing "from spontaneous resistance to conscious struggle."

Yet, by moving the plot and characters of The White-Haired Girl further and further away from their origins, preventing the mixed elements of human emotions to find expression, the final staging of the ballet has returned to the age-old element of legend. With the girl no longer lifelike, but a heroine of almost superhuman proportions, she has moved closer to the folkloric tradition of mythology. The heroic myth of the white-haired girl who roams the wild mountainside has transformed her into a Red Goddess with white hair.

ACT I

Time: Winter, 1935.
Place: Yangko Village in Hopei. There is a plain in front of the village, and hills behind.

SCENE I

[*It is New Year's Eve, and heavy snow is falling.* HSI-ERH, *daughter of the tenant peasant* YANG, *comes on through the snowstorm carrying maize flour.*]

HSI-ERH [*sings*]

> The north wind blows, the snow flakes whirl,
> A flurry of snow brings in New Year.
> Dad's been hiding a week because of his debt,
> Though it's New Year's Eve, he's still not back.
> Aunty's given me maize flour, and I'm waiting
> For Dad to come home and spend New Year.

[*Pushing open the door, she goes in. It is a humble room, containing a stove with a kitchen-god beside it and firewood and pots stacked in one corner. On the stove stands an oil lamp.*]

HSI-ERH   Now it's New Year's Eve, everybody's steaming maize cakes and dumplings, burning incense and pasting up door-gods for New Year. Dad has been away for a week, and still isn't back. We've nothing in the house for New Year. [*Pauses.*] There are only Dad and I at home: my mother died when I was three. My father cultivates one acre of land belonging to rich Landlord Huang. Dad works in the fields with me at his heels, in the wind and in the rain. . . . Every year we're behind with our rent, so just before New Year he always leaves home to escape being dunned. [*Anxiously.*] Now it's New Year's Eve, and getting quite dark—why isn't he back yet? Oh, I went to Aunty's house just now, and she gave me some maize flour which I'm going to mix with bean cake to make cakes for Dad to eat when he comes back. [*She fetches water, mixes the dough and starts making cakes.*]

[*The wind blows open the door.* HSI-ERH *runs over, but finds no one there.*]

HSI-ERH   Oh, it's the wind that blew open the door. [*Sings*]

> Wind whirls the snow against our door,
> Wind batters the door till it flies wide open.
> I'm waiting for Dad to come back home,
> And step inside the room again!

When Dad left, he took beancurd to sell. If he's sold the beancurd and brings back two pounds of flour, we could even eat dumplings. [*Sings*]

> I feel so restless waiting for Dad,
> But when he comes home I'll be happy.
> He'll bring some white flour back with him,
> And we'll have a really happy New Year!

[*She continues making cakes.*]

[*Enter* YANG *covered with snow. He has his pedlar's pole and kit for carrying beancurd, and over his shoulders the cloth used to cover the beancurd. He staggers along.*]

YANG [*sings*]

> Three miles through a snowstorm I've come home,
> After hiding a week from the duns.
> As long as I can get by this time,
> I don't mind putting up with hunger and cold.

[*After looking round apprehensively he knocks at the door.*] Hsi-erh! Open the door!

[HSI-ERH, *overjoyed, opens the door.*]

HSI-ERH   You're back, Dad!
YANG   Yes. [*He signs to her not to talk so loudly.*]
HSI-ERH [*brushing the snow from her father's clothes*]   It's snowing very hard outside, Dad! Look how thickly you're covered!
YANG   While I was away, Hsi-erh, did the landlord send anyone to press for payment?
HSI-ERH   On the 25th, Steward Mu came.
YANG [*taken aback*]   Oh? He came? What did he say?
HSI-ERH   When he found you were away he left again.
YANG   And then?
HSI-ERH   He hasn't been back since.

YANG [*rather incredulous*] Really?

HSI-ERH Yes, Dad.

YANG [*still unconvinced*] Are you sure?

HSI-ERH Why should I fool you, Dad?

YANG [*reassured*] Well, that's good. Listen, Hsi-erh, how strong the wind is!

HSI-ERH And it's snowing so hard!

YANG It's growing dark too.

HSI-ERH And the road is bad, Dad.

YANG I don't think Steward Mu will come now. I owe the landlord one and a half piculs, and my debt with the interest amounts to twenty-five dollars; but this time I've got by.

HSI-ERH [*happily*] So we've got by again, Dad!

YANG Hsi-erh, fetch some firewood so that I can dry myself. Have you still not finished that maize flour?

HSI-ERH I finished that long ago. This is some Aunty Wang gave me just now.

YANG So you've been to the mountain for firewood again in such cold.

HSI-ERH I went just now with Ta-chun. [*She fetches firewood.*] You must be hungry, Dad.

YANG [*warming himself by the fire*] I'm hungry all right. [*Chuckles.*]

HSI-ERH The cakes are mixed, I'm going to steam them.

YANG Just a minute, Hsi-erh. What do you think this is? [*Producing a wallet from his pocket.*]

HSI-ERH [*clutching at it in delighted surprise*] What is it, Dad?

YANG [*sings*]

> With the money I made by selling beancurd,
> I bought two pounds of flour at the fair;
> But I didn't want Landlord Huang to see it,
> So it's been in my wallet the last few days.

HSI-ERH [*sings*]

> With the money he made by selling beancurd,
> Dad bought two pounds of flour at the fair.
> He's brought it home to make dumplings,
> So now we'll have a happy New Year!

Dad, I'll call Aunty Wang over to make dumplings.

YANG [*stopping her*] Wait a bit, Hsi-erh! Look what this is.

HSI-ERH What, Dad?

YANG [*takes a thickly wrapped paper packet from his pocket. When all the paper wrappings are removed, a red ribbon is disclosed. While taking off the wrappings, he sings*]

> Other girls have flowers to wear,
> But your dad can't afford to buy flowers;
> So I bought two feet of red ribbon
> To tie in my Hsi-erh's hair!

[HSI-ERH *kneels before* YANG *who ties the ribbon in her hair.*]

HSI-ERH [*sings*]

> Other girls have flowers to wear,
> But Dad can't afford to buy flowers;
> So he's bought two feet of red ribbon
> For me to tie in my hair!

[HSI-ERH *stands up.*]

YANG [*laughs*] Turn round and let me have a look at you. [HSI-ERH *turns.*] Good. Presently we'll ask Ta-chun and Aunty Wang to come and have a look too. [HSI-ERH *tosses her head shyly yet coquettishly.*] Oh, I brought two door-gods too. Let's paste them up. [*He takes out two pictures.*]

HSI-ERH Door-gods! [*They paste them up and sing*]

> The door-gods ride roan horses!

YANG

> Pasted on the door they'll guard our home!

HSI-ERH

> The door-gods carry such big swords!

YANG

> They'll keep out all devils, great and small!

BOTH

> They'll keep out all devils, great and small!

YANG Aha, now neither big devils nor little devils can get in!

HSI-ERH I hope that rent-collector, Steward Mu, will be kept out too!

YANG Good girl, let's hope we have a peaceful New Year.

[*They close the door.*]

[*Enter* AUNTY WANG *from next door.*]

WANG Today Ta-chun bought two pounds of flour at the fair. I'm going to see if Uncle Yang has come back or not, and if he's back I'll ask them over to eat dumplings. [*Looks up.*] Ah, Uncle Yang must be back: the door-gods are up. [*Knocks.*] Hsi-erh! Open the door!

HSI-ERH Who is it?

WANG Your aunty.

HSI-ERH [*opens the door and* WANG *enters*] See, Aunty, Dad's back!

WANG How long have you been back, Uncle Yang?

YANG Just the time it takes to smoke one pipe.

HSI-ERH Aunty, Dad's bought two pounds of flour. I was just going to ask you over to make dumplings, and now here you are. Look, look!

WANG Ta-chun has bought two pounds of flour too, child, and for half a pint of rice he got a pound of pork as well. I was going to ask you both to our home.

HSI-ERH Have them over here!

WANG No, come on over.

HSI-ERH Do stay here, Aunty!

YANG Yes, stay here.

WANG Look at you both! Why stand on ceremony with us! [*Turns and whispers to* YANG.] Uncle, after New Year Hsi-erh and Ta-chun will be one year older. I'm waiting for you to say the word!

YANG [*afraid lest* HSI-ERH *hear, yet apparently eager for her to hear*] Don't be impatient, Aunty. When the right time comes we'll fix it up for the youngsters. Ah. . . .

HSI-ERH [*pretending not to understand, interrupts them*] Aunty, come and mix the dough.

YANG That's right: go and mix the dough.

[AUNTY, *chuckling, goes to mix dough.*]

[*Enter the landlord's steward,* MU. *He carries a lantern bearing the words, "The Huang Family—House of Accumulated Virtue."*]

MU [*sings*]

> Here I come collecting rent
> And dunning for debt!
> I've four treasures as tricks of the trade:
> Incense and a gun,

Crutches and a bag of tricks.
I burn the incense before the landlord,
I fire the gun to frighten tenants,
With my crutches I trip folk up,
And with my bag of tricks I cheat them!

This evening the landlord has sent me on an errand to the tenant peasant Yang—a secret errand, not for everybody's ears! The landlord has given me instructions to take Yang to him for a talk. [*Knocks.*] Old Yang, open up!

YANG   Who is it?

MU   I, Steward Mu!

[*The three inside start, and* AUNTY WANG *and* HSI-ERH *hastily hide the flour bowl.*]

MU   Old Yang, hurry up, and let me in!

[*There is no help for it but to open the door, and* MU *enters. All remain silent.*]

MU   [*makes a round of the room with his lantern.* HSI-ERH *hides behind* AUNTY WANG]   Old Yang! [*With unusual politeness.*] Are you ready for New Year?

YANG   Oh, Mr. Mu, we haven't lit the stove yet.

MU   Well, Old Yang, I have to trouble you. Landlord Huang wants you to come over for a talk.

YANG   Oh! [*Greatly taken aback.*] But . . . but . . . Mr. Mu, I can't pay the rent or the debt.

MU   Oh no, this time Landlord Huang doesn't want to see you either about the rent or your debt, but to discuss something important. It's New Year's Eve, and the landlord is in a good humor, so you can talk things over comfortably. Come along!

YANG   [*pleadingly*]   I . . . Mr. Mu. . . .

MU   [*pointing to the door*]   It's all right. Come along.

[YANG *has to go.*]

HSI-ERH   [*hastily*]   Dad, you. . . .

MU   [*shining the lantern on* HSI-ERH'S *face*]   Oh, don't worry, Hsi-erh. Landlord Huang will give you flowers to wear. Your dad will bring them back. [*Laughs.*]

WANG   [*putting the beancurd cloth over* YANG'S *shoulders*]   Put this over you, Uncle! The snow is heavier now. . . . When you get there, go down on your knees to Landlord Huang, and he surely won't spoil our New Year.

MU That's right. [*Pushes* YANG *out.*]

[YANG *looks back as he goes out.*]

HSI-ERH Dad! . . .

[YANG *sighs.*]

MU Hurry up! [*Pushes* YANG *off.*]

HSI-ERH Aunty, my dad! . . . [*Cries.*]

WANG [*putting her arms round her*] Your dad will be back soon. Come on, come to our house to mix dough.

[*They go out.*]

[*Curtain*]

SCENE II

LANDLORD HUANG's house.

The stage presents the entrance and a small room near the reception hall, furnished with a table and chairs. The candle in a tall candlestick on the table lights up an account book, abacus, inkstone, and old-fashioned Chinese pipe.

[*Sounds of laughter, clinking of wine cups, and the shouts of guests playing the finger-game are heard offstage.* LANDLORD HUANG *comes in, cheerfully tipsy, picking his teeth.*]

HUANG [*sings*]

> With feasting and wine we see the Old Year out,
> And hang lanterns and garlands to celebrate New Year's Eve!
> There are smiles on the faces of all our guests
> Who are drunk with joy, not wine.
> Our barns are bursting with grain,
> So who cares if the poor go hungry!

[*The servant* TA-SHENG *brings in water, and* HUANG *rinses his mouth.*]

HUANG Ta-sheng, go and tell your mistress I have a headache and can't drink with the guests. Ask her to entertain them.

TA-SHENG Very good, sir. [*Exit.*]

HUANG Well, I haven't lived in vain! I have nearly a hundred hectares of good land, and every year I collect at least a thousand piculs in rent. All my life I've known how to weight the scales in my own favor and manage things smoothly both at home and outside. During the last few years our family has done pretty well. Last year my wife died. My mother wants me to marry again, but I feel freer without a wife at home. Women are cheap as dirt. If one takes my fancy, like this one tonight, it's very easy to arrange.

[MU *leads* YANG *on.*]

YANG [*sings timidly*]

> The red lanterns under the eaves dazzle my eyes,
> And I don't feel easy in my mind.
> I wonder what he wants me for?
> Hsi-erh is waiting for me at home.

MU Old Yang, Landlord Huang is here. This way.

[*They enter the room.*]

HUANG [*politely*] So it's Old Yang. Sit down, won't you? [*Indicates a seat.*]

[YANG *dares not sit.*]

MU [*pouring tea*] Have some tea.

[YANG *remains silent.*]

HUANG Have you got everything ready for New Year, Old Yang?

YANG Well, sir, you know how it is. It's been snowing more than ten days, and we have no firewood or rice at home. I've not lit the stove for several days.

MU Bah! See here, Old Yang, there's no need to complain about poverty. Landlord Huang knows all about you, doesn't he?

HUANG Yes, Old Yang, I know you're not well off. But this year is passing, and I have to trouble you for the rent. [*Opens the account book.*] You cultivate one acre of my land. Last year you were five pecks short, this summer another four and a half pecks, in autumn another five and a half pecks.

MU [*reckoning on the abacus*] Five times five . . . two fives makes ten. . . .

HUANG   And remember the money you owe us. In my father's time your wife died, and you wanted a coffin, so you borrowed five dollars from us. The year before last you were sick and borrowed two and a half dollars. Last year another three dollars. At that time we agreed upon five per cent monthly interest. At compound interest it amounts to—

MU [*reckoning on the abacus*]   The interest on the interest amounts to —five times five, twenty-five. Two fives is ten. . . . Altogether twenty-five dollars fifty cents. Plus one and a half piculs' rent.

HUANG   Altogether twenty-five dollars and fifty cents, and one and a half piculs' rent. Right, Old Yang?

YANG   Yes, sir. . . . That's right.

HUANG   See, Old Yang, it's down here quite clearly in black and white, all correct and in order. This is New Year's Eve, Old Yang: the rent must be paid. If you've got it with you, so much the better: you pay the money and the debt is canceled. If you haven't got it with you, then go and find some way of raising it. Steward Mu will go with you.

MU   So it's up to you. I'm ready to go with you. Get going, Old Yang!

YANG [*pleadingly*]   Oh, Mr. Mu. . . . Sir. . . . Please let me off this time! I really have no money, I can't pay the rent or the debt. [*His voice falters.*] Sir. . . . Mr. Mu. . . .

HUANG   Now, Old Yang, that's no way to act. This is New Year's Eve. You're in difficulties, but I'm even worse off. You must clear the debt today.

YANG   Sir. . . .

HUANG   Come, you must be reasonable. Whatever you say, that debt must be paid.

MU   You heard what Landlord Huang said, Old Yang. He never goes back on his word. You must find a way, Old Yang.

YANG   What can I do, sir? An old man like me, with no relatives or rich friends—where can I get money? [*Beseechingly.*] Sir. . . .

HUANG [*seeing his opportunity, signals to* MU]   Well. . . .

MU [*to* YANG]   Well, listen, Old Yang, there is a way. Landlord Huang has thought of a way out for you, if you will take it. . . .

YANG   Tell me what it is, Mr. Mu.

MU   You go back, and bring your daughter Hsi-erh here as payment for the rent.

YANG [*horror-stricken*]   What!

MU   Go and fetch Hsi-erh here as payment for the rent.

YANG [*kneeling beseechingly*]   Sir, you can't do that! [*Sings*]

> The sudden demand for my girl as rent—
> Is like thunder out of a cloudless sky!
> Hsi-erh is the darling of my heart,
> I'd rather die than lose her!
> I beg you, sir,
> Take pity on us, please,
> And let me off this once!
> She's all I have,
> This is more than I can bear!

HUANG [*stands up in disgust*]   Well, I'm doing you a good turn, Old Yang. Bring Hsi-erh to our house to spend a few years in comfort, and won't she be better off than in your home, where she has to go cold and hungry and has such a hard time of it? Besides, we are not going to treat Hsi-crh badly here. And this way your debt will be canceled too. Isn't that killing two birds with one stone? [*Laughs.*]

YANG   No, sir, you can't do that. . . .

MU   Well, Old Yang, it seems to me you poor people try to take advantage of the kindness of the rich. Landlord Huang wants to help your family. Just think, Hsi-erh coming here will have the time of her life. She will live on the fat of the land, dress like a lady and only have to stretch out her hand for food or drink! That would be much better than in your house where she goes cold and hungry. In fact Landlord Huang is quite distressed by all you make Hsi-erh put up with. So you'd better agree.

YANG   But, sir, Mr. Mu, this child Hsi-erh is the apple of my eye. Her mother died when she was three, and I brought her up as best I could. I'm an old man now and I have only this daughter. She's both daughter and son to me. I can't let her go . . . sir! [*Turning to* HUANG.]

HUANG [*adamant*]   Bah!

[YANG *turns to* MU *who also ignores him.*]

HUANG [*after a while*]   I'm not going to wait any longer, Old Yang! Make your choice. Give me your girl or pay the debt.

MU   Old Yang, Landlord Huang is in a good humor now. Don't offend him, or it'll be the worse for you.

HUANG [*angrily*]   That's enough! Make out a statement! Tell him to send the girl tomorrow! [*Starts angrily off.*]

YANG [*stepping forward to clutch at him*] Don't go, sir!

HUANG Get away! [*Pushing* YANG *aside, he hurries off.*]

MU All right, better agree, Old Yang. [*Goes to the table to write a statement.*]

YANG [*barring* MU's *way wildly*] You . . . you mustn't do that! [*Sings*]

> What have I done wrong,
> That I should be forced to sell my child?
> I've had a hard time of it all my life,
> But I little thought it would come to this!

MU Get wise, Old Yang. Don't keep on being such a fool. You've got to agree to this today, whether you like it or not! [*Pushes* YANG *aside and takes up a pen to write the statement.*]

YANG [*seizing* MU's *hand*] No! [*Sings*]

> Heaven just kills the grass with a single root,
> The flood just carries off the one-plank bridge.
> She's the only child I ever had,
> And I can't live without her!

MU [*furiously*] Don't be a fool! Presently if you make the master lose his temper, it'll be no joke!

YANG I . . . I . . . I'll go somewhere to plead my case! [*About to rush out.*]

MU [*banging the table*] Where are you going to plead your case? The county magistrate is our friend, this is the yamen door; where are you going to plead your case!

YANG [*aghast*] I . . . I. . . .

MU It's no use, Old Yang! You're no match for him. I advise you to make out a statement and put your mark on it to settle the business. [*Writes.*]

YANG [*stopping him again*] You . . . you. . . .

[*Enter* HUANG *impatiently.*]

HUANG [*in a towering rage*] Why are you still so stubborn, Old Yang! Let me tell you, it's going to be done today, whether you like it or not! [*To* MU.] Hurry up and make out a statement for him.

YANG [*at a loss*] Ah!

MU [*reading as he writes*] "Tenant Yang owes Landlord Huang one and a half piculs of grain and twenty-five dollars fifty cents. Since he is too poor to pay, he wants to sell his daughter Hsi-erh to the land-lord to cancel the debt. Both parties agree and will not go back on their word. Since verbal agreements are inconclusive, this statement is drawn up as evidence. . . . Signed by the two parties, Landlord Huang and Tenant Yang, and the witness, Steward Mu. . . ." Right, talk is empty but writing is binding. Come on, Old Yang! Put your mark on it!

YANG [*frenziedly*] You can't do this, sir!

HUANG What! All right, then tell Liu to tie him up and take him to the county court!

YANG [*panic-stricken*] What, send me to the county court! Oh, sir!

MU [*seizing* YANG's *hand*] Put your mark on it! [*Presses his fingers down.*]

YANG [*startled to see the ink on his finger*] Oh! [*Falls to the ground.*]

MU Aha, one fingerprint has cleared the debt of all these years. . . . [*Hands the document to* HUANG.]

[HUANG *makes a gesture to* MU.]

MU [*ascertains that* YANG *is still breathing*] He's all right.

HUANG Old Yang, you'd better go back now, and bring Hsi-erh here tomorrow. [*To* MU.] Give him that document.

MU [*helping* YANG *up*] This one is yours, here. . . . [*Hands him the document.*] Tomorrow send Hsi-erh here to give New Year's greet-ings to Landlord Huang's family. Tell her to come here to spend a happy New Year. Go on. [*Pushes* YANG *out, then shuts the door.*]

[YANG *collapses outside the gate in the snowstorm.*]

HUANG Old Mu, you take a few men there early tomorrow. We don't want the old fellow to go back and decide to ignore the debt and run away. In that case we'd lose both girl and money.

MU Right.

HUANG Another thing. For heaven's sake don't let word get about: it wouldn't sound well on New Year's Day. If those wretches spread the news, even though we've right on our side it would be hard to ex-plain. If anyone questions you, say my mother wants to see Hsi-erh and you're fetching her to give New Year's greetings to the old lady.

MU Very good. [*Exit.*]

HUANG Ah! The only way to get rich is at the expense of the poor. Without breaking Old Yang, I couldn't get Hsi-erh!

YANG [*comes to himself outside the gate, and gets up*]   Heaven! Murderous Heaven! [*Sings*]

> Heaven kills folks without batting an eye!
> The landlord's house is Hell!
> I'm an old fool, an old fool,
> Why did I put my mark on that paper just now?
> I've gone and sold my only daughter,
> Your dad's let you down, Hsi-erh!
> You're happy, waiting at home for me for New Year,
> But I'm in despair!
> With this hand I've sold my only child,
> How can I face you when I get home?

[*He staggers off.*]

[*Curtain*]

SCENE III

[YANG's *old friend, the tenant peasant* CHAO, *enters with a basket containing a small piece of meat and a pot of wine. He is taking the path by the village.*]

CHAO [*sings*]

> In the gale the snow whirls high,
> Nine homes out of ten are dimly lit;
> Not that we don't celebrate New Year,
> But the poor have a different New Year from the rich.
> There's wine and meat in the landlord's house,
> While we tenants have neither rice nor flour!

[*He hears sounds of merriment from* LANDLORD HUANG's *house in the distance.*] Bah! At New Year the rich could die of laughing, while the poor could die of despair! Old Yang's been away a week to escape paying his debt, but he ought to be back now. I've bought four ounces of wine to drink with him. Getting his troubles off his chest is the poor man's way of spending New Year. [*Sings*]

> Just as officials are all in league,
> The poor stick together too.

I'm going to spend New Year's Eve with Old Yang,
To share four ounces of cheap wine with a friend.

[*Exit.*]

[*Enter* YANG.]

YANG [*sings*]

> I feel as befuddled as if I were drunk,
> In such a snowstorm where can I go?
> The deed in my pocket is like a knife
> That's going to kill my own flesh and blood.

Where are you, Hsi-erh? You don't know what your dad. . . . [*Falls.*]

CHAO [*enters and sees a prostrate figure. When he goes to help him up he recognizes* YANG] So it's you, Old Yang?

YANG Who's that?

CHAO It's Old Chao.

YANG Oh, Old Chao, friend. . . .

CHAO [*raising him*] What happened to you, Old Yang?

YANG Ah! [*For an instant he appears to be in a frenzy, but then fights down his feelings.*] Nothing. . . . No, nothing. Just now I went to the rich man's house. . . .

CHAO Oh, so you were badly treated up there. It's snowing faster, let's go back now and talk it over. We'll have a good talk. [*Helps* YANG *along.*]

YANG Talk. . . . Talk. . . . Talk it over. . . . Have a good talk.

CHAO Here, how is it the door is closed? [*Opens the door and helps* YANG *in.*] Why is there no light? [*Gropes for the matches to light the lamp.*] Where are you, Hsi-erh?

YANG [*hearing* HSI-ERH's *name*] Ah, Hsi-erh, Hsi-erh!

CHAO What is it, Old Yang?

YANG [*controlling himself*] Nothing, Hsi-erh has gone with Aunty Wang to make dumplings.

CHAO So this New Year's Eve you have dumplings to eat? Your daughter must be happy. Old Yang, look, I've got a pound of pork for you, for you two to eat tomorrow. And I've brought four ounces of wine. Tonight the two of us can drink a few cups. [*Heats the wine.*]

YANG Right, drink. Drink a few cups. . . . Drink a few cups. [*Sits by the stove. They drink.*]

CHAO What happened, Old Yang, in the landlord's house just now?

YANG That . . . nothing . . . Old Chao.

CHAO What is it? Tell me. I'm your friend.

YANG Ah, yes. . . .

CHAO Go on, Old Yang! What's there to be afraid of?

YANG I. . . .

CHAO You'd try the patience of a saint, the way you never take other people into your confidence, but keep all your troubles to yourself! But we two have always talked frankly, and tonight you mustn't brood. Come on, Old Yang, out with it!

YANG Very well, I'll tell you. I came home today, hoping to have escaped paying the debt. Then Steward Mu called me to the landlord's house.

CHAO Yes.

YANG Landlord Huang opened the account book and Mu reckoned on the abacus, and insisted on my clearing the debt. I couldn't pay it, so he. . . .

CHAO So what?

YANG He wanted Hsi-erh as payment.

CHAO Did you agree?

YANG I. . . . No.

CHAO [*excitedly*] Good for you, Old Yang! You did right. To let Hsi-erh go to his house in payment for the debt would be like throwing your child to the wolves. As the proverb says, "Buddha needs incense, and a man needs self-respect." That's something we must fight for. You've shown the right spirit, Old Yang. [*Raises his cup.*] Come on, Old Yang, drink up.

YANG [*in agony of mind*] Old Chao . . . Old Chao, you know tomorrow—no, next year—next year the landlord will still want Hsi-erh to go.

CHAO Next year? Well, Old Yang, I'm considering that. Next year I'm not going to stay here. I'm going north.

YANG Where? Going north? Ah, even a poor home is hard to give up. If we leave, we'll starve.

CHAO Not necessarily. Here we cultivate these small plots of poor land, and can't live anyway, what with the rent. This year I worked fifty days for the landlord, but even so I didn't clear all the rent for the melon field; yesterday he was pressing me again. Bah! Why should an old man like me, all alone and without children, end my days on these small fields? I think we'd better take Hsi-erh to the north, until she's grown up. At our age, we can't expect to live long, and our death doesn't matter; but we mustn't ruin the child's life.

YANG [*sadly, weighing his words*] Our death doesn't matter, but we mustn't ruin the child's life.

CHAO Think it over, Old Yang! I consider next year, as soon as spring comes, we should take our things and go. [*Raises his cup again.*] Drink up!

YANG Ah!

[*Enter* AUNTY WANG, HSI-ERH, *and* WANG TA-CHUN, *carrying the dumplings.*]

WANG Has Uncle Yang come back, Ta-chun?

TA-CHUN I saw him coming out of the landlord's house. [*To* HSI-ERH.] Hsi-erh, the path is slippery, let me take that.

HSI-ERH I can carry it, Ta-chun.

[YANG, *hearing voices outside, hastily wipes his eyes and pretends all is well.*]

HSI-ERH [*approaching, sees a light through the door*] Aunty, I think Dad is really back. [*They enter.*]

HSI-ERH [*joyfully*] Dad, you're back!

TA-CHUN Uncle, you're back!

WANG Uncle Chao, you're here too. . . .

CHAO We two have been chatting quite a time.

TA-CHUN Uncle, what happened in the landlord's house?

YANG I went, and couldn't pay the rent or settle the debt, so he. . . .

ALL What did he do?

YANG Nothing . . . I . . . went down on my knees to him, that's all, and then came back.

TA-CHUN Really, Uncle?

HSI-ERH Really, Dad? That was all?

YANG Certainly, child. Have I ever deceived you?

CHAO That's right.

WANG [*wiping her eyes*] Thank heaven! All's well then, and we can enjoy New Year. Uncle Chao, we have a few pounds of flour not taken by the landlord, and we made some dumplings. You and Uncle Yang come and eat.

CHAO Right.

YANG Yes.

WANG Ta-chun, empty out the garlic from that bowl, and give it to Uncle Yang. Hsi-erh, you take this one to Uncle Chao.

TA-CHUN [*handing the bowl to* YANG] Try our dumplings, Uncle.

[YANG *takes the bowl in silence.*]

[*They eat.*]

HSI-ERH [*sings*]

> Dad's come home after hiding from the duns!

TA-CHUN and WANG

> We're eating dumplings for New Year!

ALL

> Old and young we're sitting around,
> Enjoying a very happy New Year!
> Enjoying a happy New Year!

WANG

> The snow's been falling for a week or more,

ALL

> But we're all safely here together!

WANG

> Hoping by the time our young folk grow up,

ALL

> We can all pass some years in peace!
> Yes, pass some years in peace!

HSI-ERH   Dad, you aren't eating!

YANG   Yes, I am.

CHAO [*reminiscently*]   Ta-chun and Hsi-erh, today we're celebrating New Year and eating dumplings, so let me tell you a story about dumplings. It was 1930, the thirteenth day of the fifth moon, the day when the War God sharpened his sword. There was a fine rain falling. That day troops appeared from the southern mountains. They were called the Red Army.

WANG   So you're harping back to that, Uncle. Better eat now.

HSI-ERH   Let Uncle Chao talk, Aunty! I like to hear.

CHAO   Yes, they had red all over them, their red sashes bound crosswise from shoulder to waist; and they were all ruddy-faced, hefty fellows, so they were called the Red Army. They went south of the city to the Chao Village. I was there then, when the Red Army came and killed that devil, Landlord Chao. Then they distributed the grain and land among the poor, so on the thirteenth of the fifth moon all poor folk had basketfuls of white flour, and we all ate dumplings. In every house I went to then they offered me dumplings to eat. . . . [*Chuckles.*]

TA-CHUN   Where did that Red Army go to then?

CHAO   They went to the city, but they hadn't held it long when some Green Army arrived; then the Red Army went to the Great North Mountain, and never came down again. And after the Red Army left, the poor had a bad time of it once more.

TA-CHUN   Tell us, Uncle, will the Red Army be coming back?

CHAO   I think so.

HSI-ERH   When will they come?

CHAO   In good time, a day will come when the War God sharpens his sword again and the Red Army comes back. [*Chuckles.*]

WANG   Don't keep on talking but eat now. [*To* YANG.] Uncle, eat. There's plenty more.

HSI-ERH   Dad, have some more.

YANG [*holding the bowl, unable to eat, after a painful pause*]   Ah, Hsi-erh, isn't Aunty good?

HSI-ERH   Yes, she is!

YANG   Aunty, isn't Hsi-erh good?

WANG   She's a good child.

YANG   Hsi-erh, tell me, is your dad good?

HSI-ERH   What a question! Of course you are, Dad!

YANG   No, no. . . . Dad's no good.

WANG   What's got into you, Uncle Yang? Why are you talking like this?

CHAO   We've been drinking, and he may have had a drop too much. . . . [*Chuckles.*] It goes without saying you two are both good, Hsi-erh and Ta-chun. It won't be long now! [*Laughs.*]

[HSI-ERH *turns away shyly.*]

WANG   Stop talking and eat!

YANG   Yes, eat. . . .

[*They all eat.*]

HSI-ERH [*sings*]

Dad's come home after hiding from the duns!

TA-CHUN and WANG

> We're eating dumplings for New Year!

ALL

> Old and young we're sitting around,
> Enjoying a very happy New Year!
> Enjoying a happy New Year!

WANG

> The snow's been falling for a week or more,

ALL

> But we're all here safely together!

WANG

> Hoping by the time our young folk grow up,

ALL

> We can all pass some years in peace!
> Yes, pass some years in peace!

[*In a state of mental agony,* YANG *cannot keep still, so he withdraws to a corner, where he clutches the document in his pocket with trembling hands.*]

WANG What are you doing, Uncle Yang! Come and eat.

YANG [*startled*] I'm looking, looking. . . . Ah, it's empty, my pocket. Not a single coin. I can't even give the two youngsters money for New Year.

WANG Come on. To have dumplings is good enough. Come and eat, Uncle.

YANG I . . . I'll eat later.

WANG Uncle Chao, have some more.

CHAO I've had enough.

WANG [*to* TA-CHUN *and* HSI-ERH] How about you two?

TA-CHUN and HSI-ERH We've had enough.

WANG Then let's clear away. [*They clear the table.*] Uncle Yang has been on his feet all day and is tired, he should rest now.

YANG [*mechanically*] Rest now.

WANG We would go on chatting forever, but we can talk again tomorrow. Tomorrow Ta-chun will come to give you New Year greetings.

CHAO I'll be going too. Hsi-erh, take good care of your dad. Old Yang, tomorrow I'll come and wish you a happy New Year. I'm off now.

YANG Good night, Old Chao.

[*Exit* CHAO].

TA-CHUN We're going too, Uncle.

YANG See your mother back carefully, Ta-chun.

HSI-ERH Are you going, Aunty!

WANG Good night. [*She and* TA-CHUN *go out.*]

[HSI-ERH *starts to close the door.*]

TA-CHUN [*at the door*] Hsi-erh, Uncle is tired! Get him to rest early.

HSI-ERH Yes. [*Closes the door.* WANG *and* TA-CHUN *go out.*]

YANG You'd better go to bed, Hsi-erh.

HSI-ERH So had you, Dad.

YANG Your dad . . . your dad will see the New Year in.

HSI-ERH I'll stay up too.

YANG Then put on some more firewood.

[HSI-ERH *adds wood to the stove and sits by the fire.*]

YANG [*coughing*] Hsi-erh, your dad is old and good for nothing.

HSI-ERH Whatever do you mean, Dad! Come and warm yourself!

[*They sit by the stove. The silence is oppressive, while snow falls outside. Time passes.*]

YANG Are you asleep, Hsi-erh?

HSI-ERH No, Dad. . . .

YANG I'll trim the lamp. [*He trims the lamp.*] [*Presently the lamp on the stove burns low, and* HSI-ERH *falls asleep.*] The wick is burnt out, and the oil is used up. [*The lamp goes out.*] The light is out too . . . Hsi-erh! [HSI-ERH *is sound asleep.*]

YANG Asleep? Hsi-erh! [*Sings*]

> Hsi-erh, my child, you're sleeping,
> Dad calls you, but you don't hear.
> You can't imagine, as you dream,
> The unforgivable thing I've done.

Hsi-erh, Dad has wronged you! Aunty Wang, I've wronged you! Old Chao, I've wronged you! I made a statement and put my mark on it. . . . When Hsi-erh's mother died, she said, "Bring Hsi-erh up as best you can." And I brought her up. Hsi-erh has had a hard time of it with me for seventeen years. Today . . . I've wronged Hsi-erh's mother, I've sold our child. . . . Tomorrow the landlord will take her away. Neither the living nor the dead, neither human beings nor ghosts can ever forgive me! I'm an old fool, a criminal! But I can't let you go! I'll have it out with them! [*He runs wildly out, to be buffeted by the wind and snow.*] Ah, magistrates, landlords! . . . Lackeys. . . . Bailiffs! . . . Where can I go? Where can I turn? [*He clutches the document.*] Ah! [*Sings*]

> Magistrates, rich men—you tigers and wolves!
> Because I owed rent and was in debt,
> You forced me to write a deed,
> Selling my child. . . .
> The north wind's blowing, snow's falling thick and fast!
> Where can I go? Where can I fly?
> What way out is there for me?

[*He pauses, bewildered.*] Ah, I still have some lye for making beancurd—I'll drink that! [*He drinks it.*] Now I'll drink some cold water. . . . [*He takes off his padded jacket to cover* HSI-ERH, *then rushes outside, falls on the snow and dies.*]

[*Crackers sound in the village, signaling the arrival of the New Year.*]

[*Curtain*]

SCENE IV

[*Crackers sound and* TA-CHUN *comes in gaily.*]

TA-CHUN Uncle Yang! Uncle Yang! I've come to wish you a happy New Year! [*He suddenly stumbles on the corpse.*] Oh! [*Clearing the snow from the face of the dead man he recognizes* YANG.] Oh! Uncle Yang! You! What's happened? [*He hurries to the door and knocks.*] Hsi-erh, Hsi-erh! Open the door, quick! [*Hastily turning toward the backstage.*] Mother! Mother! Come quick! Come quick!
HSI-ERH [*wakened from her sleep*] Dad! Dad! [*She looks for her father.*]
TA-CHUN Hsi-erh! [*Pushing open the door.*] Hsi-erh! Look! Your dad—

HSI-ERH   Has something happened to Dad? [*Runs out, and seeing her father's body, falls on it and cries.*] Dad! Dad!

TA-CHUN   What happened, Hsi-erh?

HSI-ERH   [*cries. Then sings*]

> Yesterday evening when Dad came back,
> He was worried but wouldn't tell me why.
> This morning he's lying in the snow!
> Why, Dad, why?

TA-CHUN   [*helplessly turning toward the backstage*]   Mother, come quick!

[*Enter* AUNTY WANG.]

WANG   What is it, Ta-chun?

TA-CHUN   Mum, look at Uncle Yang! He—[*Pointing to the corpse.*]

WANG   What's happened to Uncle Yang? [*She kneels beside the corpse and touches it, hoping the dead man will wake up.*] Ta-chun, go and call Uncle Chao and the others at once.

[*Exit* TA-CHUN.]

WANG   [*finding the body stiff and lifeless, wails*]   Uncle Yang! Uncle Yang!

HSI-ERH   Daddy! [*Cries.*]

[*Enter* TA-CHUN *with* UNCLE CHAO, LI, *and* TA-SO.]

CHAO   What's happened?

TA-SO   What happened, Ta-chun?

LI   It's Old Yang.

WANG   [*crying as she tells the story*]   Friends, last night when he came back he was all right. Who could imagine this morning he would— [*Unable to proceed.*]

CHAO   [*stoops and examines* YANG]   He's drunk lye.

HSI-ERH   Daddy!

CHAO   [*noticing the dead man's clenched fist*]   Ah! [*He starts forcing open the fingers.* TA-CHUN *and* TA-SO *help him, and they take the deed of sale.*]

LI   [*reading the deed.*]   Tenant Yang owes Landlord Huang rent. . . . Since he is too poor to pay, he wants to sell his daughter Hsi-erh to. . . . [*Unable to finish he lets the deed fall to the ground. They are all horror-stricken.*]

WANG   Merciful heavens! This. . . .
HSI-ERH [*shrieks*]   Oh, Dad! [*Sings*]

> Suddenly hearing that I've been sold,
> I feel as if fire were burning me!
> Could it be Dad didn't love me?
> Or thought me a bad daughter, could it be?

CHAO [*addressing the corpse indignantly*]   Old Yang, last night you only told me half! You shouldn't have died! Because you wouldn't leave your little patch of land, you let them hound you to death!

TA-SO [*loudly*]   Last night they took away my donkey! Today for this paltry rent they drove Uncle Yang to suicide! They won't let the poor live! It's too much! [*Too angry to speak, he turns to rush out.*]

TA-CHUN [*unable to suppress his anger*]   They killed Uncle Yang, and they make Hsi-erh. . . . I'm going to have it out with them! [*He rushes after* TA-SO.]

[CHAO *and* LI *pull* TA-SO *back, while* AUNTY WANG *restrains* TA-CHUN.]

WANG   Ta-chun! Ta-chun!

LI   It's no good, Ta-so, Ta-chun! It's there in black and white! Uncle Yang put his mark on it.

TA-CHUN   His mark? They forced him, didn't they? I'll send in an appeal!

TA-SO   Right!

LI [*sighs*]   To whom can you appeal? The district head? The magistrate? Aren't they hand in glove with the rich? I think we'd better accept it, if we can.

TA-SO   Accept it? I can't!

TA-CHUN   How are we poor folk to live! [*Stamps his foot and strikes his head in despair.*]

CHAO   Ta-chun, Ta-so, blustering is no use. Time's getting on, and the landlord will soon be here to fetch the girl; we'd better hurry to prepare the dead for burial, so that Hsi-erh can at least attend her father's funeral. We all know what goes on nowadays, but they've got the whip hand. Where can we turn to look for justice? . . . [*To* HSI-ERH.] This has happened today because we old people are no good: we've done you a great wrong, child! Ta-chun, Ta-so, we'd better first bury the dead! Aunty Wang, get ready quickly, and put Hsi-erh in mourning!

[*They bow their heads in silence, wiping their eyes in sorrow and anger.*]

[*Enter* STEWARD MU *with thugs.*]

MU A happy New Year, friends! I wish you good luck and prosperity!

[*They are all taken aback.*]

MU [*seeing the dead man in their midst, realizes what has happened, but feigns astonishment*] Ah! Who's that?

LI It's Old Yang.

MU What, Old Yang! Why, last night he was all right, how could he . . . ? Well, well. . . . [*Feigning sympathy.*] Who could have thought it? Such an honest fellow. . . . [*Turns.*] Well then . . . let us all help, and prepare his funeral. . . . Oh, Hsi-erh is here. Let's do it this way: let Hsi-erh come with me to beg the landlord for a coffin for her father. Come on, Hsi-erh. [*Tries to lead* HSI-ERH *off.*]

TA-CHUN [*unable to contain his anger, darts forward and shakes his fist at* MU, *who steps aside*] I know why you've come. You shan't take her!

TA-SO [*stepping forward too*] You dare!

THUGS [*stepping forward to cover* TA-CHUN *and* TA-SO *with their guns*] Hey, there! Don't move!

MU [*changing his tune*] All right, let's put our cards on the table. Old Yang has sold Hsi-erh to Landlord Huang! Here's the deed. [*Taking the deed from his pocket.*] Old Yang put his mark on it, so justice and reason are on our side. . . . Sorry, Wang Ta-chun, but Hsi-erh belongs to the landlord now.

TA-CHUN Steward Mu, you dog aping your master, bullying the poor!

MU So! You are cursing me? Very well, fellow, just wait and see!

CHAO Mr. Mu, this is too much. The child's father has just died, and you want to carry her off, on New Year's Day too.

MU Too much? [*Pointing to the deed.*] Here's our reason. Better mind your own business.

WANG Mr. Mu, let the child attend the funeral first. . . .

MU Can't be done. Landlord Huang wants the girl taken back immediately. [*Sizing up the situation, he adopts a more conciliatory tone.*] Well, actually I can't make any decisions; you must talk to Landlord Huang. Still, I think Hsi-erh will enjoy herself later on. [*He takes hold of* HSI-ERH *again.*] Come on, Hsi-erh.

TA-CHUN and TA-SO   You! . . . [*They want to rush forward again, but are stopped by the guns of the thugs.*]

[AUNTY WANG *timidly steps in front of* TA-CHUN.]

CHAO [*signing to them to stop*]   Ta-chun! Ta-so!

HSI-ERH [*shaking off* MU's *hand, darts back to* CHAO *and* AUNTY WANG] Uncle! Aunty! [*Rushing to the dead man, she cries bitterly.*] Daddy! Daddy! . . .

MU [*pulling at* HSI-ERH *again*]   Well, Hsi-erh, we're all mortal. It's no use crying, better come with me. [*Pulls hard.*]

HSI-ERH [*frightened, screams and struggles*]   Uncle! Aunty!

WANG   Steward Mu, do let the child put on mourning for her father.

MU   All right, put on mourning.

[AUNTY WANG *goes inside and fetches out a piece of white cloth which she ties round* HSI-ERH's *head.*]

CHAO [*holding* HSI-ERH, *speaks to the dead man*]   Old Yang, Hsi-erh can't attend your funeral today. This is all the fault of us old folk, we've done her a wrong. [*To* HSI-ERH.] Come, Hsi-erh, kowtow to your father.

HSI-ERH   Uncle! Aunty! [*Kneels and kowtows.*]

[MU *drags* HSI-ERH *off crying and screaming, followed by* AUNTY WANG. TA-CHUN *and* TA-SO *want to pursue them, but are stopped by* CHAO.]

CHAO   Ta-chun, Ta-so. . . . They have the whip hand, what can we do? Let us remember how many people the Huang family has killed. Their day of reckoning will come! A day will come when power changes hands. . . . [*They sob.*] Don't cry, but come and bury the dead!

[*They carry* YANG *off.*]

[*Curtain*]

ACT II

Time: As in the last scene.

The Buddhist shrine of LANDLORD HUANG's mother. Big, bright candles are lit, and incense smoke wreathes the air.

[MRS. HUANG *comes in bearing incense sticks in her hand.*]

MRS. HUANG Yesterday my son told me our tenant Yang was sending his daughter here as payment for the rent. Why hasn't she come to see me yet? [*Sings*]

> At New Year our family gains in wealth and we old folk in
>   longevity,
> Thanks to the virtues of our ancestors and holy Buddha's
>   protection.
> I carry incense to the shrine where bright candles are lit on
>   the altar,
> And bow three times in all sincerity.
> One stick of incense I offer Ju-lai of the Western Heaven—
> May we grow wealthy, and our rents increase!
> The second stick I offer Kuan-yin of the Southern Seas—
> Grant peace in the four seasons, and may all our house grow
>   rich!
> The third stick I offer Chang Hsien, giver of children—
> Protect us, and may we increase and multiply!

[*She closes the door and sits down.*]

Now money is depreciating: one maidservant costs so many years' rent! Last year was better, when we bought that girl Hung-lu for only eight dollars; while that girl bought by the northern household only cost five dollars and fifty cents. But this year everything is expensive!

[MU *comes on with* HSI-ERH.]

MU Come along, Hsi-erh. [*Sings*]

> What a queer girl you are!
> Why act so strangely here?
> Just now, when we saw the landlord,

You wouldn't look up or say a word,
And when he gave you a flower,
You wouldn't wear it!
Now that we're going to see the old lady,
You'll have to be on your best behavior!

Look happy now!

[HSI-ERH *gives a frightened sob.*]

MU   Don't cry! If you make the old lady angry, even with her fingers she can scratch holes in your face. [*They enter the room.*] Ah, Mrs. Huang, the Yang family girl, Hsi-erh, has come to give you her New Year greetings.

MRS. HUANG   Oh, it's Old Mu. Come in. [*Enter* MU *and* HSI-ERH.]

MU   [*to* HSI-ERH]   Kowtow to the mistress! [*Pushes her down on her knees.*]

MRS. HUANG   All right, get up.

MU   [*raising* HSI-ERH]   Get up, and let the mistress look at you.

MRS. HUANG   H'm, a good-looking child. Come over here.

MU   [*to* HSI-ERH]   Go on. [*He drags her again.*]

MRS. HUANG   The child looks intelligent. What's her name?

[HSI-ERH *remains silent.*]

MU   Answer the mistress. You're called . . . called Hsi-erh.

MRS. HUANG   Hsi-erh? Well, that's an auspicious name.* It needn't be altered much to match Hung-fu and Hung-lu; we'll just add the word Hung in front. Let her be called Hung-hsi.

MU   [*to* HSI-ERH]   Thank the mistress for your new name. From now on you won't be called Hsi-erh but Hung-hsi.

MRS. HUANG   How old is the child?

[HSI-ERH *remains silent.*]

MU   Seventeen.

MRS. HUANG   Ah, seventeen. Good girl, better than Hung-fu. Hung-fu is a regular scarecrow, she looks like nothing on earth! This girl is good. Old Mu, presently you tell my son, I shall keep her with me.

MU   Oh! That's too good for her.

MRS. HUANG   Well, her family is poor. Think of the hardships her father

---

* "Hsi" means "joy."

made her suffer—nothing to eat, no clothes to wear. Now that you've come to our house, Hung-hsi, you'll live in comfort. Are you glad?

[HSI-ERH *remains silent.*]

MU   Speak up. . . . You are glad, you are glad! You are a lucky girl!

MRS. HUANG   See, the girl is dressed like a beggar! Old Mu, tell my maid Chang to change her clothes and bring her cakes to eat.

MU [*calling*]   Ta-sheng! [*There is a response offstage.*] The mistress orders Chang to change Hung-hsi's clothes and bring cakes for Hung-hsi!

VOICE OFFSTAGE   "Yes, mistress! Visitors have come from the north village to pay their respects to you and Landlord Huang."

MRS. HUANG   All right. [*Stands up. To* HSI-ERH.] Hung-hsi, soon Chang will come to change your clothes and look after you. [*Starting out.*] Ah, whoever does good deeds in his life will become a Buddha and go to the Western Paradise. [MRS HUANG *and* MU *leave.*]

VOICES OFF   "We've come to pay our respects to Mrs. Huang!" "We've come to wish Landlord Huang a happy New Year!"

HSI-ERH   Oh dear! [*Sings*]

> Oh, Dad!
> I hear so many voices here,
> I'm all of a tremble!
> So many bolts, so many doors!
> I call my dad, but he doesn't answer.
> Who'll wear mourning for my dad?
> Who'll cry at his funeral?

[*Enter* TA-SHENG *holding a plate, and* CHANG *with clothes.*]

TA-SHENG   So this is Hung-hsi. Here, come and eat your cake.

CHANG   You must be hungry, have something to eat.

TA-SHENG   Hurry. I have to go and look after the guests.

[*Out of nervousness* HSI-ERH *drops the plate and breaks it.*]

TA-SHENG   What a bad girl you are, breaking a plate on New Year's Day! I'm going to tell the old lady.

CHANG   Don't, Ta-sheng! [*Picks up the broken pieces.*] The old lady's in a good temper today; don't make her angry. The girl's just come, she doesn't know how to behave. Let her off this time.

TA-SHENG   Huh, little wretch! We'll wait and see how she behaves in future. [*Exit.*]

CHANG Hung-hsi, come with me to change your clothes. [*Taking her arm.*] Child, this is not your own home, not like with your own parents; you'll have to fit in with these people's ways. . . . Come, don't be afraid. I'm Aunty Chang, I'm a servant too. We shall be together a long time; if there's anything you can't do, I'll help you. If you have any trouble, let me know. . . . Come now, come and change your clothes. [*Exeunt.*]

[*Curtain*]

SCENE II

Time One month later.
Place At the gate of AUNTY WANG's house.

[*Enter* TA-CHUN.]

TA-CHUN [*sings*]

> Uncle Yang's been dead for a month, and Hsi-erh
> In the landlord's house is treated like dirt;
> My mother's in tears the whole of the time,
> And it's harder than ever to make ends meet.
> How can I ever get even with them?
> My whole heart seems to burn with hate!
> When I went just now to look for Hsi-erh,
> Huang's thugs wouldn't let me in at the gate!

[*Stamps.*] Today I wanted to go and see Hsi-erh in my spare time, but that gateman saw me. . . . It was Ta-so who suggested that some day, when I had time, I should fetch Hsi-erh out; but although I've been there several times, I haven't been able to see her. Yesterday Landlord Huang pressed me to pay my debt, saying if I didn't pay they'd evict me, and drive me away. This evening Steward Mu's coming again. Bah! [*He pushes open the door and goes in.*] Mother! [*No one answers.*] She must have gone over to see Uncle Chao. When she gets back there'll be more sighing and sobbing. [*Enter* TA-SO.]
TA-SO Ta-chun!
TA-CHUN Who is it?
TA-SO Me! [*Coming forward.*] My! That bastard Mu has got his knife into us! Just now when I was out, he went to my home and took away

five pints of kaoliang seeds, driving my mother nearly frantic. Some day that bastard's going to get what's coming to him. . . .

TA-CHUN I've just come back from the Huang house. It was no good, I still couldn't see Hsi-erh. . . . [*Pauses.*] Presently Steward Mu is going to throw me out. . . .

TA-SO What, is he coming soon? [*Looking at the sky.*] It's getting dark. . . . [*Looking at the door.*] Is your mother home?

TA-CHUN No.

TA-SO Ta-chun, I think we ought to have a fling at him tonight!

TA-CHUN What do you mean, Ta-so?

TA-SO When the bastard comes, we'll [*makes a gesture and whispers*]. . . .

TA-CHUN [*worked up*] Yes . . . but . . . if it leaked out, my mother and Hsi-erh. . . .

TA-SO Don't be afraid. It's dark, and when we're through with the rogue we'll drag him to the North Mountain gully to feed the wolves! [*He whispers again.*]

TA-CHUN All right, we'll be ready for him this evening! [*The watch sounds.* TA-CHUN *and* TA-SO *take cover, and* TA-CHUN *fetches a rope from the house.*]

[*Enter* MU, *weaving tipsily.*]

MU [*sings*]

> Kings and queens, kings and queens,
> And all the aces too!
> I don't care for kings or queens,
> All I want, my knave, is you!

[*Laughing he reaches the gate.*] Ta-chun! Ta-chun! Why haven't you gone yet, you rascal? Clear out of the house and be off with you!

[TA-CHUN *remains angrily silent.*]

MU You want to spend all your life here, don't you, you rogue! You won't give up! Today you were hanging about the Huangs' gate again! Do you still want another man's girl? True, Hsi-erh was promised to you before, but she belongs to our Landlord Huang now. . . . Ah, that wench! Let me tell you, Landlord Huang knows you won't keep quiet, you rogue, so he says we've got to get rid of you. You clear out of this house now, and look sharp about it! [*He advances as he speaks.* TA-CHUN *does not answer, and as* MU *approaches he falls back.*] Where are you going, fellow? Why don't you say something? . . . Where are you going? [*Pressing* TA-CHUN.]

[TA-SO *suddenly seizes* MU *from behind and throws him to the ground.*]

MU Who's that?

TA-SO Don't you dare shout! [*To* TA-CHUN.] Stop his mouth, Ta-chun. [MU *struggles.*]

TA-SO You're going to dun for debts in hell! [*As they beat* MU, *two of* LANDLORD HUANG's *thugs enter.*]

THUGS What's up?

[TA-CHUN *and* TA-SO, *seeing them, start to make off but are seized. However,* TA-CHUN *breaks loose and escapes.*]

THUGS [*helping* MU *up*] Well, Mr. Mu, you've had a fright!

MU [*panting*] Lao San, Lao San—go after him! Go after Wang Ta-chun! [*Pointing to* TA-SO.] Well, so it was you, Ta-so, my fine fellow! . . . Old Liu, take him back for questioning.

[TA-SO *is pushed off by the thugs, kicking and struggling.* MU *also leaves.*]

[*The inner curtain falls.*]

[TA-CHUN *hurries in, and hammers at the door.*]

TA-CHUN Uncle Chao! Uncle Chao!

[CHAO *enters.*]

TA-CHUN Uncle Chao, where's my mother?

CHAO She's gone home, Ta-chun. Why have you got the wind up like this?

TA-CHUN Uncle, something's happened! Ta-so and I beat up Steward Mu, but we were found out, and Ta-so was caught. Now they're after me!

CHAO You young fellows! Just rashness is no use. I knew you were smoldering with rage, but our time hasn't come yet, Ta-chun. You can't stay here now; you'd better make off quickly.

TA-CHUN Uncle. . . .

CHAO Go northwest, quickly!

TA-CHUN Uncle . . . my mother and Hsi-erh. . . .

CHAO   I'll look after them. Go now. When times change, you can come
back and see your mother and me.

[TA-CHUN *runs off, and* CHAO *goes out.*]

[*Curtain*]

SCENE III

The HUANG house.

[*Enter* LANDLORD HUANG *holding a lantern.*]

HUANG [*sings*]

>   Fate's been kind to me, I'm rich and respected,
>   My barns are stuffed with grain and my chests with gold.
>   The poor, of course, must go cold and hungry,
>   Because that's their destiny, fixed by Fate!
>   If cattle won't budge, I whip them;
>   If pigs won't die, I slaughter them;
>   And if the poor set themselves against me,
>   They'll find out to their cost what fools they've been!

A few days ago Ta-so and Ta-chun refused to pay their rent, and
beat up Steward Mu. Tch! It's really preposterous! They should remember who I am. . . . Even rats think twice before coming out of
their holes. Do they think they can get anywhere by making an
enemy of me? Ta-so I have sent to the district jail. Ta-chun ran away,
but let him go! I don't think he dares to come back even if he wants
to. As for Hsi-erh. . . . [*Chuckles.*] The only trouble is she's kept
by my mother, so I've not been able to get hold of her yet, which is
beginning to make me impatient. . . . Today I went to the north
village to feast with some friends, and I'm feeling rather restless.
Now that it's dark I'll go and have another try at it—try, try and try
again! . . . [*Laughs.*]

[*The second watch sounds, showing that it is after ten.*]

[*Sings*]

>   Hearing the second watch,
>   I tiptoe to my mother's room.

I've hit on a fine plan
To get my way tonight.

[*Exit.*]

[*The back curtain rises, disclosing* MRS. HUANG's *bedroom.*]

[*Enter* HSI-ERH, *carrying broth.*]

HSI-ERH [*sings*]

The few months I've been here,
My life has been so bitter—
First I am cursed, then beaten,
They treat me all the time like dirt.
But I have to swallow my tears,
My only friend is Aunty Chang.

[*She approaches the left side of the bed, and calls timidly:* "Mistress!" *Then approaches the right side of the bed and calls again,* "Mistress! Mistress!"] Ah! [*Sings*]

Rich people are hard to please,
I haven't a minute to myself;
And if I'm careless and annoy her,
I'm afraid she may do me in!

VOICE FROM WITHIN THE BED CURTAINS   "Hung-hsi, is the lotus-seed broth ready?"

HSI-ERH   Coming, mistress! [*A hand comes out from the curtain to take the bowl.*]

VOICE FROM THE BED   "So hot! Do you want to scald me? You damn slave! Cool it!" [*She passes the bowl back.*]

HSI-ERH [*holding the bowl, sings*]

It's either too hot or too cold,
She's never satisfied.
I'm so tired and sleepy,
But it's more than my life's worth to sleep!

VOICE FROM THE BED   "Give me the broth!"

HSI-ERH   Coming, mistress! [*A hand from the bed takes the bowl.*]

VOICE FROM THE BED   "What, so bitter? You can't have taken out the roots properly. You make me furious, damn you! Kneel down!"

HSI-ERH [*frightened*]   I . . . I. . . . [*Kneels.*]

VOICE FROM THE BED   "You bitch, who can drink such bitter broth? Open your mouth!" [*Reaching out with an opium pin, she slashes at* HSI-ERH's *mouth.*]

HSI-ERH   Oh! [*Cries.*]

[HUANG *steals on, and listens at the door.*]

VOICE FROM THE BED   "Don't cry! You really are infuriating!"

HSI-ERH   I . . . I. . . . [*Cries.*]

VOICE FROM THE BED [*angrily*]   "Damn slave!" [*She parts the bed curtain and emerges.*]

MRS. HUANG   Damn slave! [*Beats her again and again with a feather duster.*]

HUANG [*coming in quickly to stop her*]   Mother, Mother, don't be angry! Mother! [*Helps her to the bed.*]

MRS. HUANG   What brings you here? . . . [*To* HSI-ERH.] Get up. [HSI-ERH *gets up.*]

HUANG   Don't be angry, Mother. You're not feeling well these days, and Hung-hsi has offended you. . . .

MRS. HUANG   What brings you here so late?

HUANG   I came to see you, and . . . I would like Hung-hsi to sew something for me.

MRS. HUANG   I need Hung-hsi to make my broth.

HUANG   Oh. . . .

MRS. HUANG   My, how you reek of wine! Better go to bed at once!

HUANG   Yes, Mother. . . . Yes . . . er . . . Mother, you rest and have some opium. Don't be angry. [HUANG *prepares the opium pipe for his mother, who smokes; then he puts down the bed curtains.*]

HUANG   Come, Hung-hsi, come.

HSI-ERH [*in alarm*]   Young master, you. . . .

MRS. HUANG   Son, what are you doing? Haven't you gone yet?

HUANG   Mother, I was saying that Hung-hsi is quite clever, isn't she [*taking* HSI-ERH's *hand*], at looking after you! . . . [*Pinches her arm.*]

[HSI-ERH *gives a scream.*]

MRS. HUANG [*angrily getting out of bed again and sitting down*]   You wretched slave, have you gone crazy again?

HUANG   Er . . . er . . . Mother, I think tomorrow I'd better ask Dr. Chen from the town to examine you again.

MRS. HUANG   Humph!

[*Enter* CHANG, *and sets a teapot on the bed.*]

CHANG [*sizing up the situation*] Has Hung-hsi offended you again, mistress? [*To* HUANG.] Why are you here, sir? It's getting late, you should rest now.

HUANG [*to himself*] Huh, this servant Chang. . . .

CHANG The old lady is not feeling well and it's getting late. . . . Better go to bed, sir.

MRS. HUANG Go to bed, son.

CHANG [*nudging* HSI-ERH] Sir, here's your lantern. [*Passing him the lantern.*]

MRS. HUANG Go on back, son. Hung-hsi, prepare that broth for me.

HUANG Well, Mother, you'd better sleep. [*To* CHANG.] Tomorrow you wash those clothes of mine.

CHANG Yes, sir.

[*Exit* HUANG.]

CHANG Hsi-erh, come and heat the old lady's broth.

[HSI-ERH *moves to take the bowl, but* CHANG *signs to her to be seated, and heats the broth herself.*]

[HSI-ERH *remains silent, and they watch the broth.*]

CHANG [*softly letting down the curtains*] How did you offend the old lady, Hung-hsi?

HSI-ERH She said I hadn't taken the roots out of the lotus seeds, and they tasted bitter; but I had picked them clean. . . .

CHANG [*indignantly*] Well! She feels bitter because she's had too much opium. . . .

VOICE FROM THE BED "Chang! What are you talking about?"

CHANG I was telling Hung-hsi not to cry, so as not to wake you. . . .

VOICE FROM THE BED "Oh. . . ."

[*Silence.*]

CHANG [*softly*] Hung-hsi, you couldn't have had enough to eat this evening. [*Taking a dumpling from her sleeve.*] Have this.

HSI-ERH [*biting eagerly into the dumpling, gives a cry because her mouth hurts*] Oh!

CHANG [*surprised*] What's the matter? [*Looks at the wound.*] Oh, so she's hurt you with the opium pin again. . . . [*Indignantly.*] Well! Presently I'll go to the kitchen and get some soup for you.

HSI-ERH [*in pain*] No . . . no need.

CHANG [*looking at* MRS. HUANG] Well, the old lady is asleep. . . . [*Sits by* HSI-ERH *and fans the fire.*] Ah, Hung-hsi, it's a hard, hard life. Only we two know it. It was because my family couldn't pay our rent either that I was sent to work here in payment for the rent. The things I've seen during these years! Every single maidservant like us has a wretched life of it. [*She sighs, then pauses.*] Hung-hsi, I'll tell you something, but you mustn't let it upset you. . . .

HSI-ERH Yes, Aunty.

CHANG Ta-chun and Ta-so, because the landlord pressed them for rent, beat up Steward Mu. Ta-so was caught and put in jail, and Ta-chun ran away. . . .

HSI-ERH Oh! [*She starts crying from the shock.*]

CHANG [*comforting her*] It happened nearly a month ago; but I didn't tell you for fear it might upset you. . . .

HSI-ERH Then . . . Aunty Wang?

CHANG Don't worry, your Uncle Chao's looking after her. . . . That's how it is, and it's no use crying over spilt milk. We're all in the same boat; although life is so hard, we have to stick it out. . . .

[HSI-ERH *cries.*]

[*The third watch sounds.*]

CHANG That's the third watch now. . . . The old lady is asleep, and the master should have gone to bed too. When the broth is ready, Hung-hsi, come back to bed; don't run around. I'll wait for you. [*Exit.*]

HSI-ERH [*goes on watching the broth, and sings*]

> It's after midnight now,
> The more I think, the sadder I grow.
> Poor Dad was hounded to death,
> And Ta-chun forced to leave home.
> Why must we poor folk suffer so?
> Why are the rich so cruel?
> How can we go on living like this?
> Will these hard times never end?

[*She dozes and the broth boils. She starts up to remove the pot from the fire, but lets it fall. The pot is broken and the broth spilled.* MRS. HUANG *snores.*]

HSI-ERH [sings]

> I'm dizzy and I feel so frightened;
> I've broken the pot and spilt the broth!
> Now I've done such a dreadful thing,
> I'm afraid I shan't escape with my life!
> Where can I hide myself?
> Oh, Heaven, save me!

[As she runs out, the back curtain falls. HSI-ERH re-enters from the side of the curtain, and sings]

> At dead of night it's so dark,
> The road is black and everywhere there are dogs.
> I can hear someone coming after me;
> I can't escape this time!

[Enter HUANG with a lantern to confront her. HSI-ERH halts in dismay.]

HUANG [overjoyed]   Aha, what luck! What brought you here, Hung-hsi?

HSI-ERH [frightened]   I . . . I. . . . [Wants to leave.]

HUANG [seizing her]   Ah! Hung-hsi, sew something on for me! I need it now. Come, come on over! [Pushes open the door. The back curtain opens. He pushes HSI-ERH in and bolts the door behind him. This is LANDLORD HUANG's study. A painting of a big tiger hangs there. The tiger is crouching, ready to spring.]

HSI-ERH [terrified]   Oh! [She turns to fly, but is pushed aside by HUANG.]

HUANG [seizing HSI-ERH's hand]   Come, Hung-hsi. [His eyes gleam with lust, as he pushes HSI-ERH.] Come on!

HSI-ERH   Oh! [Struggling.] Aunty! Aunty! [She starts running, but is pushed into the inner room.]

HUANG   You! Ha! Still shouting! You won't escape now! Come on! [Follows HSI-ERH inside.]

[The fifth watch is heard. Day gradually dawns.]

[Curtain]

SCENE IV

[CHANG *enters hurriedly.*]

CHANG   Hung-hsi! Hung-hsi! [*Sings*]

> Last night she was beaten and frightened,
> So I stayed with her till it was late.
> Only when all was quiet, at midnight,
> And she had calmed down, I came back.
> But this morning she's not to be found,
> Though I've looked for her everywhere.
> Hung-hsi! Hung-hsi! [*Exit.*]

[*Enter* HSI-ERH *with dishevelled hair and crumpled clothes. Her face is tear-stained, and she walks with difficulty.*]

HSI-ERH [*comes to the door, but shrinks from opening it. Sings*]

> Heaven!
> You could kill me with a knife or axe,
> But you shouldn't have shamed me!
> I little thought of this
> When I came to the Huang house. . . .
> Mother bore me, Dad brought me up,
> Was it all for nothing?
> Now—how can I face people?
> How can I live on?

Oh, Dad, Dad, I've let you down! Aunty Wang, Ta-chun, I can never face you again! [*Having decided to commit suicide, she finds a rope in a corner of the room, and picks it up.*] Oh, Dad, Dad, I'm coming. [*Ties the rope to a rafter.*]

[CHANG *enters and sees her through a crack of the door.*]

CHANG   Hung-hsi, let me in!
HSI-ERH [*startled*] Oh! [*The rope falls from her trembling hands.*]
CHANG   Hung-hsi! Open the door for me, quickly!
HSI-ERH [*opens the door, and runs to* CHANG *as she enters*] Aunty! [*Cries.*]
CHANG   Hung-hsi! You—
HSI-ERH   I . . . I. . . .
CHANG [*seeing the rope, understands*] Hung-hsi, how could you ever think of such a thing? You must never . . . never. . . .

HSI-ERH Aunty! [*Cries.*]

CHANG Child, how could you be so foolish as to think of such a thing! You must on no account do that.

HSI-ERH Aunty, I . . . I can't face people any more.

CHANG I understand. It's my fault for not looking after you better.

HSI-ERH Aunty, I can't go on living. . . .

CHANG Don't talk nonsense, child. What's done is done, but you have to live anyway. You're young, child, and there is hope. I'll look after you, and later on we two will live together. The day will come when we shall avenge your father. . . . [*Helps her up, wiping her eyes.*]

[HSI-ERH *remains silent.*]

CHANG Stop crying now, and come and rest.

[TA-SHENG *enters.*]

TA-SHENG Hung-hsi, Hung-hsi! [*Seeing them.*] Oh, there you are, Hung-hsi! Last night you made such trouble, the old lady is asking for you!

[HSI-ERH *looks frightened.*]

CHANG Go now.

HSI-ERH Aunty! [*She clings to* CHANG.]

CHANG I'll go with you, Hung-hsi. [*They go out together.*]

[*Curtain*]

ACT III

SCENE I

Time: Seven months after the Second Act.
Place: MRS. HUANG'S room.

[*Enter* HUANG *and* MU *carrying wedding invitation cards. The servant* TA-SHENG *follows, holding a teapot; and after him come thugs dressed in military uniform.* CHANG *comes on carrying colored silk.* MRS. HUANG *enters holding a teacup from which she is sipping. The atmosphere is lively.*]

HUANG [*sings*]

Cassia trees in autumn—

ALL [*sing*]

Make the whole courtyard fragrant!

HUANG [*sings*]

Preparing for the wedding—

ALL [*sing*]

We all work with a will!

MU   Our young master is now promoted captain of the militia, and getting married. This is truly a double happiness!

HUANG and MRS. HUANG [*sing*]

The masters are busy!

ALL [*sing*]

The servants are busy!
All busy and happy together!

MU   The preparations for our master's wedding have made every member of the household happy, whether young or old, master or servant!

MRS. HUANG [*sings*]

New clothes and coverlets must be quickly made!

[CHANG *and* TA-SHENG *tear up the silk, while* HUANG, MRS. HUANG, *and* MU *sing cheerfully.*]

TOGETHER [*sing*]

Red silk and green, like ten thousand flowers!

MRS. HUANG [*sings*]

Measure it quickly! Cut it straight!

ALL [*sing*]

Some for our master and some for his bride!
And some for quilts and covers for the bed!
To deck the bride!

> To spread the bed!
> Let's all hurry to get them made!

MRS. HUANG [*sings*]

> Send cards at once to our relatives!

MU [*sings*]

> I take my pen and quickly write!

HUANG   To Secretary-General Sun of Kuomintang County Headquarters, to Magistrate Liu and Captain Li. . . .
MRS. HUANG   To the Seventh Aunt, and to Uncle. . . .
MU [*sings*]

> One card is written and then another. . . .

ALL [*sing*]

> When the time comes, guests will gather,
> Men and women, old and young,
> To feast here in our hall together!

MRS. HUANG   Chang, go to the servants' quarters, and see how the sewing is getting on.
CHANG   Yes, mistress.
MRS. HUANG   Ta-sheng, go and see how the preparations for the feast are going forward.
TA-SHENG   Yes, mistress.
MRS. HUANG   Old Mu, you speed them all up.
MU   Yes, mistress.
ALL [*sing*]

> Cassia trees in autumn make the whole courtyard fragrant,
> The whole household's busy preparing for the wedding!
> We're just waiting for the happy day to come,
> When with flutes and cymbals we welcome the bride home!

[MU, CHANG, *and* TA-SHENG *leave.*]

MRS. HUANG [*in a low voice*]   Son, has that procurer from the city arrived?
HUANG   Not yet. I'm so worried, yesterday I sent for him again.
MRS. HUANG   Better hurry. Her condition is more obvious every day,

and your wedding is drawing near. If you don't make haste, and word gets out, our family reputation will be ruined.

HUANG   How about this, Mother—for the next day or two let Old Mu keep an eye on her, and stop her running around. Later we can find a quiet place, and lock her up.

MRS. HUANG [*approvingly*]   Good. [*Exeunt.*]

[*Enter* MU.]

MU [*picking up the invitations and glancing round prior to going out again*]   Ah, here comes Hung-hsi. Landlord Huang told me to keep an eye on her. Let's see what she's up to. . . . [*Hides behind the door.*]

[*Enter* HSI-ERH, *carrying a wooden pail. She is seven months pregnant, looks haggard, and walks with difficulty.*]

HSI-ERH [*sings*]

> Seven months have passed—
> Like a twig crushed beneath a stone,
> I bear the shame, swallowing my tears.
> I can't say how ill I feel.
> Things have gone so far, there's no help for me,
> I'll just have to bear it and swallow my pride.

[*Entering the room she sees the red silk and invitation cards on the table.*]

HSI-ERH   Ah, there's going to be a wedding. Does it mean Landlord Huang? . . .

[MU *coughs.* HSI-ERH *steps aside. Enter* MU.]

MU   Oh, Hung-hsi, what are you doing here?

HSI-ERH   Fetching hot water for the old lady.

MU   You must be happy now. What do you think I'm doing?

HSI-ERH   How should I know?

MU   Well, look at this! [*Picking up the invitation cards.*] What are these?

HSI-ERH   Those?

MU   Wedding cards, for the wedding! Ah, these days we're all busy preparing, didn't you know? As for you . . . you ought to be pleased now! You ought to be laughing! The old lady says you mustn't run around these days. . . . Just wait! [*Exit.*]

HSI-ERH   What? Steward Mu said I. . . .

[*Enter* HUANG.]

HSI-ERH [*seeing* HUANG]   Oh, it's you.
HUANG   Ah, Hung-hsi! [*Wants to turn back.*]
HSI-ERH [*stopping him*]   You—wait! I want to ask you something. . . .
HUANG   Well, but I'm busy now, Hung-hsi. . . .
HSI-ERH   Let me ask you—
HUANG   All right. [*Taking up an invitation card, and listening help-lessly.*]
HSI-ERH   I'm growing bigger every day, what can I do? People laugh at me and despise me. But I can't die, however much I want to. Tell me, how shall I live on? . . .
HUANG   Er. . . . [*Wanting to make off.*]
HSI-ERH [*stopping him*]   Sir, you. . . . [*Weeps.*]
HUANG   Now, Hung-hsi, don't cry. Er, you know, Hung-hsi, the time has nearly come. Just keep calm. Keep quiet, Hung-hsi, and don't run about. I'm going now to make preparations. [*Exit hastily.*]

[*Enter* CHANG *with silk.*]

HSI-ERH [*bewildered*]   Aunty. . . .
CHANG   So you're here.
HSI-ERH   What's that you're carrying, Aunty?
CHANG   Clothes I made for the bride.
HSI-ERH   Is there going to be a wedding, Aunty?
CHANG   I was just going to talk to you, Hung-hsi. Come along to our room for a talk. . . .

[*She leads* HSI-ERH *out of the door, to their own room. The back curtain falls.*]

HSI-ERH   Aunty—
CHANG   You know, Hung-hsi, the time is getting near. . . .
HSI-ERH   I know.
CHANG   You ought to realize.
HSI-ERH   I do realize, Aunty: it's seven months now. But what can I do? At least now he's. . . .
CHANG [*surprised*]   What are you talking about, Hung-hsi?
HSI-ERH   Just now Landlord Huang said he was going to marry me. . . .

CHANG   What! You're dreaming, Hung-hsi! You've got it wrong, child!
HSI-ERH [*greatly taken aback*]   What do you mean, Aunty?
CHANG   [*sings*]

> Oh, Hung-hsi, you foolish child,
> He's not going to marry you,
> But a girl called Chao from town;
> Her family's rich and powerful. . . .
> Child!

Just think, Hung-hsi, how could he dream of marrying a servant like
you or me?
HSI-ERH   No need to go on, Aunty. I lost my head for a moment. Landlord Huang is my enemy; even if he married me, he would make me
lead a wretched life. Oh, it's just because I'm getting bigger every
day, and can't do anything about it. So I thought—
CHANG   Ah, I meant once the child was born you should give it to me
to bring up for you; then one day when you left the Huang family
you could marry someone else. I didn't think to tell you about the
wedding. Who could imagine you would suppose. . . .
HSI-ERH   I understand now, Aunty. Now he's going to be married, and
he's cheating me too. What a devil he is! I'm not a child. He's ruined
me, so that I can't hold up my head again; but I'm not like my father!
Even a chicken will struggle when it's killed, and I'm a human
being! Even if it kills me, Aunty, I'm going to speak my mind!
CHANG   [*crying*]   I never thought of you as a child, love. I like your
spirit—
HSI-ERH   Aunty! [*Too moved to speak she falls into* CHANG's *arms.*]
VOICE OFFSTAGE   "Aunty Chang, the mistress wants you."
CHANG   Someone's calling me. Wait a little, Hung-hsi. I'll be back
soon. [*Crossing the threshold she turns back.*] Don't go out again.
[*Exit, closing the door.*]

[HSI-ERH *watches* CHANG *go. Presently she can no longer contain herself for anger, and rushes out, just as* HUANG *enters from the other side.*]

HSI-ERH   [*fiercely*]   Sir!
HUANG   [*startled*]   Hung-hsi, why are you here?
HSI-ERH   [*stepping forward*]   Sir, you. . . .
HUANG   Now, Hung-hsi, go back quickly. It doesn't look good if you're
seen in the courtyard.
HSI-ERH   [*loudly*]   Landlord Huang!

HUANG [*startled*]   What! You—

HSI-ERH   On New Year's Eve you forced my dad to commit suicide! On New Year's Day you got me to your home. Since I came you've never treated me as a human being, but as dirt beneath your feet! Your mother beats and curses me! [*Coming nearer.*] And you—you ruined me!

HUANG   You . . . why bring that up now?

HSI-ERH [*coming nearer*]   I'm seven months gone, but you're getting married and deceiving me! I ask you, what do you mean by it! [*Bites and tears at him.*]

HUANG [*throwing* HSI-ERH *down*]   You fool! Mad! [*He shakes her off and hurries out.*]

HSI-ERH [*getting up*]   I'll have it out with you! I'll have it out with you! [*Runs out after him.*]

[*Curtain*]

SCENE II

[MRS. HUANG's *room.* HUANG *enters hastily.*]

HUANG   Mother! Mother!

MRS. HUANG [*putting down her opium pipe*]   What is it, son?

HUANG   Mother, I was too careless. I didn't have Hung-hsi watched, and now she's making trouble.

MRS. HUANG [*sitting on the bed*]   What's she been doing?

HUANG   She's after me now! Look, Mother, she's coming here! The guests will be here directly. If this gets known, it will be too bad.

MRS. HUANG   The fool! She must be mad! Well, you go. Send Old Mu here.

[*Exit* HUANG.]

[MRS. HUANG *picks up a broomstick and stands waiting angrily.* HSI-ERH *runs in.*]

HSI-ERH   I'll have it out with you! . . . [*Enters the room.*]

MRS. HUANG   Silly girl! You are mad! Kneel down!

HSI-ERH   You! [*Refusing to kneel.*]

MRS. HUANG [*fiercely*]   Kneel down!

[HSI-ERH *looks at her angrily, trembling with hate.*]

MRS. HUANG   Wretched girl! Do you admit your guilt? I ask you, who got you with child?

HSI-ERH   What!

MRS. HUANG   Wretched girl! Carrying on with men, you've spoiled our family's reputation. Speak! Who is your lover? Speak up, who is it?

[MU *comes in behind* HSI-ERH's *back.*]

HSI-ERH   [*loudly*]   It's your son! [CHANG *is listening from one corner and* HUANG *from another.*]

MRS. HUANG   [*furiously*]   What! You liar! You are accusing my son? You are asking for trouble! [*Steps forward to strike her.*]

HSI-ERH   [*starts to rush forward but is seized by* MU. *She shrieks*]   It's your son! It's your son! You've ruined my whole family! There isn't one good person in your Huang family! Not a single man or woman in your family for generations has been any good! You're all bitches and. . . .

MRS. HUANG   Old Mu! Old Mu! Stop her mouth, quickly!

[MU *gags* HSI-ERH *with a handkerchief.*]

MRS. HUANG   Quickly shut her in the inner room and whip her!

[MU *drags* HSI-ERH *to the inner room and whips her. The strokes of the lash and muffled cries are heard.*]

MRS. HUANG   [*listening*]   Good, good. Today she must be well beaten.

[CHANG *listens in distress outside the door.*]

[*There is a pause.*]

MRS. HUANG   [*taking out a lock*]   Old Mu, lock the door for me.

[*As* MU *locks the door* HUANG *enters hastily.* CHANG *hides herself and listens at the door.*]

HUANG   Mother, it's time now. I think we'll have to find a way to get rid of her. The guests will soon be here. If outsiders hear of this, it will be too bad.

MRS. HUANG   You're right. The bride is coming. If the bride's family hears of it we'll be in an awkward position. . . . Old Mu, is there anybody outside?

[*As* MU *looks outside the door* CHANG *hides herself.* MU *re-enters the room, closing the door, and* CHANG *listens again.*]

MU   No one.

MRS. HUANG   Good. We mustn't lose any time. Tonight when they are all asleep, Old Mu, you get a horse and take her away.

HUANG   Yes, Old Mu. When you get to the city, take the girl to the procurer for him to get rid of quickly. On no account must people know.

MU   Very good, sir. I'll do that. [*Exit.*]

HUANG   Don't be angry, Mother. Let's go to inspect the preparation of the bridal chamber. [*Takes his mother's arm to help her out.*]

[CHANG *hides herself as* HUANG *and* MRS. HUANG *leave. Then she runs into the room and tries to open the inner door, but finds it locked.*]

CHANG   The key? [*She looks for the key on* MRS. HUANG's *bed, and finding it opens the door. A voice is heard offstage:* "Aunty Chang!" *Enter* TA-SHENG. CHANG *hides the key, and pretends nothing is amiss.*]

TA-SHENG   Aunty Chang! [*He comes in.*] Oh, there you are, Aunty Chang. The mistress wants you to go to supervise the sewing.

CHANG   All right, I'm coming. [TA-SHENG *goes out, followed by a distracted* CHANG.]

[*Voices are heard offstage*]:

MU   Old Kao, what a drunkard you are!

KAO   It's the young master's wedding. Why shouldn't I drink?

MU   Saddle a horse for me at once. Quickly!

KAO   Why do you want a horse so late?

MU   Never you mind. Just get it ready.

KAO   All right. All right.

[CHANG *re-enters, carrying cakes, and hastily closes the door. She puts the cakes on the table, then opens the door of the inner room.*]

CHANG   Hung-hsi! Hung-hsi! [*After dragging* HSI-ERH *out, she locks the door and puts the key back on the bed.*]

CHANG   Hung-hsi! [*Undoing the rope binding* HSI-ERH's *arms.*] Hung-hsi! Hung-hsi! [*Removing the gag from her mouth.*] Hung-hsi! Wake up, Hung-hsi!

HSI-ERH [*coming to herself*]   Who are you?

CHANG [*softly*]   It's Aunty.

HSI-ERH   Ah, Aunty! . . . [*Falls on* CHANG.]

CHANG   Hung-hsi, Hung-hsi, I know all that happened. [*Helping her up.*] You must go quickly. They want to ruin you.

HSI-ERH Ah!

CHANG They're murderers! They've sold you! They'll be coming to fetch you, you must go at once! If you fall into their hands, you'll never escape again.

HSI-ERH Aunty, they . . . they. . . . [*She wants to rush out.*]

CHANG [*pulling her back*] Don't be foolish, Hung-hsi. You're no match for them. Go quickly. You must fly for your life.

[HSI-ERH *says nothing.*]

CHANG Go by the back door. Along the gully. I've opened the door for you. Quick! [*They start out.*]

VOICE FROM OFFSTAGE "Aunty Chang! Aunty Chang!"

[*Taking fright they hide. The voice grows fainter.*]

CHANG [*urgently*] Hung-hsi, soon you won't be with me any more. In future you'll have to make up your own mind. I can't go with you. They're calling me.

HSI-ERH Aunty!

CHANG [*giving* HSI-ERH *the cakes from the table*] Here are some cakes to eat on the road. Mind you only drink running water. However hard life is, you have to go on living. Remember how they destroyed your family. A day will come when you can avenge yourself.

HSI-ERH I shall remember, Aunty.

CHANG [*giving* HSI-ERH *money*] Here's some money I've saved. You'll need it on your journey. Soon I'll be leaving their family. One day we shall meet again.

HSI-ERH [*takes the money and kneels down*] Aunty—

CHANG Ah, Hung-hsi, get up. Go quickly. [*Opens the door and runs out, leading* HSI-ERH.]

VOICE FROM OFFSTAGE "Aunty Chang! Aunty Chang!"

[*After a while* CHANG *comes back by the way she went out, walking calmly. The third watch sounds. Enter* HUANG *and* MU.]

HUANG [*taking the key from his mother's bed, unlocks the inner room, goes in, and discovers* HSI-ERH *has gone. In surprise*] What! Where's Hung-hsi? She's disappeared!

MU What!

HUANG Old Mu, Hung-hsi has escaped! The back window is open. She must have climbed out through the window. Go and catch her, Old

Mu. When you've caught her, strangle her with a rope and throw her into the river, so we won't have any more trouble.

[*They leave the room.*]

MU She won't dare leave by the front gate, sir. Let's go by the back gate. [*Exeunt.*]

[*Curtain*]

SCENE III

[HSI-ERH *is escaping by the back gate. There are stars in the sky.*]

HSI-ERH [*falls down and gets up again. Sings*]

> They want to kill me, to murder me,
> But I've escaped from their tigers' den!
> Mother bore me, Dad brought me up,
> I want to live, I want to live!

[*She runs off.*]

[HUANG *and* MU *enter in pursuit, carrying ropes.*]

HUANG Hurry up after her, Old Mu!

MU Right.

HUANG If she took this road, there's a big river in front, and she can't get away.

[*They pursue. A mountain looms in front. On one side is a rushing river flanked by marshland.* HSI-ERH *hurries in.*]

HSI-ERH [*sings*]

> I'm going on, I'll not turn back,
> I've been wronged and I want revenge!
> They killed my dad and ruined me,
> I'll remember it in my grave!

[*The sound of running water is heard.*]

> I can hear running water,
> There's a river gleaming under the stars;
> It's a great river flowing east,
> I've lost my way—where shall I go?

[*Suddenly the sound of heavy footsteps behind throws her into a panic.*] Ah! I'm being followed! [*She stumbles and falls in the mud. When she extricates herself her shoes have fallen off; but her pursuers are near, and she has no time to pick up her shoes.*] There are some reeds. I'd better hide myself there. [*She crawls into the reeds.*]

[*Enter* HUANG *and* MU.]

HUANG Can you see her, Old Mu?
MU No. [*They search.*]
HUANG The river's in front. Where could she have gone?
MU The mountains on both sides are steep, and there's no path.
HUANG A girl, and so near her time, where can she go?
MU She won't get away, sir. [*They search again.*]
MU [*suddenly discovering a shoe*] Ah, sir, isn't this Hung-hsi's shoe?
HUANG [*taking the shoe*] Yes, it's hers all right.
MU Then she must have jumped into the river.
HUANG Ah, well, she brought it on herself. Well, that saves us trouble. Let's go back, Old Mu. If questions are asked, we'll just say she stole things and ran away. Don't let anyone know the truth.
MU Right. [*They leave by the way they came.*]
HSI-ERH [*emerges from the reeds and sings*]

> They want to kill me, how blind they are!
> I'm water that can't be drained dry!
> I'm fire that can't be quenched!
> I'm not dying, I'm going to live!
> And live to be avenged!

[*She hurries into the mountains.*]

[*Curtain*]

ACT IV

SCENE I

Three years later—the autumn of 1937.

On the hillside overlooking the river, not far from the Goddess' Temple. It is dusk. The sun is setting.

[*Enter* UNCLE CHAO *with a long whip, leading his flock.*]

CHAO [sings]

> Year after year passes,
> And the road's overgrown with wild grass;
> Houses crumble and the place is empty,
> Some have died and some have gone.
> When cold winds blow, the lonely grieve;
> Water flows eastward never to return.

[He stands at the river's edge watching the water flow eastward, then speaks with feeling.] Ah, how quickly time passes. It's three years since that child Hsi-erh drowned herself in the river. . . . [Sits on a boulder.]

[Enter LI from one side carrying incense.]

LI [seeing CHAO] Ah, Uncle Chao, watching the flock?

CHAO Well, Li, where are you off to?

LI I'm going to burn incense before the White-haired Goddess.

CHAO Burn incense before the White-haired Goddess? . . . Oh, yes, it's the fifteenth of the moon again today. . . .

LI [sitting down beside CHAO] It's quite some time now since the White-haired Goddess appeared in these parts. . . .

CHAO Well, we shall see. Something must be going to happen. . . . [Leans forward a little, as if he heard something.]

LI [suddenly standing up] Listen, Uncle Chao!

CHAO [after a pause] Oh, it's only the wind in the reeds.

LI [relaxing. Softly] Tell me, Uncle, have you seen it?

CHAO Seen what?

LI The White-haired Goddess, Uncle. Old Liu met her once in Uncle Yang's land, and Chang Szu saw her when he was cutting wood in the North Mountain gully. They say she was all white, in the shape of a woman; but she was gone in a flash. . . . [Shivers.]

[Pause.]

CHAO [thinking back] Ah, if the White-haired Goddess were any good, then Hsi-erh's family should have been avenged.

LI May the fairy help us! [Pauses.] Say, Uncle, wasn't it that autumn Aunty Chang sent Hsi-erh. . . .

[CHAO hastily stops him and looks around.]

LI [in a lowered voice] Didn't you say Aunty Chang sent her away?

CHAO Ah, how could a girl run far? She drowned herself in the river, poor thing. . . .

LI [*sighs. They are silent. He looks at the sky*] Uncle, I must go to burn incense now. A storm is coming. [*He moves toward the temple.*]

CHAO [*sighs sadly. Sings*]

> Is there no good judge
> To right the wrongs of old?
> What we suffered in the past
> No words can tell!
> But if the goddess were any good at all,
> She'd avenge the ghosts of those unjustly killed!

[AUNTY WANG, *leaning on* AUNTY CHANG's *arm, enters from the direction of the temple.*]

CHANG Uncle Chao!

CHAO Oh, Aunty Chang, Aunty Wang! You've been all that way to burn incense?

CHANG Well, Aunty Wang insisted I come with her. Ah, when you're brooding over something, you can't forget it.

WANG [*crying*] Uncle Chao . . . I want nothing else, great goddess, but let my child come back. . . . I've never done a bad deed in my life. Why should this have happened to me? All these years have passed, Uncle Chao, yet every day as soon as I close my eyes, I see Hsi-erh on one side and Ta-chun on the other. Oh, son, why have you forgotten your mother? Poor children! One drowned herself, and the other ran away. . . . [*Cries bitterly.*]

CHANG Now don't cry, Aunty Wang. [*Comforting her.*] Don't take on so, Aunty Wang.

CHAO Nothing can bring the dead to life. What's the use of crying? . . . Although Hsi-erh died, she died well. . . . As for Ta-chun, although there's been no news of him since he left, he'll come back some day. . . .

CHANG That's right. Every day since I left the Huang family, I've reasoned with her, saying, "Wait, Aunty. Although Hsi-erh is dead, Ta-chun is sure to come back. Don't complain of fate. Our fate is the same. I'll help you, and you help me. Then we shall struggle along in spite of difficulties."

CHAO [*nodding sadly*] Struggle along, struggle along. One day Heaven will stop being blind.

[LI *enters hurriedly, in consternation. There is a gust of wind.*]

LI [*looking pale*] Uncle Chao! Uncle Chao!

CHAO What is it?

LI She's coming! She's coming!

THE OTHERS What is it?

LI Behind the temple! White! All white! The White-haired Goddess!

THE OTHERS [*panic-stricken*] What, is it true? Let's go quickly!

[*They run off.* CHAO *follows with his sheep. The sky grows dark, thunder rolls, and the storm breaks.*]

A CHORUS SINGS OFFSTAGE

> The storm is coming,
> The storm is coming,
> THE STORM IS COMING!
> Heaven and earth grow dark
> With lightning and with thunder!
> Heaven and earth grow dark
> With lightning and with thunder!
> God has grown angry,
> And the world's in chaos!
> A gale has sprung up, and from the mountain
> The White-haired Goddess is coming down!

[*A great clap of thunder and flash of lightning.*]

[*Enter the* WHITE-HAIRED GODDESS—HSI-ERH—*with disheveled white hair, rushing through the storm.*]

HSI-ERH [*sings*]

> I came down to gather fruit and berries,
> When this sudden thunderstorm broke.
> The mountain's steep and the path is slippery,
> I can't get back to my cave, so I'll take shelter
> In the Goddess' Temple nearby.

[*She slips and falls, and her fruit rolls to the ground. She hastily picks it up.*] I've spent more than three years out of the sun. Today I came out to get some maize and potatoes, and steal some food from the shrine for my winter store. . . . [*Thunder and a downpour,* HSI-ERH *sings*]

Lightning makes me close my eyes,
Thunder makes me lower my head,
Wind tries to sweep me off my feet,
And I'm drenched in the pouring rain!
But never mind the thunder and lightning,
The wind and the pouring rain!
I clench my teeth
And step by step
Push on—
The temple's close ahead!

[*Exit in the direction of the temple.*]

[MU *enters running through the storm with a lantern and umbrella.*]

MU [*sings*]

Thunder's crashing, lightning's flashing,
This storm broke out of the blue!
Master went to town on business,
What's keeping him so long?

[*At a clap of thunder he crouches down.*] Ah, what weather! . . .
Really, what is the world coming to! Recently I heard the Japanese
fought their way across from Lukouchiao and have occupied Paoting.
They may even be here in a few days. Landlord Huang went to town
for news. He ought to be back by now. . . . [*He is restless and anx-
ious. Thunder rolls again. He stares ahead, not knowing what to do.*]
Ah, during the last few years the villagers have been talking about
some white-haired goddess, and ghostly noises are heard at midnight. [*Sighs.*] What can I do? . . . [*Shivers. He suddenly sees a
shadowy figure on the left, and gives a start.*]Who is it?

[*After a pause,* LANDLORD HUANG's *voice is heard in the dark:* "Oh. . . .
Is it Old Mu?"]

MU [*reassured*] You're back at last, sir!

[HUANG *hurries in holding an umbrella, followed by* TA-SHENG.]

MU Are you all right, sir?
HUANG Things look bad, Old Mu! [*Sings*]

I set out for the county town
The day before yesterday;
But I'd only reached the market town
When I heard some dreadful news!
The Japanese have taken the county town,
So I hurried right back,
Hurried back like mad today!

MU [*startled*]   What! Is it true?

TA-SHENG   Yes.

HUANG   It's appalling! The Japanese kill people and set fire to houses!
All my in-laws have fallen into their hands!

MU [*more alarmed*]   Heavens! Then what can we do, sir?

HUANG [*reassuringly*]   Don't worry, Old Mu. Whatever changes take
place, we'll always be able to find a way out. Come on, let's go home
first.

[*There is a clap of thunder, and the rain pours down more heavily.*]

MU   The storm's growing worse, sir. Let's take shelter first in the
temple. [*The three battle their way toward the temple. On the way
they meet* HSI-ERH. *A flash of lightning lights up the* WHITE-HAIRED
GODDESS.]

HUANG [*panic-stricken*]   What!

[*There is another flash of lightning, and* HSI-ERH *recognizes* HUANG.]

HUANG   Ghosts! Ghosts!

[*The three men hide in terror.*]

HSI-ERH [*in rising anger rushes at* HUANG *and the others, throwing the
sacrificial fruit at* HUANG *and shrieking*]   Ah!

HUANG and MU [*flying in terror*]   Help! . . . Help! . . . Ghosts!
Ghosts!

[*They rush off, followed by* TA-SHENG.]

[*A pause.*]

HSI-ERH [*halting in alarm and uncertainty*]   Ghosts? Ghosts? [*She
looks round, then is silent for a moment.*] Oh, you mean I'm a ghost?
[*She looks at her hair and clothes.*] So, I don't look like a human
being! [*Her voice trembles with indignation and grief.*] This is all
your doing, Landlord Huang! You brought me to this! And you call
me a ghost? . . .

[*Wind, rain, and thunder are heard, and lightning flashes, as* HSI-ERH *sings.*]

> I'm Hsi-erh whom you ruined,
> I'm not a ghost!

[*Thunder crashes even closer.*]

> . . . I've lived in a cave for more than three years,
> Gritting my teeth for misery;
> Hiding by day for fear folk see me,
> While at night there are tigers and wolves;
> I've only rags and leaves to wear,
> Only temple offerings and berries to eat,
> So my hair and skin have turned white!

[*Accusingly*]

> I was brought up by parents too,
> But now I've come to this pass!
> It's all through you, Landlord Huang,
> You brought me to this, yet now you call me
> A ghost! All right—
> I'm a ghost!
> The ghost of someone cruelly killed!
> The ghost of someone hounded to death!
> I'm going to scratch and pinch you!
> I'm going to bite you!

[*Shrieks.*]

[*She rushes headlong into the storm.*]

[*Lightning and sheets of rain.*]

[*The chorus sings "The Storm . . ." offstage, the sound gradually dies away in the distance.*]

[*Curtain*]

SCENE II

The following afternoon.
Under a big tree at one end of the village.

[OLD CHAO *and two peasants enter. They are obviously upset.*]

ALL [*sing*]

> A storm's sprung up. The world's
> In a bad way, we can't live in peace.

FIRST PEASANT

> Landlord Huang has practically squeezed us dry!

SECOND PEASANT

> The White-haired Goddess is making trouble!

CHAO

> The Japanese are fighting their way over!

PEASANTS

> It's said they've taken Paoting city!

FIRST PEASANT

> Hu-tzu has gone to town for news,

SECOND PEASANT

> Why isn't he back yet?

ALL

> It's enough to distract one, such goings on!

CHAO   Ah, Hu-tzu went to town three days ago; how is it he's not back yet?
FIRST PEASANT   Could he have met the Japanese?
SECOND PEASANT   Surely they can't be there already? [*Sighs.*]

[*As the three are waiting impatiently,* AUNTY CHANG *hurries in.*]

CHANG   Oh, you're here. Have you heard the news?
ALL [*startled*]   What's happened?
CHANG   Yesterday evening when Landlord Huang was coming back from town and took shelter in the temple from the rain, he saw a ghost!
ALL [*amazed*]   Really?
CHANG   It's true. He's ill now from the shock.
CHAO   Well! Now the Huang family's sins are finding them out, if ghosts come out to confront him!

CHANG   And I heard those Japanese have occupied the county town!
ALL [*startled*]   No! Then what's to be done?
CHAO [*stamping impatiently*]   Why isn't Hu-tzu back yet?
FIRST PEASANT   Oh, look! Isn't that Hu-tzu coming?
ALL [*shouting*]   Hu-tzu! Hu-tzu!

[HU-TZU *hurries in.*]

HU-TZU [*panting*]   You're all here. Things are in a bad way! [*Sings*]

> The Japanese have taken the county town,
> And smashed the Kuomintang troops!
> The county head's fled, the commissioner too,
> Leaving just the people, with nowhere to turn!

ALL   Ah! Only the people are left to bear the brunt!
HU-TZU [*sings*]

> When the Kuomintang troops fled from the market town,
> There was cursing, conscripting, beating, and looting!
> And when the Japanese come, so they say,
> There's always burning, raping, shooting!

ALL   Heavens! Only the people are left with no one to care for them!
HU-TZU [*sings*]

> But I heard some good news too—
> Troops have come from the west, with banners flying.
> They'll fight the Japanese and save us all!
> They can march sixty miles in a single night,
> They're super men and officers, they really fight!

ALL [*astounded*]   Really?
HU-TZU [*sings*]

> At Pinghsing Pass they won a great victory,
> Killing several thousand Japanese,
> Then fought their way north. . . .

ALL   What army is that?
HU-TZU [*sings*]

> They call it the eight—eight—
> Eighth Route Army!

ALL [*at a loss, echoing him*]   What—the Eighth Route Army?

HU-TZU [*emphatically*]   Yes. They're called the Eighth Route Army. I heard they're very good to the people—

[LI *rushes in before* HU-TZU *has finished, carrying a hoe.*]

[*The "Eighth Route Army March" is heard.*]

LI [*showing amazement*]   Quick! Quick! I was just coming in from the fields, when I saw troops coming down the Southern Hill!
ALL [*alarmed*]   What! Troops?
FIRST PEASANT   Could it be the Japanese?
LI   No, they didn't look like Japanese. They're Chinese troops!
SECOND PEASANT   Ah, they must be retreating.
LI   They don't look like retreating either. You look! [*All stare in the direction he points.*] They're in good order, heading briskly due north.
ALL [*looking*]   Ah, there are so many of them!
LI   Ha! That's a funny army! They're all youngsters, wearing big straw hats, and with no puttees, only shoes. And there's a figure "eight" on their sleeves.
ALL [*in unison*]   Oh, they must be the Eighth Route Army!

[*The martial music grows louder.*]

[*They watch anxiously.*]

SECOND PEASANT [*suddenly catching sight of them*]   Ah! Here they come! Here they come!
AN ARMYMAN'S VOICE OFFSTAGE   "Hey! Countryman—countrymen!"

[*They all take cover in fright.*]

[*Enter* TA-SO, *ragged and unkempt, leading a soldier who proves to be* TA-CHUN.]

TA-SO   By calling out like that, Ta-chun, you frightened them all away! Say, Ta-chun, just now there was someone here who looked like Uncle Chao.
TA-CHUN   Let's call him then.
TA-SO   Uncle Chao! Uncle Chao!
TA-CHUN [*calling too*]   Uncle Chao!

[*After a pause,* CHAO *and others enter; but the sight of the soldier makes them fall back a few steps in fear.*]

TA-CHUN [*advancing*]   Uncle Chao, don't you know me? I'm Ta-chun!
TA-SO   I'm Ta-so!

ALL [*incredulously*]   What?—Ta-chun!—Ta-so! [*After a second they recognize them, and are overjoyed.*] Well! Well! Ta-chun! Ta-so! You've come back! [*Other peasants crowd in.*]

[*They sing happily in unison*]

> A clap of thunder,
> And then a sunny sky!
> The stars in heaven
> Are falling from on high!
> Ta-chun! [*Some:* Ta-so!] You've been away so long,
> Who could tell you would come home today!

[*Enter a peasant:* "Ta-chun! Your mother's coming!"]

[TA-CHUN *goes to meet her.*]

ALL [*following* TA-CHUN *to meet her, sing*]

> Now mother and son will meet,
> And be together from now on!
> All we country folk are happy too;
> All we country folk are happy for you!

[AUNTY WANG, *calling* "Ta-chun! Ta-chun!" *runs in.*]

TA-CHUN [*shouts*]   Mother!
WANG [*unable to believe her eyes, hesitates, then rushes forward, crying*]   Ta-chun! My boy!
TA-CHUN   Mother! [*He breaks down too.*]
SOME PEASANTS [*comfortingly*]   Aunty Wang. . . . [*Sing*]

> Don't take on so!

OTHERS [*sing*]

> Don't be so upset, Ta-chun!

CHANG   Don't make your mother sad, Ta-chun!
CHAO [*wiping his eyes*]   Don't take on so, Aunty. Ta-chun's back, isn't he?
WANG [*wiping her eyes*]   Oh . . . I'm not . . . not sad. [*Cries again.*]
CHAO   Well! [*Sings*]

> You waited day after day so many years,
> Now Ta-chun's here, isn't he?

ALL [*sing*]

> Isn't it grand that he's back!

CHANG   Your day of rejoicing has come, Aunty.
CHAO   Tell us, Ta-chun, how did you come back?
TA-CHUN and TA-SO   Right!
TA-CHUN   Mother, Uncle—
TA-SO   Aunty Chang, neighbors—
TA-CHUN and TA-SO [*sing*]

> When we left that year,
> Landlord Huang—

TA-CHUN

> Drove me out with nowhere to go!

TA-SO

> Threw me into the county jail!

TA-CHUN

> I fled to Shansi province,
> And joined the army there!

TA-SO

> Life was misery in that jail!

TA-CHUN

> Today our troops have come to the front,
> Determined to fight the Japanese invaders!

TA-SO

> They stormed the county town and opened the jail doors,
> Letting us out after all we'd suffered!

BOTH

> So we came back together,
> Home to see our old neighbors!

ALL [*to* TA-CHUN]   What army do you belong to then?
TA-CHUN [*sings*]

> I'm in the Eighth Route Army.

TA-SO [*simultaneously*]

He's in the Eighth Route Army!

ALL [*delighted, crowding round him*] Oh, so you joined the Eighth Route Army then! [*Sing*]

The Eighth Route Army! The Eighth Route Army!
You've come from the west!
It was you who won the battle of Pinghsing Pass,
You're the army with the super officers and men!

TA-CHUN Yes, the Eighth Route Army, led by the Communist Party, is like one family with the common people. Do you remember, Uncle Chao, you used to talk about the Red Army? That Red Army is the present Eighth Route Army!

CHAO Eh? What's that you say? The Eighth Route is the same as the Red Army? [*Wildly happy, to all.*] Ho! Have you all forgotten the Red Army that came to Chao Village on the thirteenth of the fifth moon that year, the day the War God sharpened his knife? . . . It's too good to be true! It's too good to be true! Everything will work out all right now. The Red Army's come back again!

TA-CHUN [*correcting him*] The Eighth Route Army—the Eighth Route Army's come back!

ALL [*in unison*] The Eighth Route Army—the Eighth Route Army's come back! Now there'll really be a change for the better!

[*Laughter.*]

[*The "Eighth Route Army March" sounds loudly offstage.*]

[*All go to meet the troops.*]

[*Curtain*]

A C T   V

SCENE I

Spring, 1938.
Under the big tree in front of the village. The tree has come into leaf. This village has become one of the Eighth Route Army's anti-Japanese

bases behind the enemy's lines. The early morning sun lights up the sentry box of the Self-Defense Corps. From a tree beside it hangs a reading board on which is written: "Resist Japan and Reduce Rents."

[HU-TZU, *carrying a lance with a red silk tassel, is on sentry duty.*]

HU-TZU [*sings*]

> The first clap of thunder in spring!
> The first lamp lit in the valley!
> The poor are going to be masters,
> Now the Communist Party's come!
> We mustn't be afraid, we must fight
> To build up our new people's power.
> Since the government's ordered rents reduced,
> We must all rally round and work hard!

[*Cheerfully.*] Ah! At last the time has come for us poor folk to be masters! Last year when Ta-chun was transferred here from the army he became assistant officer of our district. When the village held an election for political officers in the first moon, Uncle Chao was elected village head and Ta-so chairman of the Peasants' Union. Now an order has come that rents be reduced, so we shall have to settle old scores with Landlord Huang. [*Sighs.*] Only the villagers don't all see eye to eye yet. Folk are still so afraid of Landlord Huang and that "White-haired Goddess" that nobody dares stick his neck out. There was to be a meeting today, but I'm sure they won't all come. [*Walks to one side to look round.*]

[*Enter* UNCLE CHAO *and* TA-SO.]

CHAO and TA-SO [*sing*]

> If everyone rallies round,
> Our struggle is sure to succeed!
> The government will back us up,
> They're sending us cadres today.

TA-SO Hu-tzu!
HU-TZU [*turning round*] Oh, Ta-so! . . . Oh no—[*Hastily correcting himself.*] Peasant Union Chairman and Village Head. [*Laughs.*]
CHAO [*laughing too*] Have you seen anybody from the district, Hu-tzu?
HU-TZU [*impatiently*] Not yet!

TA-SO They said they'd come today; why aren't they here yet? [*Goes to one side to look.*]

CHAO Hu-tzu! This time we're going to demand rent reduction and settle old scores with Landlord Huang. How about it, youngster, do you dare stand out and speak up?

HU-TZU Need you ask, Village Head? Of course I want to attack Landlord Huang. [*Raising his thumb.*] I'll be the first! . . . But one person isn't enough. See here, this looks bad: a meeting was announced for today, but so far nobody's shown up! Bah! I think it'll be a washout.

CHAO [*reassuringly*] Now, Hu-tzu, don't you worry. It's always darkest before dawn. Today cadres are coming from the district with Ta-chun, we've already thought out a good plan, and we're not afraid of Landlord Huang's tricks! . . . Keep cool, youngster, and wait and see. It won't be long now!

HU-TZU All right. [*Smiles contentedly.*]

TA-SO [*seeing figures on the road to the village*] Hey, Uncle Chao, is that Ta-chun and the district head there?

[CHAO *and* HU-TZU *look.*]

HU-TZU Yes, it is. It's Ta-chun. And the district head!

[*Two figures approach, and they go eagerly to meet them, calling "District Head!" "Ta-chun!"*]

[*The district head and* TA-CHUN *walk briskly in.*]

HU-TZU Hey! Ta-chun. . . . Oh no, it's our Assistant Officer Wang who's come!

[TA-CHUN *mops his head and smiles at* HU-TZU.]

CHAO [*to the district head*] We've been waiting a long time. Why are you so late?

DISTRICT HEAD [*wiping his face*] Ta-chun and I came by way of Liu Village, otherwise we'd have been here much earlier.

CHAO How about it? I suggest we go first to the village office.

TA-SO Yes, let's go to the village office first.

[*They start for the village.*]

[*Sound of villagers singing in unison offstage.*]

DISTRICT HEAD [*seeing the villagers approaching*] Hullo! What are these folk doing?

HU-TZU [*stepping forward*] Bah! They're going again to sacrifice to the "White-haired Goddess," damn them! See, there's that rogue Steward Mu too!

TA-CHUN [*to the district head*] Suppose we step out of sight for a second, District Head, and watch them?

CHAO Yes, just come over here. [*They hide on one side.* HU-TZU *takes cover too.*]

[*Enter the villagers—an old man, an old woman, two peasants, and two women, carrying incense and offerings.* MU *follows.*]

ALL [*sing*]

> The world is out of joint,
> And troubles never cease;
> But the White-haired Goddess has power
> To protect and give us peace!

MU [*seeing there is no one about, addresses them craftily*] Ah, do you know? Another strange thing happened yesterday evening!

ALL [*startled*] What?

MU The White-haired Goddess appeared again! [*Sings*]

> Yesterday, at the dead of night,
> The White-haired Goddess appeared again!
> "You shan't reap what you've sown," she said.
> There's great trouble ahead!
> Ruin will stalk the land,
> Everywhere men will die,
> Everywhere fires will break out,
> The sound of weeping will reach the sky!

ALL [*aghast*] Oh! What can we do?

MU [*sings*]

> Then she warned men:
> To be safe and sound,
> You must do good deeds!
> Don't meddle in things that aren't your concern,
> And offer more incense in the temple.
> If you do this you'll be safe!

ALL [*pray*]   Oh, Goddess, help us!
MU   And the goddess said too—[*Sings*]

> The Eighth Route Army won't last long,
> It'll vanish like dew in the sun!
> When the sun comes out the dew disappears,
> And the Eighth Route Army will soon be gone!

[HU-TZU *has already appeared behind* MU. *Now he rushes forward, snatches* MU's *incense and candles, and dashes them to the ground.*]

HU-TZU   You bastard, what rumors are you spreading?
MU [*taken by surprise, is at a loss for words*]   I . . . I. . . . [*Stoops to pick up his incense and candles.*]
HU-TZU   Get out! [*Kicks him off, stamping on the candles and incense.*]

[*Exit* MU *in alarm.*]

[*The others make as if to leave, but* HU-TZU *stops them.*]

HU-TZU [*angrily*]   Stop! No one must pass! Well! When you are summoned to a meeting you won't come, but you have plenty of time for burning incense.
CROWD [*protestingly*]

> What are you doing, Hu-tzu?
> What if you offend the goddess?
> This concerns us all, not just you.

HU-TZU [*not yielding*]   The goddess, indeed! Where is the goddess? No, I won't let you go! [*He is spoiling for a fight.*]

[*The district head,* TA-CHUN, CHAO *and* TA-SO *come in hastily.* CHAO *pulls* HU-TZU *aside and restrains him.*]

CHAO   Hu-tzu. . . .
TA-SO   Don't be angry. No need to get excited.
DISTRICT HEAD   That's right, friends. Don't get heated. . . .

[*The crowd quiets down.*]

OLD MAN   Now the district head is here.
CROWD   Ah, District Head, Ta-chun. . . .
DISTRICT HEAD   Friends, weren't you talking about the White-haired Goddess? Let's hear what miracles the goddess has worked.
TA-CHUN   That's right. Just what?

OLD MAN District Head, Ta-chun. . . . [*Sings*]

> The White-haired Goddess often shows herself,
> It's three whole years now we've seen her.

FIRST PEASANT [*sings*]

> We've all seen her,
> She comes and goes without a trace. . . .

SECOND PEASANT She's all in white! A flash—and she's gone! [*Sings*]

> She's often in the Goddess' Temple,
> Where she comes out at dead of night!

THIRD PEASANT [*sings*]

> The sacrifice set out one day
> Will be gone by the next!

FOURTH PEASANT [*sings*]

> She declares truths in the temple,
> Every word can be heard distinctly!

FIFTH PEASANT It's true. She said—[*Sings*]

> Men are wicked, sinful creatures,
> That's why we can't have peace!

SIXTH PEASANT And Steward Mu told us—[*Sings*]

> The White-haired Goddess is so powerful,
> We must all mend our ways!

ALL [*sing*]

> Otherwise we'll offend her, and that'll be the end of us!

HU-TZU [*impatiently*] That's a pack of lies! Where is the White-haired Goddess? Why haven't I seen her?

[*The crowd shows fresh indignation.*]

FIRST How can you say that, Hu-tzu?
SECOND Everybody knows how powerful the goddess is.
THIRD Who will bear her anger if you offend her?
DISTRICT HEAD [*intervening persuasively*] Friends, don't lose your heads. Let's look into the business of the goddess. We must get to the bottom of it. . . . If you want to burn incense, we won't stop

you. But I hope you'll give some thought too to the matter of re-
ducing rents. Our government will always work for the people.

TA-CHUN   Just think what we've suffered all these years. Now the communists are here, leading us to become our own masters. We must
stand up and act!

OLD MAN   Well, yes, District Head, Ta-chun. . . . We'll leave you
now.

DISTRICT HEAD   All right. In a few days we'll get together and have a
talk.

[*The villagers leave.*]

DISTRICT HEAD [*to* CHAO *and* TA-SO]   Village Head, Ta-so, it's clear
what's happening. We've studied the relevant materials in our office too. [*In a low voice.*] This is no simple matter. . . .

TA-CHUN [*following him up*]   That's right. Landlord Huang is involved. The district office has decided to get to the bottom of the
mystery of the "White-haired Goddess." . . . Tonight there'll be a
full moon. I think Ta-so and I should go to the Goddess' Temple. . . .

[*They confer in whispers.*]

DISTRICT HEAD [*to* CHAO *and* TA-SO]   What do you think? Do you agree?

CHAO   Yes. A good idea.

TA-SO   Right, let's see what happens tonight.

DISTRICT HEAD   Better be on your guard, Village Head.

CHAO [*eagerly*]   That goes without saying. . . . [*Turns to* HU-TZU.]
Hu-tzu, you keep a sharp watch in that direction tonight. Our day of
vengeance is coming, youngster.

TA-CHUN   Then let's go quickly and prepare.

[*They walk briskly out.*]

[HU-TZU, *holding his red-tasseled lance, climbs onto a mound to stand
guard.*]

[*Curtain*]

SCENE II

Evening.
The Goddess' Temple. There are offerings on the shrine. It is dark
and eerie.

[*Enter* TA-CHUN *carrying a pistol, and* TA-SO *with an unlighted torch and a big knife. Approaching the door, they look around, then whisper together and enter the temple.* TA-CHUN *points out a corner to* TA-SO, *and both hide themselves.*]

[*The wind roars. The temple lamp sheds an eerie light.*]

[*Pause.*]

[TA-CHUN *peers out from the gloom, then shrinks back into the shadows.*]

[*There is musical accompaniment throughout.*]

TA-SO [*nervously*]   Ta-chun! Ta-chun!

TA-CHUN [*stopping him*]   Quiet! [*Makes a gesture, and they keep silent again.*]

[*Enter the "White-haired Goddess" from outside. She darts behind the shrine. After a while, seeing there is nobody there, she comes out to collect the sacrifices on the shrine.*]

[TA-CHUN *and* TA-SO *leap out from the darkness.*]

TA-CHUN [*shouting*]   Who are you?

HSI-ERH [*taken by surprise, is bewildered. She shrieks and rushes at* TA-CHUN]   Ah!

[TA-CHUN *fires.* HSI-ERH *is hit in the arm and falls, but she gets up and runs out in fright.*]

TA-CHUN   Ta-so! After her, quick!

[*The scene changes. On the mountain path.*]

[HSI-ERH, *clutching her wounded arm, runs with difficulty, and jumps over a ditch and runs off.*]

[TA-CHUN *and* TA-SO *follow.*]

TA-SO   Which way? She's vanished again!

TA-CHUN [*looks around and down at the ground*]   The trail of blood has disappeared too.

TA-SO [*looking down*]   There's a valley beneath us. We have come a long way.

TA-CHUN [*making a discovery*]   Look, Ta-so! There's a gleam of light!

TA-SO   Ah, it must be a cave!

[*The crying of a child is heard.*]

TA-CHUN [*listening hard*]   There seems to be a child crying. . . . Let's go after her, Ta-so.

[*The two jump across the ditch.*]

TA-CHUN   Ta-so, light the torch! [*Exeunt.*]

[*The music continues. There is a gust of wind.*]

[*The scene changes again. Inside the cave. An oil lamp gleams on a ledge of the rock, its flickering light revealing the gloom and horror of the cave. On one side are piled firewood, wild fruit, maize and temple offerings. The child is struggling and crying on the firewood as* HSI-ERH, *panic-stricken, crawls into the cave, and blocks the entrance with a rock. Seeing its mother the child crawls over, crying "Ma!" Outside the cave* TA-CHUN's *voice is heard "Ta-so! Here! Here!" They push at the rock, which crashes down. They enter the cave,* TA-SO *holding the torch.* HSI-ERH *hastily steps to one side to shield her child with her body.*]

TA-CHUN [*covering* HSI-ERH *with his pistol*]   Are you man or spirit? Speak!
TA-SO   Quickly! Man or spirit?
TA-CHUN   Speak or I'll fire!
HSI-ERH [*with hatred, fiercely*]   I. . . .
TA-CHUN   Speak! Speak and I'll let you go.
HSI-ERH   I . . . I. . . . [*Explosively.*] I'm human, human, human! [*Sings*]

> I'm flesh and blood! I've a heart like you!
> Why do you say I'm not human?

TA-CHUN   Where did you come from?
HSI-ERH [*sings*]

> Under the mountain a stream flows by,
> From Yangko Village my family!

TA-CHUN and TA-SO [*startled*]   Then how did you come here?
HSI-ERH   All because of your Huang family! [*Sings*]

> You hounded my dad to death!
> You forced Ta-chun to leave home! [TA-CHUN
>   *and* TA-SO *stand dumbfounded.*]

You want to kill me, but I won't die!
I came and lived in this cave,
Each day I traced a line on the stone,
But they're not enough to express my hate!
Such hate, such burning for revenge
Is cut in my bones and engraved on my heart!
Ah! [*Cries.*]
Did you think I was dead?
You were wrong, wrong! [*Laughs loudly.*]
I'm a fire you'll never put out!
I'm a tree you'll never uproot!

TA-CHUN and TA-SO   What is your name?
HSI-ERH [*sings*]

I'm the fire in the waste, I'm the tree on the hill!
And I am Hsi-erh—who is living still!

[TA-CHUN *and* TA-SO *exclaim in amazement.*]

HSI-ERH   Well, now you've come again, I'll have it out with you! I'll
have it out with you! [*Rushes wildly at them.*] [TA-CHUN *and* TA-SO
stand there at a loss. The torch in TA-SO's *hand is still burning, and
by its light she sees* TA-CHUN's *face.*] Ah, you, you! [*To her amazement she recognizes* TA-CHUN.] Are you Ta-chun? [*Faints.*]

[*The child cries over her.*]

[TA-CHUN *and* TA-SO *step forward hastily and look at her.*]

TA-CHUN [*speaking as if in a dream*] Yes. . . . It is Hsi-erh. [*He
pauses, not knowing what to do, then sees the wound on her arm.*]
Ah! [*Taking a towel, he binds it up very sadly, calling softly.*]
Hsi-erh!
TA-SO   Hsi-erh!

[*The pain of her wound brings* HSI-ERH *to herself. She sighs and opens
her eyes. When she sees* TA-CHUN *she knows all is well, and listlessly
closes her eyes again.*]

[*Musical accompaniment.*]

TA-CHUN [*looks from* HSI-ERH *to the cave. He remembers all the past,
and his tears flow. Then he grows angry.*]   Now I understand every-

thing! Ta-so! Go back quickly to tell the district head. Have Land-lord Huang arrested! Tell Old Chen to report to the district!

TA-SO Right!

TA-CHUN Hold on! And tell my mother and Aunty Chang to bring some clothes to fetch Hsi-erh back!

TA-SO Right! [*Hurries off.*]

TA-CHUN [*to* HSI-ERH] Hsi-erh! Hsi-erh! [HSI-ERH *comes to herself.*] We've come to ask you to go back.

HSI-ERH Eh? To go back? [*Shakes her head.*]

TA-CHUN [*vehemently*] You don't realize, Hsi-erh, how things have changed outside. Do you remember the Red Army Uncle Chao spoke about that year? Well, now the Red Army's come—it's called the Eighth Route Army now. They've come, and we poor folks have become masters! You must go out, we must take revenge!

HSI-ERH [*after a pause, in a low voice*] Ah . . . changed . . . changed! Revenge! [*She nods.*] Revenge!

[TA-CHUN *takes off his jacket and puts it over* HSI-ERH's *shoulders, then picks up the child and leads* HSI-ERH *out of the cave. Dawn is breaking and birds can be heard. There is sunlight outside the cave.*]

[*Singing offstage*]

> The sun's come out! The sun's come out!
> The sun so bright—a blaze of light!
> For generations till today
> We suffered pain and grief;
> But today we've seen the sun rise
> To drive away the gloom of night!
> Where did our Hsi-erh disappear to?
> She's left us many a year.
> But today—
> We'll trample down the hill,
> We'll tear open the mountain cave,
> To rescue Hsi-erh!
> To rescue her!

[TA-SO *leads the district head,* AUNTY WANG, AUNTY CHANG, OLD CHAO, *and others up the mountain path. They enter singing.*]

ALL [*sing*]

> Where is Hsi-erh?
> Where is Hsi-erh?

TA-SO Over there—ah, look!

ALL [*sing*]

> Hsi-erh has come! She's coming home!

[*They advance in welcome.*]

[HSI-ERH's *appearance dumbfounds them. After a moment* AUNTY WANG *goes up to her.*]

WANG Hsi-erh!

CHANG [*going to her*] Hsi-erh!

CHAO Hsi-erh!

[*Seeing these familiar faces,* HSI-ERH *is at first unable to speak. Presently she calls:* "Uncle Chao! Aunty Chang! Aunty Wang!" *Finally she falls into* AUNTY WANG's *arms and sobs bitterly. All are moved to tears.* AUNTY WANG *and* AUNTY CHANG *straighten* HSI-ERH's *hair.*]

DISTRICT HEAD Don't be sad, friends! Today we've rescued Hsi-erh! That's good! Tomorrow we'll hold a mass meeting to accuse Landlord Huang, avenge Hsi-erh, and vent our anger. Let's go back now!

ALL [*sing*]

> Country folk, comrades, don't shed tears!
> The old life forced men to turn into ghosts,
> But the new life changes ghosts back into men,
> It's saved our unhappy sister here!
> The new life changes ghosts into men,
> She's been restored to us again!

[*While singing they help* HSI-ERH *off.*]

[*Curtain*]

SCENE III

The following morning at sunrise.

At the gate of the HUANG family ancestral hall, chosen as the meeting place for the peasants' mass meeting.

[*Gongs sound offstage. Shouts are heard:* "Come to the meeting!" "The meeting's at the gate of the Huang family ancestral hall."]

[*Singing offstage*]

Age-old injustice must be avenged,
And a thousand years' wrongs be set right!
Hsi-erh, who was forced to become a ghost,
Becomes human again today!
Crushing rents must be reduced,
The grain extorted must be restored!
Those who suffered their whole lives long,
Will stand up and become the masters today!

How much of our blood have you sucked?
How much have you drunk of our sweat?
How much of our grain did you steal?
How much of our gold did you get?
How long have you tricked and oppressed us?
How many deaths lie at your door?
Today we shall settle scores with you,
Settle every old score!

[*The curtain parts.*]

[*Innumerable peasants have stood up to accuse* LANDLORD HUANG.]

[*The district head,* TA-CHUN, UNCLE CHAO *and others are standing on the platform. Self-Defense Corps guards, armed with red-tasseled lances and swords, surround the meeting place.* LANDLORD HUANG, *in mourning for his mother, stands with bent head below the platform, while* STEWARD MU *has hidden under the table.*]

[HUANG *has just spoken, and now it is the turn of the masses to question him. Feeling is running high.*]

FIRST PEASANT [*sings*]

You pretend to reduce the rent, but it's all a lie!

ALL [*in chorus*]

You pretend to reduce the rent, but it's all a lie!

SECOND PEASANT [*sings*]

You take the land back on the sly!

ALL [*in chorus*]

You take the land back on the sly!

THIRD PEASANT [*sings*]

> When you've rumors to spread, you rattle away!

ALL [*in chorus*]

> When you've rumors to spread, you rattle away!

FOURTH PEASANT [*sings*]

> When you hound folk to death, you've nothing to say!

ALL [*in chorus*]

> Then you've nothing to say!
> Then you've nothing to say!
> So much rent you squeezed, so much money too,
> There's no counting the tragedies caused by you!
> *Speak, Landlord Huang! Speak up, you!*

[HUANG *mumbles and wants to justify himself. The crowd grows angry.*]

CHAO [*sings*]

> Landlord Huang, do you argue still?
> To pretend to be crazy will serve you ill!

ALL [*in chorus*]

> Serve you ill!

TA-CHUN   Landlord Huang, I tell you—[*Sings*]

> The bad old times have got to stop!
> We common folk are up on top!

ALL [*in chorus*]

> Today the world is ours instead!
> Murderers must atone for the dead!
> Pay what you owe to the folk you've bled!
> We'll have your blood for the blood you've shed!

[*Two peasant women rush forward.*]

FIRST WOMAN [*sings*]

> That year—in the ninth moon,

SECOND WOMAN [*simultaneously*]

> That year—in the twelfth moon,

FIRST WOMAN [*sings*]

> You came to our door for the rent!

SECOND WOMAN [*simultaneously*]

> You came to our door for the debt!

FIRST WOMAN [*sings*]

> You beat my boy till he nearly died!

SECOND WOMAN [*simultaneously*]

> You beat my dad till you broke his legs!

TOGETHER [*sing*]

> We'll have your blood for the blood you've shed!

ALL [*sing*]

> Murderers must atone for the dead!
> Pay what you owe to the folk you've bled!
> We'll have your blood for the blood you've shed!

[THIRD *and* FOURTH PEASANTS *rush forward.*]

THIRD PEASANT [*sings*]

> The wrong you did me I'll never forget!

FOURTH PEASANT [*simultaneously*]

> The hatred I bear you I'll never forget!

THIRD PEASANT [*sings*]

> My son must repair the dike, you said!

FOURTH PEASANT [*sings*]

> My brother must build you a tower, you said!
> My brother fell to his death from the tower!

THIRD PEASANT [*sings*]

> My son was swept off and drowned in the flood!

TOGETHER [*sing*]

> Your crimes will be visited on your head!

ALL [*sing*]

> Murderers must atone for the dead!
> Pay what you owe to the folk you've bled!
> We'll have your blood for the blood you've shed!

[*The crowd roars:* Make Landlord Huang speak! Landlord Huang! Answer us!]

[HUANG *continues to mutter.*]

CHAO [*loudly*]   Neighbors! Since he won't confess, let's not waste our breath on him! Hu-tzu! You fetch Hsi-erh here!

ALL [*echoing him*]   Right! Fetch Hsi-erh!

[HU-TZU *runs off.* HUANG *and* MU *stand aghast.*]

PEASANT WOMEN [*tearfully, sing*]

> Hsi-erh! . . .

ANOTHER GROUP OF WOMEN [*sing*]

> Hsi-erh! . . .

PEASANTS [*sing*]

> Hsi-erh! . . .
> Hsi-erh! . . .

PEASANT WOMEN [*sing*]

> The poor child suffered bitterly,
> But a new life starts for us poor folk today!

ALL [*sing*]

> A new life starts! A new life starts today!

[HU-TZU's *voice offstage:* "Hsi-erh is coming!"]

[*All turn to see* HSI-ERH. *Sing*]

> Today the world belongs to us,
> We'll take revenge for past wrongs!

Past wrongs!
We'll accuse!
We'll accuse!
And avenge Hsi-erh for all past wrongs!

[*Enter* AUNTY WANG *and* AUNTY CHANG *supporting* HSI-ERH, *who is wearing a new dress.*]

THE CROWD [*shouts*]   We want vengeance for Hsi-erh!

[*Seeing* HUANG, HSI-ERH *rushes across like a mad thing to scratch him, but her thirst for vengeance overcomes her, so that she falls fainting into the arms of* AUNTY WANG *and* AUNTY CHANG.]

[*Pause.*]

CHAO [*moved to tears*]   Child, don't be upset! The time has come for you to speak!
TA-CHUN   Hsi-erh! Did you hear? The time has come for you to speak!
HSI-ERH [*as if in a dream*]   What? The time . . . has come . . . for us to speak?
ALL [*thunderously*]   Yes! Hsi-erh, the time has come to speak!
WANG and CHANG   Speak, child!
HSI-ERH   I'll speak, I'll speak, I—will—speak!

[*Sings*]

> I want vengeance for all that happened,
> My wrongs are too many to tell!
> They're a mountain that can't be leveled,
> A sea that can't be drained!
> But what's caused such a great change
> That I can beard my enemy today?
> Landlord Huang—
> To be cut into pieces is too good for you!

ALL [*sing*]

> To be cut into pieces is too good for you!
> To be cut into pieces is too good for you!
> To be cut into pieces is too good for you!

HSI-ERH [*sings*]

> That year—[*Her voice falters.*]

WANG [*sings*]

> That year on New Year's Eve,

HSI-ERH [*sings*]

> In storm and snow—

WANG [*sings*]

> Mu came and pressed for rent!

HSI-ERH [*sings*]

> And hounded my dad to death!

WANG [*sings*]

> Our good Old Yang was hounded to death!

ALL [*sing*]

> Those hounded to death
> Are too many to count!
> Too many to count!

HSI-ERH [*sings*]

> On New Year's Day—

CHANG [*sings*]

> They took her to the Huangs' house that day—

HSI-ERH [*sings*]

> I led a wretched life there—

CHANG [*sings*]

> She was raped by Landlord Huang!

PEASANT WOMEN [*shocked, sing*]

> Ah! Ah!

HSI-ERH [*cries and sings*]

> Ah! . . .

CHANG [*sings*]

> Then they wanted to sell her—

HSI-ERH [*sings*]

> As a prostitute!
> Landlord Huang! Landlord Huang!
> Murderous brute!

ALL [*sing*]

> You man-devouring beast!
> The day of reckoning has come!

[*Unable to control their anger, the villagers rush forward to beat* HUANG.]

[*The district head and others stop them.*]

DISTRICT HEAD   Friends, don't beat him yet! Let Hsi-erh finish.

HSI-ERH [*sings*]

> But Aunty Chang, she saved me,
> So I could leave the tigers' den.
> It was pitch black!

ALL [*sing*]

> It was pitch black!

HSI-ERH [*sings*]

> And the way was dark!

ALL [*sing*]

> And the way was dark!

HSI-ERH [*sings*]

> I didn't know where to turn!

ALL [*sing*]

> Where did you go?

HSI-ERH [*sings*]

> I stayed in a cave in the mountain,
> Far from people and out of the sun,
> Eating raw fruit and offerings,
> Till I seemed neither ghost nor man!

But I refused to die,
Though stones rot or streams run dry!
I bore my hardships till today,
And today they have vanished away!

WANG, CHANG, and PEASANT WOMEN [*sing*]

In the light of the sun. . . .

HSI-ERH [*sings*]

Let vengeance be done!

PEASANT WOMEN [*sing*]

She'll be avenged in the light of the sun!

ALL [*sing*]

Now our time has come,
We must be revenged!
We want justice done,
Hsi-erh must be avenged!

[*No longer to be stopped they rush forward and beat* HUANG *and* MU.]

[*The district head and other cadres try to stop the crowd. The district head stands on a table.*]

DISTRICT HEAD [*shouts*]   Friends! I represent the government. I support your charges against Landlord Huang. We will certainly avenge Hsi-erh. First let us arrest Huang and Mu for public trial according to proper legal procedure.

[*All cheer excitedly.*]

[*Members of the Self-Defense Corps tie up* HUANG *and* MU.]

ALL [*sing*]

Landlord Huang, you have bowed your head!
You quake with dread!
You have bowed your head!
You quake with dread!
Age-old feudal bonds
Today are cut away!

Crushing iron chains
Will be smashed to bits today!

[*The song is repeated.*]

[*The sun rises. It shines brightly on* HSI-ERH *and the surging crowd, who shout for joy and sing*]

We, who suffered in days bygone,
Shall be our own masters from now on!
Shall be our own masters from now on!
Our—own—masters—from—now—on!

[LANDLORD HUANG *crouches before the crowd like a felled tree.*]

[*The peasants stand proudly under the sun, countless arms raised high.*]

[*Curtain*]

The
Red
Detachment
of
Women

Ballet Slippers and Rifles

The greatest international attention shown any recent cultural event in China was directed to The Red Detachment of Women. *The show, described in program notes as a model of the "revolutionary modern ballet," was viewed in Peking by then President Richard Nixon on February 22, 1972; a filmed version was shown on U.S. television by the National Broadcasting Company on March 12. Western critics of the ballet tended to alternate between admiration of the technical side of the performances and an ironic view of its all-too-obvious political message.*

Norman Webster, Peking correspondent for The Globe and Mail, *the Toronto daily newspaper, reported on the opening performance of the ballet in November 1969, noting at the outset that "the heroes were suitably heroic," the "villains—a cruel landlord and his mercenaries—were sneaky, nasty, cowardly degenerates." He said that the ruling élite, whose fate used to dominate Peking opera in the past, were now only "black foils against which workers, peasants and soldiers strike bright sparks of goodness."*

As Webster saw the plot, it involved the daughter of a poor peasant in the days before the Communist victory in China, when she was "enslaved and viciously beaten by an evil landlord and the leader of his mercenaries (or, as the Chinese program put it, his running dog). The girl finally escapes, encounters a handsome member of the Red Army political cadre, and makes her way to the camp of a Red women's fighting force. She is taught the rationale of the revolution and joins the detachment." The summary continues:

"Later, sent on a scouting mission into the landlord's headquarters, she comes upon the hateful man. Unable to control herself, she

shoots him, thus prematurely giving her comrades the signal to attack. Although victorious in the ensuing skirmish, the detachment fails to capture the landlord: only wounded, he makes his escape. The heroine's pistol is taken away from her because of her rashness, and she receives it back (with tears of gladness) when she has realized that making revolution is much more than just settling personal scores.

"Battles follow, Communist soldiers, men and women, against 'Kuomintang bandits,' and the Communists roll up victory after victory. But the handsome party man is wounded and captured and, scorning a chance to save his life by signing a document proffered by the landlord, walks bravely to his death in a great bonfire. The Red Army soon liberates all the oppressed peasants. The heroine personally kills the landlord and, learning of the party man's fate, does a dance of grief. She then becomes party representative with the women's movement."

Reporting on the Peking audience's first reaction to the new ballet, Webster observed that it "was with the show from the start." The crowd ranged from children to grandmothers, and its interest was kept riveted on the dancing, the "excellent special effects (thunder and rain, exploding grenades), colorful costumes and exaggerated acting." He reported that the landlord was the "prime creation" of the ballet, whether he was acted as "the perfect Western-style villain in Panama hat, gold watch chain and black and white oxfords, or oozing evil Oriental style in magnificent subtly colored robes. At first huge and arrogant, with cruel mustache and sideburns, he became by the end a fearful, broken creature scrabbling frantically about the stage as the Red Army moved in. The audience, which had hated him from the start, now found him a hugely amusing spectacle. Applause broke out when he was shot down."

When President Nixon saw The Red Detachment of Women *in Peking, other analyses of the ballet were published in the West. The New York Times, on February 23, 1972, published commen-*

taries on the ballet by Faubion Bowers, an authority on the performing arts in Asia, and on the music by its staff reviewer Harold C. Schonberg. Mr. Bowers wrote that, "whatever the Chinese may feel toward the Russians nowadays, one debt of gratitude" is owed, enabling them to "combine toe slippers and rifles, and with splendid effect." He recalled that the Soviet Union had sent some of its best Bolshoi teachers to Peking. With the cooperation of the then Minister of Culture Mao Tun, they laid the groundwork for what became the Peking Ballet Troupe and its Shanghai equivalent. Bowers said that Shih Ching-hua, who played the heroine in the ballet which Mr. Nixon saw, as well as in the film version, is "the prima ballerina" of Peking, although "the star system is eschewed as bourgeois." He added: "She can do anything—a split during a leap in the air, combining a back bend in which her head nearly touches her knee, for example—and do it as well as any dancer with a Russian name."

Mr. Schonberg observed that the musical score of The Red Detachment of Women does not give a composer's name, and that the ballet's music "sounds like Russian academicism with a touch of Oriental exoticism." He added: "Harmonically, 'Red Detachment of Women' is unadventurous. It stays close to D minor and related keys. It uses a few leit-motifs that represent various characters. The scoring is competent but unimaginative. Largely the score is poster music, of a movie background nature, with a great climax toward the end that sings the praises of the workers and peasants." The reviewer found some interest in the music's native elements. The scene of the ballet is the island of Hainan, and Schonberg wrote that "the composer, or arranger, has made full use of Chinese percussion instruments," which provide "an unusual touch to an otherwise conventional example of Moscow Conservatory scoring, 1935 vintage."

An unsigned article in the Peking Review of March 22, 1968, noted that "the composers have used a great deal of Hainan folk song rich in local color," thereby transforming "the ballet art which was once exclusively in the service of the foreign feudal and bourgeois lords" into an art that is close to the common people of China. In its choreography, the article stated, the ballet "has swept away the decadent, ethereal, fairy-like poses of the ballet," weaving "elements of the Chinese classical dance and folk dances into the ballet style." The Peking periodical's analysis said that the music was "militant, with its emphasis on the portrayal of characters," expressing "the bravery of the women soldiers" in its theme song.

Behind this finished product lay a "fierce struggle," Peking Review continued. Without naming the role of Russian ballet instructors or of Mao Tun, it noted that "ballet has a history of less than 20 years in China." Without naming deposed Communist Party Secretary Liu Shao-chi by name, the periodical summarized his alleged cultural conflict with Mao's wife, as follows:

"When the ballet troupe was dominated by the counter-revolutionary revisionist line in art, it did exactly what troupes in capitalist and modern revisionist [a reference to the Soviet Union] countries have done. It put on ballets like Swan Lake, The Corsair, Giselle and Notre-Dame de Paris (Esmeralda). The revolutionary members of the troupe finally refused to tolerate this any longer and rose to make a revolution in art. Yet the top Party capitalist roader [Liu] pontificated: 'The reflection of contemporary life cannot be forced. It is not certain whether the ballet and foreign opera can reflect it.' In 1964, he even raised the cry that ballet should not be reformed and must remain a completely Western form. Comrade Chiang Ching sharply rebutted these reactionary fallacies. She said: Ballet has been performed in foreign countries for several hundred years. But now Western ballet is decaying and dying. It falls to us to raise and carry the red banner of revolution in the ballet. She encouraged the members of the troupe to serve, not a handful of persons, but the people of the entire coun-

try as well as the revolutionary people of Asia, Africa and Latin America."

An even more pointed account of the background struggle involving the production of The Red Detachment of Women *was provided by Wu Hsiao-ching in an article entitled "A Great Victory in 'Making Foreign Things Serve China,'" which appeared in* Chinese Literature, *No. 5, 1969. Wu put the underlying problem bluntly: "The ballet is a classical art form foreign to China. How to deal with classical Western culture, particularly this so-called 'exclusive area in art' hitherto monopolized by the bourgeoisie, involves two diametrically opposed policies. Should we remould it, occupy it and conquer it, or should we bow to tradition and allow it to go on serving the bourgeoisie?" The author gives the following version of the behind-the-scenes conflict:*

"The 'wholesale westernization' advocated by the big renegade Liu Shao-chi and his agents in the field of literature and art, Chou Yang and company, goes contrary to this revolutionary principle [Mao's saying, 'Make foreign things serve China.']. The revisionists babbled that the ballet is 'the acme of art, something that cannot be surpassed,' and that the ballet should be 'thoroughly western,' 'downright western' and 'western enough to be systematic.'

"This policy of 'wholesale westernization' in literature and art shows up vividly the slavish mentality of Liu Shao-chi, Chou Yang and their ilk who are flunkies of imperialism and focuses a spotlight on their wild ambition to turn China again into an 'adventurers' paradise' for the western bourgeoisie by carrying out the line of 'making China foreignized' in both art and politics. What they meant by 'thoroughly western' was that the characterization, theme and presentation should be all 'western': only aristocrats, swans and immortals should be portrayed but not the workers, peasants and soldiers; only so-called 'eternal themes' such as 'love,' 'life and death,' 'virtue and evil' should be depicted and not the revolutionary struggle of the proletariat.

"What they meant by 'downright western' implied, in the characterization of foreign roles, entering into these roles so that you not only 'act foreign characters but become like foreign characters.' For them a western Swan Lake or Notre Dame, or the love story of Romeo and Juliet are not enough. To foster bourgeois attitudes they said that 'China's first ballet must be Liang Shan-po and Chu Ying-tai (a story of love between pampered children of the rich in ancient China).' They seemed determined to marry China's native lords and ladies to western capitalism."

The article further alleged that proponents of "westernization" sought to have "scholars" and "ladies" occupy "our theatrical stage, corrupt our masses and sabotage our socialist economic base." It accused them of wanting the ballet "to remain forever a tool used by the bourgeoisie to enslave people mentally," make "history go backwards," and thus advance "a thoroughly counterrevolutionary revisionist line in literature and art."

The Peking Review article, quoted earlier, asserted that a struggle for characterization of the central heroine in The Red Detachment of Women, Wu Ching-hua, reflected high-level disagreements. The periodical said that the young woman was "one of the laboring people who suffered bitterly in the old society" and that the ballet should therefore "depict her resistance and struggles and how she matures under the Party's leadership." It accused the supporters of Liu Shao-chi of trying to base the presentation of her personality on a "feudal court favorite," named Zarema, who had appeared in an earlier ballet, Fountain of Bakhchisarai. "They wanted," according to the article, "to impose on her movements of the 'spirit,' sentiments of 'pity and weariness, sadness and grief,'" which was "an attempt to frustrate the transformation of ballet."

The narration of events in Chinese Literature referred to the period of this conflict as "those days when the air was murky with their vicious babbling" and said that this was when "our beloved Comrade Chiang Ching, holding high the great red banner of

Mao Tse-tung's thought, fought against the evil wind and adverse waves to set a new course." She was working not only in the interest of the people of China, the article said, but also for the three billion "revolutionary people in the world," so that "the theme of armed struggle which the ballet Red Detachment of Women presents is actually an extremely important subject in the international communist movement in the twentieth century" and a beginning in "the remolding of the world's theatrical stage with the thought of Mao Tse-tung."

This "remolding," in Wu Hsiao-ching's words, "boils down to the question of the proletariat seizing control of the situation and triumphing over the bourgeosie in the realm of literature and art." He asks whether the character of the heroine, Wu Ching-hua, and the Communist Party leader Hung Chang-ching could possibly be portrayed "with bourgeois and petty bourgeois thinking and emotions?" He answers: "No! Is it possible to use the dance movements of male and female roles in the old ballet without making any changes whatsoever? No! The principles on which our ballet is based are the political and artistic criteria of the proletariat. We select the best dance movements, the highlights, and the most vivid stage arrangements to depict these heroic figures, so that they appear 'On a higher plane, more intense, more concentrated, more typical, nearer the ideal, and therefore more universal than actual everyday life.' " This final quotation is taken from Mao Tse-tung's writings. Specifically, these principles were, consciously and in planned detail, applied as follows:

"The ballet Red Detachment of Women in its characterization of heroic figures was adept in combining certain features of the Chinese drama and folk dance while critically using the old art form of the ballet and on this basis was able to create a brand-new ballet choreography. For instance, when the heroes appear, they all do a liang-xiang (take a conventional stance or pose in such a way as to let the audience gain a clear concept of the character right *from the start), which has been adopted from old Chinese opera, but these are the* liang-xiang *of the ballet and no longer that of old opera."*

When Wu Ching-hua appears, dashing out of a coconut grove, her pose is "fleeting but impressive, like a flash of lightning." When party leader Hung appears, disguised as an overseas merchant to get into the landlord's manor, he is "like a ray of brilliant sunshine brightening the darkest corners." The article describes these poses as "fine, expressive figures" that resemble "sculptured statues in a magnificent setting."

When the heroine is captured and flogged, her dances dramatize that she "remains unvanquished," as "her vigorous leaping movements, particularly in spinning somersaults when she is being flogged, show her fiery rebellious character." Standing "resolute and indomitable," the characterization "is a clear break from the presentation of feminine fragility characteristic of the old ballet." Further. "In the scene of Wu Ching-hua pouring out her bitterness before she joins the Red Army, she flings herself on the red flag and, full of animation, strokes it and the red armband. Then, in a lively pas seul, *she raises her blood-stained arms and with fury condemns Nan Pa-tien's [the landlord's] cruel oppression." In the final scene, when Wu kills the landlord, the ballet "creates a unique dance which utilizes the 'reclining fish' movement of Peking opera in a leap" designed to dramatize "the heroine's political maturity and her military skill and judgment."*

The polarization of characters in ballets such as The Red Detachment of Women *is achieved, according to the article in* Chinese Literature, *through innovations that contrast "beauty and evil, in using negative characters to highlight the heroes." Specifically, "what is fine appears more beautiful, while the evil comes out more vicious this way." To bring out "the great fearless spirit of Hung Chang-ching," the party leader, "who is determined to vanquish all enemies and never to yield, the choreography gen-*

eralizes his revolutionary heroism and optimism into an integrated dance of leaping, splitting, and spinning movements which portray this spirit of his thorough emphasis, varied tempo, and changes in position." The contrast is further emphasized: "On the other hand, the enemy is arranged around him in stooping movements, in contrast to his nobility. This stage pattern presents a vivid contrast of Hung Chang-ching in a series of jumps over the heads of the stooping enemy, so that he appears like an eagle spreading its wings against the storm, while the crawling enemy appears like a pack of stray dogs."

Linking the polarization within the ballet's choreography to the ideological conflict from which it emerged, the article states: "This graphic composition, brimming with revolutionary romanticism, makes us envisage our proletarian revolutionary heroes as a towering Mount Tai in spirit, while the renegade Liu Shao-chi and his ilk, who trumpet about a 'philosophy of survival' in life, are in contrast but a stinking heap of rubbish at the foot of Mount Tai."

One Western observer, Klaus Mehnert, who is equally familiar with the Soviet Union and Communist China, has given his impression of a Peking performance of The Red Detachment of Women *in his book,* China Returns *(1972). He saw the performance in a theater in the southern part of the capital, the Tientsao, or "Bridge of Heaven." The crowds and the gigantic portrait of Mao reminded him, not of present-day Moscow, "but rather of those first performances I had attended in the Soviet Union" in 1929 and 1931. He found that the audience really were "the Masses, the people Mao talks about." The ballet itself also reminded Mehnert of "the early days in the Soviet Union," being "totally political theater glorifying deeds of legendary heroism in a civil war."*

Klaus Mehnert noted that, at the conclusion of the ballet, the head of Mao appeared against the backdrop, "wearing a military cap, encircled by a bright red halo." Everybody called out three

*times, "Long live Mao Tse-tung!" and then the curtain fell. Mehn-
ert commented: "What reminded me so strongly of Russia in the
1920s was not only the proletarian audience; it was the absolute
black-and-white of the plot, the pathos of the gestures and the un-
abashed glorification of violence. In Moscow at the time, the
avant-garde theater of [Vsevolod E.] Meyerhold and Alexander
Tairov was already in decline, and heroic naturalism was the order
of the day. The new theory was that art should have no subtleties;
rather it should exert a strong persuasive influence on people's
thinking. The same was true here."*

PROLOGUE   Filled with Hatred, Wu Ching-hua Flees the Tiger's Jaws
SCENE ONE   Wu Ching-hua Is Helped by Hung Chang-ching to Reach
the Revolutionary Base
SCENE TWO   Wu Ching-hua Denounces the Tyrant for His Crimes, and
Joins the Red Army
SCENE THREE   Night Raid on the Tyrant's Manor
SCENE FOUR   The Party Fosters Heroes; the Army and the People Are
United as One
SCENE FIVE   Intercepting the Enemy at a Mountain Pass
INTERLUDE   Pursuing the Enemy Troops
SCENE SIX   Forward Along the Path Crimson with the Blood of Martyrs

PROLOGUE

The Second Revolutionary Civil War Period [1927-1937]. Hainan Island. Night. THE TYRANT OF THE SOUTH's dungeon.

[*The curtain rises.*]

Chained to a post is WU CHING-HUA, daughter of a poor peasant. She
hates being a bondmaid, a slave. Several times she has run away, but
each time she has been caught, brought back, and cruelly beaten. She
stands with head and chest high, her eyes blazing with hatred. If only
she could smash the bloody shackles which bind her and wreck the lair
of these man-eating beasts!

With her in the dungeon are two other peasant women, locked up by THE TYRANT because they have been unable to pay their land rent. They too have been beaten savagely. Fists clenched, they pour out their hatred.

[*The two women dance.*]

LAO SZU, THE TYRANT's bailiff and bully, enters with a guard. He has been ordered to take CHING-HUA out and sell her.

He unlocks the shackles, releasing CHING-HUA. Strong class feeling makes her forget her painful injuries and rush to her cellmates. She urges them to fight THE TYRANT to the end.

LAO SZU comes after her and threatens her with his whip, pushing her toward the dungeon door.

Catching him off guard, CHING-HUA seizes the whip and kicks him to the ground. [*At the door, she does "gong jian bu." Her arms forcefully spread, she glares at* LAO SZU, *and performs "liang xiang."*]

He starts to rise. The two women throw themselves on him and the guard and hold them fast.

CHING-HUA watches in concern. The women urge her to flee.

She dashes out of the tiger's maw with determination.

SCENE ONE

Immediately following the prologue. Late at night in the dark coconut grove.

[*Lanterns marked "South Manor" gleam.*]

LAO SZU and a gang of guards are in pursuit of CHING-HUA. Carrying whips and ropes, they prowl like beasts of prey among the coconut trees, but in vain. LAO SZU is fuming with rage. He orders his men to scatter and search.

[*Dance of* LAO SZU *and the guards.*]

CHING-HUA is hidden behind a tree. After the gangsters leave, she emerges quickly. [*She does "zu jian gong jian bu liang xiang."*]

[*Solo dance.*]

She advances swiftly in big strides. [*Then she rapidly does "zu jian sui bu—pas couru," and "pi cha tiao—pas de chat," followed by "pu bu.*"] Separating small trees with her hands, she cautiously peers in all directions, then runs deeper into the grove. The enemy's chase intensifies her hatred. If they don't catch her, she'll flee. If they do, she'll fight. Rather death than slavery! [*She does "ping zhuan—chaîné," "ye tui zhuan—tour en dedans," "xian shen tan hai—attitude basse" and "dao ti zi jin guan."*]

Discovering "civil guards" coming her way, CHING-HUA nimbly hides behind a tree.

Two of the men furtively search.

She cleverly eludes them but in the darkness bumps into LAO SZU. They grapple in a desperate struggle.

[*Struggle dance.*]

CHING-HUA turns and jumps up. Flinging off his arms, she swings one leg in a sweeping kick. LAO SZU leaps to avoid it. She turns and runs. Pursuing, he grabs her left arm. She angrily pushes down on him. Neither give way. [*They do "xi tui la zhuan—tour lent à deux."*]

She breaks loose. Again he pounces on her. She fights fiercely. [*She does "pi cha," "jiao zhu," "jian shi bian shen tiao—jeté entrelacé," and "diao yao," then performs "liang xiang."*]

"You're coming back with me," LAO SZU yells.

She furiously raises her head. "I'll die first!" LAO SZU is weakening. CHING-HUA's courage doubles. She twists his arm, bites him fiercely and kicks him to the ground.

She runs, but the vicious guards catch up and surround her. They are too many for her. She again falls into their clutches.

THE TYRANT OF THE SOUTH rushes in, followed by "civil guards" and bondmaids. The sight of CHING-HUA's stubborn resistance enrages him. He cruelly presses her temple with the tip of his cane. She is adamant and refuses to bow her head. He strikes her savagely. She seizes one end of the cane. She will fight even if it costs her life. [*They do "chuan fan shen."*] THE TYRANT trembles with rage. He orders his guards to drag CHING-HUA aside. "Beat her to death!" he howls.

Whip blows are heard. The hearts of the bondmaids, who share the same suffering and hatred as CHING-HUA, burn like fire. They are torn by anxiety for her. The tearing cuts of the whips seem to be ripping their own flesh. If only they could save their class sister!

[*The bondmaids dance.*]

THE TYRANT decides to make CHING-HUA an example to cow the others.

He orders that she be dragged in and beaten to death before their eyes.

CHING-HUA refuses to yield. She continues to fight courageously as the lackeys rain blows on her with their whips. [*She does "tan hai fan shen" and "guo bao."*] She struggles, chest high and fists raised, until they beat her unconscious.

LAO SZU announces that she is dead. "Anyone who resists or tries to escape," THE TYRANT grates threateningly to the bondmaids, "will meet the same fate."

Thunder rumbles. A storm is brewing. THE TYRANT, LAO SZU, and other lackeys hastily leave. Heartbroken, the bondmaids rush toward CHING-HUA. The "civil guards" drive them away.

Lightning flashes, thunder rumbles. A violent storm shakes the coconut grove.

In the deluging rain, CHING-HUA slowly revives.

[*Solo dance.*]

Her body a mass of excruciating wounds, weak from hunger and cold, where can she go in this dark night? Is there no end to the coconut grove? [*She does "zu jian sui bu—pas suivi."*] Is there no road open to oppressed slaves? Haltingly, she stumbles forward, forward. . . . Then the pain overcomes her and she falls in a faint.

The rain passes, the sky clears. Dawn breaks through the mist. Sunlight slants into the coconut grove.

Red Army cadre HUNG CHANG-CHING and his messenger PANG enter, disguised as peasants. They are on a scouting mission.

[HUNG *and* PANG *dance.*]

Bold, steady, and alert, a bamboo hat in hand, HUNG advances, examining the surroundings. [*He does "ji bu yuan chang," inclined forward to look around, then performs "liang xiang."*] He peers everywhere with flashing eyes. [*Lightly he does "qian yue—sissonne ouverte," "cuo bu—chassé," "shang bu fan shen," and performs "liang xiang."*]

He and PANG discover the fainted CHING-HUA. They run over and lift her up. She gradually comes to. On seeing two strangers, she struggles to run away.

"Don't be afraid," they say kindly. "We're poor working people just like you."

Dizzy from her exertions, CHING-HUA nearly falls. HUNG quickly supports her. He sees the bloody weals on her arms. Shocked, he gently pats them with the towel from around his neck.

Class hatred flames in his heart. "Who beat you like this?"

His simple, earnest manner dispels CHING-HUA's suspicions. She angrily points toward where THE TYRANT has gone. "That fiend who kills without blinking an eye—the Tyrant of the South!"

"The Tyrant of the South," HUNG and PANG repeat in fury. "That butcher! We'll make him pay for his countless bloody crimes."

In concern HUNG asks: "Where will you go now? Where is your home?"

"Home? I have no home. . . ."

HUNG is filled with deep proletarian feeling for this poor peasant's daughter who has suffered so bitterly. He points and says: "Beyond the coconut grove, on the other side of the mountain, red flags wave in the bright sun. The armed forces of us workers and peasants are there. Go and join them and get revenge."

CHING-HUA, though lacerated and bruised all over, is greatly inspired. "No matter how many hardships and dangers, that's the road I will take."

[HUNG, CHING-HUA, *and* PANG *dance.*]

The men, fists clenched, take leaping steps to urge CHING-HUA on. [*They do "xi tui tiao—temps levé, jambe repliée."*] She is tremendously encouraged. [*She does "he li xuan zhuan—grande pirouette attitude."*] In the bright morning sunlight, HUNG enthusiastically points out the road to revolution. [*The three perform "zao xing."**]

HUNG takes two silver coins from his pocket and gives them to CHING-HUA. "Here is something for the road."

Silver! The girl stares, astonished. [*She does a startled stance on points.*]

CHING-HUA, CHING-HUA, a tender shoot who sprouted from under a stone, who grew steeped in bitter water, who has worked since childhood like a beast of burden, a girl who never had a home or saw a dear one. [*Agitated, she moves backward on "sui bu—pas couru."*]

"Is . . . is this for me?"

HUNG nods. "For you."

CHING-HUA doesn't know what to do. Tears in her eyes, she gazes fixedly at HUNG, filled with gratitude.

Such kindness is much too profound for her!

* A sculptural dancing pose struck by the artists in the course of a dance or during a pause in order to present a harmonious unity of physical appearance and mental world of the characters.

She wipes her hands on the front of her tunic and, trembling, accepts the silver. She gives HUNG a deep bow, then flies off in the direction he has indicated.

HUNG and PANG watch till she is out of sight. Then, alertly scanning the dense grove, they continue scouting. [*They perform "liang xiang."*]

[*Curtain*]

SCENE TWO

[*Vigorous, ringing, the "March of the Women's Company."*]

Forward, forward!
Important the soldiers' task, deep the women's hatred.
Smash your shackles, rise in revolution!
We're the Women's Company, taking up arms for the people.
Forward, forward!
Important the soldiers' task, deep the women's hatred.
Communism is the truth, the Party leads the way.
Slaves will arise, slaves will arise!
Forward, forward! . . .

A morning several days later, on the drill field in a Red base.

[*The curtain rises.*]

[*Fleecy white clouds dot the clear blue sky, colored flags flutter in the breeze, songs fill the air. A lofty kapok tree is in bloom with a profusion of red flowers.*]

A happy crowd of local people have gathered by the kapok tree to celebrate the formation of the Red Army Women's Company. There are young and old, Red Militia, girls of the Li nationality. . . .

[*Group dance.*]

[*"March of the Women's Company" again rings forth.*]

Bright and brave, the Red women soldiers, with PARTY REPRESENTATIVE HUNG and THE COMPANY COMMANDER at their head, march briskly to the drill field. The peasants are overjoyed, children jump merrily, welcoming cheers resound.

HUNG and THE COMPANY COMMANDER solemnly proclaim the formal

establishment of the Red Company of Women of the Chinese Workers' and Peasants' Red Army!

THE COMPANY COMMANDER orders a practice drill. The girls perform a spirited rifle drill [*"zu jian sui bu—pas suivi"*] to the commands of their leader.

[*Target practice dance.*]

HUNG brandishes a sword vigorously with the fearless heroism of revolutionary soldiers.

He advances with firm, broad steps. [*He does "dao hua," and performs "liang xiang" with sword raised.*] He leaps into the air boldly. [*He does "she yan da tiao," "bei dao fei jiao," "yan shi tiao," "xiao beng zi—série de renversés" and "la tui beng zi—grand jeté en tournant," and performs "liang xiang" with a sword slash.*]

Women soldiers, also flourishing swords, fly back and forth on the stage, steel blades flashing, militant cries ringing.

[*Women's sword dance.*]

A little girl soldier, sturdy and nimble, spiritedly practices with hand grenades.

[*The little girl soldier solo.*]

Women soldiers, bright and bold, do a bayonet drill. It ends with shouts of fierce class hatred.

[*Bayonet dance.*]

Five brawny Red Guard men dash out from the crowd with a five-inch dagger in each hand. They perform a dance full of leaps and twists, brave and clever, manifesting the great strength of the people's forces.

[*Dagger dance.*]

The soldiers and civilians are of one heart. Everyone is stirred. Children perform a mime in dance showing the overthrow of THE TYRANT OF THE SOUTH. The whole place is in a ferment.

[*Dance by the entire ensemble.*]

Suddenly, a Children's Corps sentry rushes in and announces: A girl who has run away from Coconut Grove Manor is here.

She's arrived at last! CHING-HUA, having overcome severe hardships, walks stumbling forward. Everyone surrounds her in concern and supports her. Kids in the Children's Corps tell her: "This is a Red base. See, the red flag!"

Red flag! CHING-HUA stares at the rippling banner with deep emotion. She staggers forward and presses it against her cheek. Tears roll down her face.

"Red flag, oh, red flag, today I've found you! . . ."

Soldiers and peasants crowd around. In agitation she looks at the women soldiers in their new uniforms, at the red star on their caps, the red tabs on their collars, their red armbands. . . . She excitedly touches the girls by the hand.

"I want to be a soldier too!"

HUNG and THE COMPANY COMMANDER and PANG the young messenger come forward. CHING-HUA immediately recognizes her benefactors and is very excited. HUNG enthusiastically presents her to THE COMPANY COMMANDER and the peasants. "This class sister has been cruelly oppressed and her hatred is strong. She was nearly killed several times, but finally managed to escape from the hellish Coconut Grove Manor."

All the soldiers and peasants give CHING-HUA a hearty welcome.

THE COMPANY COMMANDER hands her a bowl of coconut milk. "Drink. This is your home now. We are all your class sisters."

Coconut milk! The cool, sweet liquid is infused with deep class feeling. For more than ten years CHING-HUA had been a bondmaid, a slave. No one treated her like a human being. But today beneath the red flag, how warm the sunshine, how friendly the people! She raises the bowl with both hands and drinks.

THE COMPANY COMMANDER notices the weals on her arms and asks her about herself. For generations CHING-HUA's family suffered bloody oppression. Fury wells up in her heart. She pours out the story of the crimes of THE TYRANT OF THE SOUTH.

[*Solo dance.*]

She pulls up her sleeves and reveals the whip marks covered with blood. [*She does "ce shen xi tui," "zhan chi dun zhuan" and "bei shen gui bu."*] She tells of the tortures she endured in THE TYRANT's dungeon. [*From "pang yue bu—jeté fermé" she turns to "zu jian bing li—soutenu en tournant." In the "zao xing" she shows how she was chained in* THE TYRANT's *dungeon.*] She tells how she was nearly beaten to death by THE TYRANT in the coconut grove. [*She does "tan hai fan shen" and expresses her fury in "liang xiang."*]

HUNG points out the cruelties inflicted on CHING-HUA's family for generations as a lesson to the soldiers and peasants, saying:

"Her suffering is ours. Her hatred is ours. Slaves must arise. But only by taking up guns and waging revolution under the guidance of our great leader Chairman Mao and the Chinese Communist Party can we win a new world and liberate hundreds of millions of suffering people." [*He does "xi tui da tiao," and "kong zhuan—tour en l'air" and performs "liang xiang" with an arm extended.*]

Tremendously aroused, the masses hold up banners reading: "Down with the tyrants! Share out the land!" "Capture the Tyrant of the South." They are determined to overthrow THE TYRANT and liberate Coconut Grove Manor.

HUNG and THE COMPANY COMMANDER approve CHING-HUA's request to join the army. THE COMPANY COMMANDER hands her a rifle.

CHING-HUA excitedly accepts it. Proud and elated, she takes her place in the fighting ranks of the Red Company of Women.

[*Curtain*]

SCENE THREE

Dusk. The courtyard of THE TYRANT's manor.

[*The curtain rises.*]

It is THE TYRANT's birthday. The manor is a scene of revelry and carousing. "Civil guards" carry pots of wine, platters of meat, expensive gifts. Some noisily drive across the yard a number of Li nationality girls they have seized. Local tyrants, evil gentry, Kuomintang scoundrels, and bandit chieftains arrive to join in the festivities.

THE TYRANT emerges from the manor house to greet his guests. Local tyrants and Kuomintang scoundrels present gifts, bow and offer birthday greetings. Highly elated, THE TYRANT invites them into the banquet hall.

His wife orders the bondmaids to serve fruit and cakes.

[*The bondmaids dance.*]

"Civil guards" with whips compel the Li girls to dance for the birthday banquet. Filled with loathing for THE TYRANT and his despotic landlord and gentry guests, the girls are forced to comply.

[*Li nationality dance.*]

A "civil guard" hurries in with a red calling card which he hands to THE TYRANT, announcing: "A distinguished guest has arrived."

THE TYRANT looks at the card. A big merchant from overseas! He doesn't know him. What brings him here? The gentry discuss this, but cannot agree on a reason. Dizzied by the prospect of lavish gifts, THE TYRANT is not willing to let the opportunity slip by. He orders his guards to line up and present arms in welcome to the distinguished guest.

The "distinguished guest" is none other than HUNG, Party representative in the Women's Company. After several days of scouting he has learned the enemy's situation and has worked out a plan. That is, he will take advantage of the festivities of THE TYRANT's birthday party and enter the enemy's lair disguised as a big merchant, accompanied by PANG and other fighters, also in disguise. At midnight, shots will be fired as a signal for the Red Army to attack from the outside while he and his group strike from within. In this way they will wipe out THE TYRANT and his gang.

Calm and dignified, HUNG strides into the courtyard. [*Loftily, he performs "liang xiang."*]

THE TYRANT hastily comes forward to greet him. HUNG orders his "retainers" to present the gifts. THE TYRANT stares greedily. With excessive courtesy he bids his guest take a seat of honor.

To impress HUNG with his authoritativeness, he directs LAO SZU and the "civil guards" to put on military display.

[*"Civil guards" dance with halberds.* LAO SZU *executes a boxing dance.*]

HUNG flings them a handful of silver. They scramble avidly for the rolling coins. THE TYRANT, embarrassed, invites HUNG into the banquet hall.

It is now late at night. The manor looks exceedingly gloomy.

CHING-HUA and another girl soldier steal in, disguised as bondmaids. They want to make contact with PANG. At the doorway, they quietly dispose of the sentry, then look around carefully. CHING-HUA explains the layout of the manor to the other girl.

Footsteps are heard approaching. The girls turn quickly and alertly hide behind a rockery.

Two "civil guards" pursue and savagely beat a little bondmaid. She falls senseless to the ground. They carry her off.

[*Dance of "civil guards" and little bondmaid.*]

CHING-HUA watches in a fury. She charges out to save her suffering class sister. [*She does "ying feng zhan chi—arabesque," "jian shi bian shen tiao—jeté entrelacé" and "pi cha tiao—pas de chat."*] The other girl stops her.

PANG cautiously approaches in the dark. He gives the secret signal CHING-HUA has been waiting for. [*He does "kua ye tui kong zhuan," and "zan bu," landing in a "pu bu" followed by a "guo men kan."*]

[PANG *solo.*]

CHING-HUA hears his signal and goes to him. He tells her there has been no change in the enemy situation. They will proceed according to plan, and strike when HUNG fires the shot. PANG swiftly returns to his own post.

Loud voices in the banquet hall. THE TYRANT and the guests come out. He is seeing them off.

At the sight of THE TYRANT, CHING-HUA's whole being cries out for vengeance. She has only one thought: "Kill the Tyrant of the South! Get revenge! Revenge!"

[*She and her companion dance.*]

CHING-HUA leaves her companion and rushes out. [*She does "dao ti zi jin guan" and "pien tui zhuan."*] The girl tries to hold her back. CHING-HUA is in an uncontrollable rage. [*She does "xian shen tan hai—attitude basse" and "ying feng zhan chi—arabesque."*] Pushing her companion aside, she turns abruptly and fires two shots, wounding THE TYRANT. CHING-HUA has prematurely given the signal.

The startled enemy come swarming out. CHING-HUA's companion pulls her into cover.

Shots crackle on all sides. The Red Army unit has surrounded the bandit lair. Terrified, the wounded TYRANT jumps into a concealed tunnel with LAO SZU and flees.

HUNG swiftly emerges from the hall and calmly prepares to cope with the unexpected change. He makes a rapid appraisal, then orders PANG and the others to kill the "civil guards" in coordination with the Red Army's assault from the outside.

The "civil guards" break and scatter in cowardly flight.

The flag of victory waves over the manor. Tears in their eyes, the peasants surge into the courtyard. HUNG and THE COMPANY COMMANDER tell them: "We've opened the Tyrant's granary. All that grain was the product of the sweat and blood of the poor. It's now going to be returned to you."

Cheering, the peasants race toward the granary.

PANG comes forward with THE TYRANT's cane. "The bandit chieftains, big and small, have all been wiped out," he says. "Only the Tyrant and Lao Szu are missing." THE COMPANY COMMANDER and PANG go to search the rear courtyard.

The peasants, on receiving grain, are overjoyed, HUNG carries in a big basketful. Warmly, fondly, he delivers it into the hands of an old farmhand. With uplifted bags of golden grain, the peasants cheer again and again: "Long live Chairman Mao!" "Long live the Communist Party!" "We thank our dear ones—the Workers' and Peasants' Red Army!"

[*A grain distribution dance by the masses.*]

PANG and THE COMPANY COMMANDER bring in an old despotic landlord they have found in the rear courtyard. In response to HUNG's stern queries, he tremblingly reveals THE TYRANT's tunnel.

CHING-HUA realizes that THE TYRANT has escaped. Enraged and impatient, she is about to plunge, gun in hand, into the tunnel, but HUNG stops her.

THE COMPANY COMMANDER severely criticizes her for breaching discipline, and relieves her of her gun. CHIN-HUA is very upset.

In concern, HUNG asks her how it happened.

[*Curtain*]

SCENE FOUR

Early morning. Rosy clouds fill the sky. A Red Army camp by the Wanchuan River.

[*The curtain rises.*]

On a blackboard beneath the coconut trees is written: "Only by emancipating all mankind can the proletariat achieve its own final emancipation." HUNG is conducting a political class for the women soldiers.

[HUNG *solo.*]

With grand sweeping gestures he points to the distance, indicating the great goals of the proletarian revolution and the responsibilities of revolutionary fighters. "Revolution is not simply a matter of personal vengeance," he says. "Its aim is the emancipation of all mankind." [*He does "yi di xi tui kong zhuan—saut de basque," "duo ni," "pang tui kong zhuan—grand temps levé en tournant à la seconde," and performs "liang xiang."*]

Revolutionary truth illuminates the fighters' hearts like the sun. Standing before the ranks, HUNG encourages them to unite closely, shoulder to shoulder and hand in hand, under the leadership of Chairman Mao and the Chinese Communist Party, and join in the revolutionary torrent which will sweep away the old world.

Class is dismissed. CHING-HUA remains behind. She studies the shining words on the blackboard, then walks, and sits on a stump.

[CHING-HUA *solo.*]

She rises again slowly, her mind in ferment, and tries to grasp the significance of what the Party representative has just said. [*She does "zu sian sui bu—pas suivi," followed by a "she yan" stance in a kneeling position.*]

Regretfully, she recalls her mistake in opening fire without permission in Coconut Grove Manor. "In the whole world is there any proletarian who hasn't been steeped in blood and tears? Why do I think only of vengeance for myself?" [*With a quick succession of "zao xing" on points, she demonstrates how she shot at THE TYRANT OF THE SOUTH.*]

She runs to the blackboard, reads it carefully. Suddenly, she understands. [*She turns forcefully, does "ling kong yue—grand jeté," "he li shi—attitude" and "xian shen tan hai—attitude basse."*] She strides resolutely to greet the rising sun. Fist raised she vows: "I will follow Chairman Mao and the Chinese Communist Party forever and be a conscious proletarian vanguard soldier fighting all my life for the liberation of mankind!"

THE COMPANY COMMANDER, returning from target practice, fondly hails her. CHING-HUA, ashamed, walks over and criticizes herself. Pleased to see CHING-HUA maturing politically, THE COMPANY COMMANDER cannot restrain her affection for the stubborn new fighter. She urges CHING-HUA to continue raising her proletarian consciousness and to transform her hatred for the class enemy into combat skill in annihilating them. Under THE COMPANY COMMANDER's instructions, CHING-HUA practices shooting and grenade throwing.

[*They dance.*]

HUNG arrives and is happy to see CHING-HUA determined, militant, and in high spirits. He tells THE COMPANY COMMANDER to return the gun to CHING-HUA. Greatly moved, the girl expresses her revolutionary determination to THE PARTY REPRESENTATIVE and THE COMPANY COMMANDER.

In the sunshine of the revolutionary base, the heroic Red Army Women's Company is united, alert, earnest, and lively. It has a flourishing and youthful spirit.

Soldiers return from drill with captured enemy rifles and report to HUNG. He chats with them and urges them to capture still more weapons and wipe out still more of the foe.

Several women soldiers enter, carrying fish and vegetables they have grown themselves. HUNG goes to work with the soldiers.

A girl soldier mends an army tunic for one of the men. Two soldiers are absorbed in exchanging experiences of target practice. A group of soldiers patrol along the bank of the river, vigilantly guarding the Red base.

A few girl soldiers, washing vegetables by the river, notice the head cook approaching with a pair of buckets on a shoulder pole. They mischievously block him, snatch the buckets and cheerfully fetch water for him.

[*Dance of the girls and the head cook.*]

Merry songs of approaching peasants can be heard in the distance. HUNG and THE COMPANY COMMANDER go with soldiers to meet them.

Peasants enter with bamboo hats they have woven and lichee nuts they have picked, and present them to the Workers' and Peasants' Red Army.

Holding the hats, the peasant girls dance and sing of the close ties between the soldiers and the civilians.

[*Song*]:

> The river water is clear, oh clear,
> Hats we weave for the Red Army dear,
> Our armymen love the people, we support them delighted,
> As one family we are with them united.
>
> The river water is clear, oh clear,
> Hats we weave for the Red Army dear,

Our armymen love the people, we support them delighted,
Together we strike the foe benighted.

Our Red base is beautiful, we closely cohere,
The river water is clear, oh clear,
Hats we weave for the Red Army dear,
Together we'll march ever on, no fear.

HUNG thanks the peasants on behalf of the army for their warm support. He says the fighters will win more victories to manifest their gratitude.

In response to the peasants' enthusiastic welcome, THE COMPANY COMMANDER and CHING-HUA lead the women soldiers in a joyous dance.

HUNG and the Red Army men dance boldly, staunchly, with vigorous strides and powerful arm movements, with soaring leaps and stalwart gestures. [*They do "xi tui tiao—temps levé, jambe repliée," "bian shen tiao—grand fouetté," "kong zhuan—tour en l'air" and perform "liang xiang."*] These show the all-conquering power and invincible courage of the Workers' and Peasants' Red Army.

[*Dance of* HUNG *and Red Army men.*]

Happy soldiers and civilians, close as one family, gaily dance and sing.

[*Dance of the entire ensemble.*]

Suddenly they hear the approaching beat of galloping hoofs. PANG the messenger enters with an order from headquarters.

Cannon boom in the distance. The Kuomintang troops have launched a major offensive against the base area.

It is a tense situation. HUNG and THE COMPANY COMMANDER decide that they should set out immediately.

The fighters of the Red Army and Red Guards are promptly assembled. They march with firm strides, bidding farewell to dear ones as they hasten to the battlefield.

[*Curtain*]

SCENE FIVE

Shortly before dawn. A battle position in a mountain pass.

[*The curtain rises. Racing clouds, towering cliffs, rolling gunsmoke, leaping flames.*]

In order to wipe out the enemy effectives, the main force of our army is rapidly sweeping around to their rear. THE COMPANY COMMANDER is leading a group from the Women's Company in this maneuver. An intercepting platoon of Red Army soldiers and Red Guards under HUNG is holding the mountain pass to give our army time to complete its move in safety.

Heavy fire is heard at the foot of the mountain, as the crafty enemy attempts a pincers assault. HUNG sizes up the situation and decides to take a few comrades to protect the flank. He orders CHING-HUA to command the holding action in the pass.

"We will complete our mission," CHING-HUA and the soldiers vow.

The enemy charges the pass. Making use of the favorable terrain, CHING-HUA and her comrades give the enemy a head-on blow. Their hate-laden bullets angrily pour down, their hand grenades burst amid the enemy. The fighters are brave and staunch. Solidly united, they give each other cover. [*They do "hua cha" and "gui zhuan."*] They beat back the enemy's frenzied assault.

[*Dance of* CHING-HUA *and the fighters.*]

The little girl soldier is hit, but she continues to fight. CHING-HUA hurries over and bandages her wound.

Having defeated the enemy's flanking attempt, HUNG leads the soldiers back to the position. He shows warm concern for the wounded girl. She vows she will not leave the firing line.

Again the enemy is stirring. They gather additional soldiers and attack once more. The Red Army men tell HUNG: "Our ammunition is nearly finished."

Outnumbered, running out of bullets, HUNG calmly calls the fighters together and says: "Now is the time to prove our worth to the Party. When our bullets are gone, we'll still have our swords and rocks. We must defend the position with our blood and lives!"

The fighters whip out their swords and pick up rocks. Sternly they wait.

The enemy swarm up the slopes, snarling and baring their talons. HUNG and his comrades swing their swords, heave their rocks, and send the foe reeling.

CHING-HUA, who suffered much and has strong class hatred, is firm and courageous, thanks to the education the Party has given her. She hotly battles the attacking diehards.

[*Dance fight of* CHING-HUA *and a "civil guard."*]

Gripping her sword with both hands, she slashes. The enemy hastily wards off the blow. In the heated duel CHING-HUA's blade flies out of her grasp. Fearless, she rushes him, empty-handed, and grabs him by the neck. [*She does "ying feng zhan chi—arabesque," lands in "shuai cha," then rises and performs "liang xiang."*]

She fights with growing strength. One kick sends the guard's halberd sailing, and they grapple. She nimbly trips him down. [CHING-HUA does *"qian qiao" and trips the guard, landing him in a "ke zi." Pressing down on him, she does "xuan zi."*]

The guard weakens. She steps on him, seizes his dagger, and stabs the scoundrel to death.

Red Army soldiers and Red Guards battle shoulder to shoulder, striking terror in the hearts of the enemy.

[*Dance fight of two soldiers and two "civil guards."*]

Amid a hail of bullets and rolling smoke, CHING-HUA, PANG, and the fighters beneath the fluttering red flag valiantly fight the foe. Their courage is enormous. It grows as they battle, and soon the red flag of victory waves on high.

The enemy forces have scattered and retreated, and the heroes remain in control of the position.

HUNG looks at his watch. Excitedly, he announces: "By now our main force has moved out according to plan. Our intercepting platoon has successfully completed its delaying action." Smiles of triumph appear on everyone's face.

As the platoon prepares to leave, the enemy springs another assault. HUNG decides to remain behind and cover the withdrawal of his troops. He orders CHING-HUA to lead the comrades out immediately.

She pleads that she be allowed to stay. CHING-HUA has already been admitted to the Communist Party on the firing line. HUNG solemnly unstraps his dispatch case and gives it to her. "If we should lose contact, deliver this to the battalion Party committee."

He peers down at the enemy at the foot of the mountain. CHING-HUA again goes to him and begs that he let her stay and fight. HUNG waves a resolute hand. "Carry out orders!" She reluctantly leads the comrades from the position.

Only HUNG, a Red Army fighter, and a Red Guard are left. They steadfastly hold out against the foe.

[*They do a militant dance.*]

The enemy feverishly attack. Completely in command of the situation, HUNG battles the foe furiously on every side. [*He does "ping zhuan—chaîne," "kong zhuan—tour en l'air," and flings a grenade. Then he does "ling kong yue zhuan—jeté par terre en tournant" and throws another.*]

The Red Army soldier is hit, wounded. HUNG orders the Red Guard to support him. The Red Guard fighter spots a bandit soldier aiming at HUNG. He rushes him and takes the bullet in his chest.

Two enemy soldiers charge. HUNG, now alone, fights valiantly, with the typical courage of a proletarian revolutionary soldier who has an indomitable spirit and is determined to vanquish all enemies.

[*Dance fight of HUNG and the two enemy soldiers.*]

Swinging his sword, he fights the diehards. [*One enemy soldier falls in "gao pu hu." HUNG whirls and puts his foot on him.*]

The other enemy soldier attacks. HUNG jumps up and slashes at them with his sword and kills them. [HUNG *does "yan shi tiao" and "shuang beng zi—double spirale." He slashes left and right and then performs "liang xiang" with his sword raised.*]

More enemy soldiers swarm in and surround HUNG. He pulls out his last hand grenade, yanks the firing string, and raises it menacingly. The attackers scramble and flee. HUNG flings the grenade after them. It explodes, and they topple to the ground, dead.

Supporting his two comrades, HUNG starts moving out through the pass. They are met by a fusilage of bullets. HUNG is severely wounded. His two companions are killed. With his remaining strength, he gently lowers them to the ground. Holding himself erect by sheer force of will, he gazes after the departing Red Army platoon. A smile of satisfaction appears on his face as the platoon reaches safety.

His wound gives a sharp stab of pain, and he falls in a faint.

Dark clouds gather. Thunder rumbles.

THE TYRANT OF THE SOUTH and a Kuomintang army officer enter with a gang of bedraggled-looking soldiers. Trembling, they crawl to the top of the rise, where they discover HUNG. They fearfully surround him.

HUNG revives. He indignantly pushes the enemy soldiers aside and rises before the clifftop like a towering pine. Lightning rips across the cloudy night sky, illuminating HUNG's militant figure. His angry piercing gaze quells his attackers. Terrified, they dare not look up.

Thunder and lightning rock the firmament.

[*Curtain*]

INTERLUDE

[*The curtain rises.*]

With the momentum of an avalanche the main force of the Red Army advances swiftly in pursuit of the enemy troops.

[*Dance of the Red Army men.*]

Preceded by a flame-red battle flag, the Red Army units, powerful and courageous, cross over mountains chasing the foe.

They press forward as irresistibly as molten steel, speeding like arrows from a bow. [*They do "pi cha da tiao—grand pas de chat."*]

[*Dark change*]

SCENE SIX

Dusk. Rear courtyard of THE TYRANT OF THE SOUTH. Oppressive overcast sky. Dim and gloomy. A huge banyan tree, tall and spreading.

News of one victory after another by the Red Army creates panic in the enemy lair. LAO SZU runs in and threatens the "civil guards" with his gun, trying desperately to halt the collapse.

A Kuomintang army officer, who has been knocked dizzy by the blows of the Red Army, refuses to heed the pleas of THE TYRANT that he remain. He runs for his life, followed by the beaten remnants of his troops.

THE TYRANT'S WIFE is frantically busy, ordering the servants to move her valuables. She stumbles about, ready to flee.

Seeing his power slipping away, THE TYRANT beats his chest, stamps his feet, and roars in frustration. LAO SZU lyingly vows that he will go with his master and fight to the end. They snarl and bare their talons for a last-ditch struggle.

[THE TYRANT *and* LAO SZU *dance.*]

The "civil guards" keep running in to report the approach of the Red Army. Trapped, THE TYRANT decides on a last resort. "Put the manor on full alert," he orders. "Pile brushwood beneath the banyan tree, and bring in HUNG."

Four "civil guards" push HUNG into the courtyard.

Head and chest high, HUNG is calm. He looks contemptuously at the enemy diehards. [*He performs "liang xiang."*]

THE TYRANT holds out a sheet of paper. In a vain attempt to save himself from total defeat, he orders HUNG to write a "recantation."

HUNG throws off the "civil guards" with a shake of his arms. The rascals fall back in alarm.

[*He dances.*]

HUNG glances scornfully at the brushwood and torches beneath the banyan tree. He steps forward with firm strides, his strong arms outstretched. He looks at the sky and surrounding countryside, his determination soaring: How beautiful is our native land! How fertile and vast. For the past hundred years, fiends have been running amok, spreading ruin. But now the building of a revolutionary base in the Chingkang Mountains has opened new vistas. Chairman Mao has pointed the way to victory—armed revolution, the wresting of political power. No one can stop a spreading prairie fire!

Raising his right arm, he stands in the middle of the execution grounds thinking, listening, his mind far away. He seems to hear the battle song of the Red Company of Women, he seems to see the people's armed forces mowing down the enemy. His tightly clenched right fist waves slightly in rhythm to the battle song, his eyes shining.

The execution grounds are a battlefield. As if with a weapon in his hand HUNG marches straight up to THE TYRANT. The landlord and LAO SZU cringe before his piercing gaze and fearless manner. [HUNG *does "jian shi bian shen tiao—jeté entre lacé," sailing scornfully over* THE TYRANT *who kneels in a frightened crouch.*]

Swinging his arms, HUNG sweeps across the execution grounds like a whirlwind, terrorizing the foe. [*He does "fei jiao," "pien tui—grand rond de jambe en dehors," and "kong zhuan—tour en l'air." Furiously he does "ping zhuan—chaîné" in a rapid movement, then turns sideways to perform "liang xiang."*] With the utmost contempt and hatred for the class enemy, he grabs the sheet of paper, rips it to shreds, and flings it in the face of THE TYRANT.

What does death matter? The communist creed is the truth! HUNG points at the villains in a rage. "Communists are not afraid to die! You'll never escape the people's punishment!" He soars over the heads of the foe like an eagle in the sky. [*He does "xuan feng kong zhuan—grand assemblé en tournant," "yan shi tiao," "pang tui zhuan—grande pirouette à la seconde" and performs "liang xiang" with an arm in the air.*] The bandits fall prostrate and trembling in the face of the Communist's splendid courage and heroism.

To the grand strains of the *Internationale*, HUNG angrily shakes off the guards who try to seize him and with majestic calm mounts the pyre beneath the banyan tree. He extends his left hand, as if to caress the beautiful motherland. Gazing far, he sees the glorious, triumphant New China that is to come. Standing in the flames, he raises his right fist and shouts: "Down with the Kuomintang reactionaries! Long live the Chinese Communist Party! Long live Chairman Mao!"

HUNG, the Communist, towers above the blaze, his spirit magnificent as the mountains and rivers.

[*Dark change*]

Rosy dawn streaks the sky. Dark clouds scatter, revealing a glowing sun rising in the east.

Red flags waving, bugles blaring, the Red Army surges into Coconut Grove Manor.

[*A Red Army battalion commander waves his men forward.*]

[*Peasants armed with weapons of every sort advance quickly, led by the commander of the Women's Company.*]

[*The Red Army catches up with the retreating shattered foe. They fight. The enemy soldiers are annihilated.*]

Under cover of chaos, LAO SZU, clutching the money box of THE TYRANT'S WIFE, runs into the fleeing TYRANT. They battle ferociously. LAO SZU kicks the landlord to the ground and tries to escape.

CHING-HUA rushes in and kills LAO SZU with one shot. She whirls and again kicks down THE TYRANT who is trying to rise, threatening him with her gun.

Pretending to be subdued, the kneeling TYRANT begs for his life. Stealthily, he pulls out a dagger and swings a vicious blow at CHING-HUA. She dodges and sends the dagger flying.

He runs in haste. With two shots she ends the life of the crime-steeped counter-revolutionary chieftain.

Red Army soldiers rush in. They pour a volley of bullets into THE TYRANT'S body, avenging the laboring people he had oppressed.

The rising sun lights up the land. Liberation has come to the long-suffering people of Coconut Grove. They and the soldiers joyously congratulate one another.

The Red Army men free peasants who had been immured and beaten in THE TYRANT's dungeon, and knock off their shackles. A white-haired grandfather is reunited with a granddaughter THE TYRANT had snatched away. Peasants angrily relate to the Red Army THE TYRANT's evil deeds. With tears of happiness in their eyes, they express from the bottom of their hearts their boundless love for and gratitude to our great leader Chairman Mao, the Chinese Communist Party, and the Workers' and Peasants' Red Army.

CHING-HUA and THE COMPANY COMMANDER inquire everywhere about HUNG. A bondmaid from the manor sorrowfully points to the banyan tree and *tells of* HUNG's heroic death. This news comes as a terrific blow.

Grief-stricken, CHING-HUA runs to the tree.

[CHING-HUA *and* COMPANY COMMANDER *dance.*]

Wiping away their tears, clenching their fists, they call on the fighters to convert sorrow into strength, to carry on the cause of the fallen hero and wage revolution until final victory. [*They do "pan feng shi—écarté," "ling kong yue—grand jeté" and "he li shi—attitude" and end by performing "liang xiang" with their heads raised.*]

The powerful strains of the *Internationale* swell forth. Red Army soldiers and the liberated laboring masses gather before the banyan tree and bid sorrowful farewell to their beloved comrade-in-arms: "Comrade Hung, you shall live forever in our hearts!"

The battalion commander announces that CHING-HUA has been appointed Party representative of the Women's Company. CHING-HUA solemnly accepts HUNG's dispatch case which the battalion commander hands her. "Oh, Party, you rescued me from an abyss of bitterness," she says, "you raised me to maturity in the flames of class struggle. I pledge to model myself after Comrade Hung. I shall be a revolutionary and never leave the battlefield until the red flag waves over the Five Continents and Four Seas!"

HUNG has given his life, but millions of new revolutionaries rise. Beneath the red battle flag, the hard-working women who have just been freed step forward to join the ranks of the Red Company of Women.

The people's army grows in size and strength. Revolution's torrent cannot be stemmed. In the bright sunlight, the swelling ranks stride forward along the path crimson with the blood of the fallen.

Onward, onward! Under the banner of Mao Tse-tung, onward to victory!

[*Final curtain*]

Taking the Bandits' Stronghold

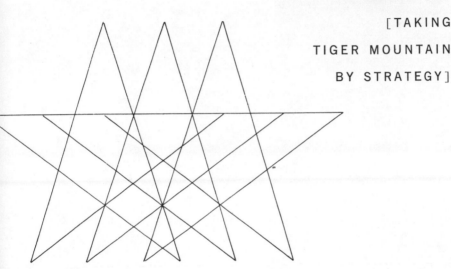

Eagle into Vulture

What's in a name? The play Taking the Bandits' Stronghold *was rewritten several times, until it emerged under the title* Taking Tiger Mountain by Strategy. *One minor but significant change was that of the name, or nickname, of the Nationalist commander —the chief of the "bandits"—from "Eagle" to "Vulture." The change clearly symbolizes the aim of the overall revision of the play: to make its villains more villainous, even in their labels, so that there could be no possibility of misinterpretation; and to make its heroes more overwhelmingly heroic.*

If one goes by subsequent accounts in newspapers and periodicals, Taking the Bandits' Stronghold *was the center of a fierce struggle between those who wanted to use the play to propagate a "return to capitalism" and those who saw it as a vehicle for emphasis on "class" divisions. Although in most instances this volume presents the most up-to-date texts of Peking operas and other stage vehicles, the following pages contain an earlier version. The reader will, nevertheless, find a text that has already undergone many revisions and was regarded as ideologically refined and appropriate as late as 1968. In this version, the antagonist is still identified as "Eagle, bandit chieftain of Tiger Mountain, leader of the Kuomintang's 'Fifth Peace Preservation Brigade.'" Actually, Eagle had been his name in the novel* Tracks in the Forest Snow (1962), *by Chu Po, on which the play is based. The initial version, prepared and produced by the Peking Opera Troupe of Shanghai in 1958, also retained the group name for the commander's assistants, "The Eight Invincibles"; this was later changed to "The Eight Terribles." The soldier called "Big Pockmark" is later identified only as "Bandit Chief of Staff," thereby removing a human point of identification, although a somewhat negative one.*

*The plot centers around the shrewdness, skill, and nerve of Yang
Tzu-jung, a Red Army scout. The "strategy" to which the new title
refers is his infiltration of the "bandit" headquarters on Tiger
Mountain in disguise and with a convincing cover story. Yang
brings with him a much-coveted secret Contact Map and is accepted by "Eagle," or "Vulture." He persuades the commander
that the mountain is unassailable, and when the Kuomintang
soldiers celebrate their chief's fiftieth birthday Yang manages to
get them drunk. He has also persuaded them to light up the
mountain with torches for the celebration of the "hundred chickens feast," a signal for the People's Liberation Army (PLA) to
overrun the headquarters.*

*During the ideological discussions of the play, accusations were
made that the original text, until revised in 1963, had made Yang
a picture of "dare-deviltry and dashing roughness" with "bandit-
like airs." If so, the characterization was not changed much in the*
Taking Tiger Mountain by Strategy *script, which was revised col-
lectively by the Peking Opera Troupe of Shanghai in July 1970.
Yang comes across as a crack-shot, for example, who impresses
Eagle-Vulture and his cronies with his ability to hit two lamps
with one shot from his gun; his ability to fool the villains of the
play, and to outthink as well as outshoot them, is reminiscent of a
Western motion picture—Western in the sense of a cowboy-and-
sheriff movie.*

As a matter of fact, the polarization of such stage productions as
Taking Tiger Mountain by Strategy, *for all its ideological under-
pinning and behind-the-scenes conflict, is strikingly similar to an
old-fashioned genre: the magnificent hero undoing the evil villain.
The image of Yang as a sort of Superman was described by the
Shanghai Troupe in a commentary, "Strive to Create the Brilliant
Images of the Proletarian Heroes," which appeared in the booklet*
To Find Men Truly Great and Noble-Hearted, We Must Look
Here in the Present *(Peking, 1971). This is their view of Yang's*

role in the play: "While defining his ideal of the Chinese revolution, we also referred to his ideal of the world revolution. While delineating his indomitable courage and soaring spirit, we also gave expression to the steadiness and poise, the sagacity and alertness in his makeup. The description of these facts in his character rests firmly on one essential point, the soul of the hero Yang Tzu-jung, and that is 'the morning sun in his heart'—a red heart that is infinitely loyal to Chairman Mao and Mao Tse-tung Thought. Thus Yang Tzu-jung appears before us as a fearless proletarian revolutionary hero, with largeness of mind and a thoroughgoing proletarian revolutionary spirit, one who in all circumstances gives prominence to proletarian politics. It is a brilliant image of a hero who is at once lofty and mature."

According to this version of the play's history, the pre-1963 version had pictured Yang as having a flirtation with Vulture's foster-daughter Rose, and had him telling "ribald stories in the bandits' stronghold." The Shanghai Troupe added: "The result was that they turned Yang Tzu-jung into a filthy-mouthed desperado and a reckless muddle-headed adventurer reeking with bandit odor from top to toe. Such a character can only be a living sample advertising Liu Shao-chi's reactionary military line of putschism, adventurism and warlordism."

The Shanghai Troupe revised the play to bring out "the essential sides" of the hero's character, "class love and class hatred." His arias in Scenes Three and Five were designed to convey the character's "deeper ideological meaning," to show that Yang "is the representative of millions of worker-peasant soldiers who, nurtured by Mao Tse-tung Thought, have grown up and been steeled in revolutionary wars." The original script, the Troupe recalled, "did not even mention Mao Tse-tung Thought for once." To make up for this, Yang now sings an aria in Scene Eight, "The Morning Sun of My Heart."

The Shanghai commentary added that, on his way up the moun-

tain, Yang had been worried and expressed such thoughts as "In the endless sea of forest I have only my shadow as a companion," and "Besides skeletons and bloodstains, not a human being I see." The Shanghai Troupe recast Scene Five and instead gave Yang a long aria "to express his great and far-sighted ideal and lofty revolutionary ambitions," on the theme "Let the red flag fly all over the world." The commentary stated: "We hold that a powerful portrayal of the noble communist ideal cherished at heart by a hero is an important content of combining revolutionary realism with revolutionary romanticism."

Some of the theatrically most effective scenes of the play rest on carefully constructed ideological bases. The Shanghai Troupe described why and how it put the hero into specific settings and gave him a number of stage tasks:

"To reveal the two aspects of Yang Tzu-jung's character—his dash and courage as distinct from his sagacity and alertness—is also a point that should not be neglected. In order to demonstrate his courage and great aspiration—'Shake the heights with my will' and 'with my courage the valleys fill'—we added a new prelude to Scene Five, which begins with stirring music illustrative of the hero galloping on a fine horse through a blinding snowstorm, followed by a new-type er huang dao ban [ballad form] of leisurely singing to the quick rhythm of percussion instruments to produce the effect of a valiant, singing Yang Tzu-jung entering at flying speed on horseback. In this way the audience will see with the mind's eye, even before the entry of the leading character, a dashing and dauntless hero approaching on horseback, whip in hand. We also designed for him a militant and sprightly riding dance and tiger-killing dance after his entry to emphasize his courage and daring spirit."

Klaus Mehnert, giving his impression of a performance in Peking, wrote in China Returns (1972) that Yang's riding scene came across "with particular vividness," with the hero wearing a thick *fur hat, a tigerskin jacket, black trousers, light brown high boots, and a heavy, dark leather coat trimmed with white lambskin that "catches the light dramatically each time he moves." Mehnert wrote: "He rides, but there is no horse: in traditional Peking opera style, the ride is simply suggested by his carrying a whip. So Yang 'gallops' through the woods, over obstacles, across ravines, till suddenly the horse rears wildly, and we hear the angry roar of a tiger. The hero jumps off the horse and kills the (invisible) tiger with two shots from his pistol. Alerted by the shots, the Vulture's soldiers appear on the scene; they admire Yang's heroic feat, and simply assume that he is one of their own."*

Mehnert regards the Red Army soldiers' race through the snow as "the greatest piece of acrobatic pantomime." There are no skis, but the pantomime-dance gives the impression that the soldiers "race over the snow, with short rapid steps or long high leaps" and "they swarm from the rocks to the left of the stage, taking off like ski jumpers, sailing headlong through the air in incredible elevations, disappearing in a green-and-white cascade of moving bodies, only to reappear immediately, three rows deep, facing the audience" and moving toward the front of the stage.

The booklet that contains the Shanghai Troupe's account of the opera's evolution also has a commentary by Hung Cheng, which speaks of the tiger-killing episode in the revised version as follows: "His [Yang's] aria, as well as his accompanying acrobatic dance, fully convey to the audience the hero's lofty spirit before battle. 'Killing the tiger,' which follows immediately, further highlights Yang Tzu-jung's dauntlessness, auguring well for his penetration into the bandits' lair. When the bandits come onto the scene, the expression of fright on their faces at the dead tiger and their silly and disgusting manner in questioning Yang Tzu-jung stand in sharp contrast with the courage Yang shows even after killing the tiger."

The Shanghai Troupe provides a separate analysis on "Using the

*Dance in Depicting Proletarian Heroes," which describes under-
lying ideological concepts of the riding and tiger-killing scenes:*

"In the 'riding dance,' for instance, when the horse bolts at the
roar of the tiger, Yang's daring and courage can be seen in the
way he firmly and agilely controls his mount. His facial expression, the look in his eyes and the sureness of his movements also
show his coolness, cautiousness and wisdom. The panicky horse
shies and prances, but its rider remains calm. The fright of the
horse prompts Yang to a series of swift movements, which in turn
reflect both the degree of the animal's fright and the steadiness
of Yang."

*Concerning the Skiing Dance, the Shanghai Troupe writes that it
took "considerable pains to create appropriate choreography" and
stated: "In Scene Nine we represent swift skiing and the scaling
of steep cliffs by 'showing repose through action and seeking action in repose.' By various movements within different areas of
space, our dance conveys the impression of skiing, scaling cliffs
and descending slopes." The dance is designed to show the detachment's "fearlessness of hardships or death" and its "revolutionary heroism and revolutionary optimism."*

*The dances are designed to show the relationship between heroes
and "negative characters" as "one class annihilating another in
desperate struggle." The Shanghai Troupe writes: "In the socialist
theater, negative characters are always a foil for the positive characters. The latter must dominate the former in manner and in
position. This is the major principle guiding creation in proletarian
literature and art."*

*The analysis becomes specific: "Take the choreography of Scene
Six. How do we make Vulture serve as a foil for Yang Tzu-jung?
Obviously, to let him swagger like a conquering hero would not
be suitable. On the other hand, if we made him completely incom-
petent, he wouldn't be much of a foil. If we cast him as a 'clown'*

in the manner of the old operas, the result would be even worse. It would detract the audience's attention from the hero and focus on the villain, vitiating the intensity of the whole atmosphere of fierce class struggle." Nevertheless, Lois Wheeler Snow, widow of the author Edgar Snow, writes in China on Stage *(1972) that to her "Western, bourgeois eyes, the evil ones" in Peking operas "are often more successful than the heroes." She found the actor playing Vulture in Peking "superb in his role" and wrote: "His physical dexterity and grace added a supernatural quality as he literally rose in the air or bounced on his rocky throne in the throes of wily wickedness, like an Oriental Nome king. It is difficult to achieve the portrayal of complete bad or complete good on stage. Somewhere in conveying badness an interesting contrast is bound to appear, even if it is only unintentional humor. All good is sometimes all bore." But she reminded her readers that one must keep in mind "for whom" (in Mao's questioning phrase) these stage productions are meant, and that "audiences whose heritage is deep suffering from Kuomintang bandits, invaders, imperialists, landlords, war lords, traitors, spies, and the like, are [more] apt to accept—and relish—absolutely drawn heroes and villains than bourgeois theatre audiences in the U.S.A. or Europe, thousands of miles and ideological light years away from such immediate suffering."*

The choreography of the scene in which Yang brings out the secret map is designed to dramatize the contrast between the two adversaries. The Shanghai Troupe notes that the audience applauds enthusiastically "when Vulture circles madly around Yang after Yang produces the Contact Map." This, according to the analysis, is not done in appreciation of the dance movements, but because the dance "demonstrates that Yang has the will and wit with which to overcome all enemies no matter what the difficulties, because it embodies the audience's own desires."

The music used in Taking Tiger Mountain by Strategy *(formerly,*

Taking the Bandits' Stronghold) *is examined by three writers: Tang Ho, Hung Yuan, and Jen Min, members of the Comrade-in-Arms Troupe of the Peking Command. The analysis begins by referring to Chiang Ching's efforts to counteract "the arch-renegade Liu Shao-chi and his agents in Peking opera circles," who try to reduce the role of Yang, sought to "smear him as a bandit," and "screamed" that "Yang Tzu-jung sings too much!" Prompted by Mao's wife, "musical images of positive characters" were stressed, with particular attention to Yang; the hero's portrayal projected him "in rough, broad outlines," combined with "fine delineation, just as his gallant, soaring singing alternates with moving lilting."*

The use of instrumental music is summarized as follows: "In the music highlight the singing, in the orchestra highlight the three major instruments [first and second fiddles and moon guitar], in the Western instruments highlight the strings and oppose foreign flavor, heaviness, freakiness and confusion." These principles are designed to eliminate "all the heterogeneity, cacophony and loose structure in music." The analysis concludes that "for the sake of creating the musical images of proletarian heroes," this particular stage production has "carried out a successful revolution in Peking opera music, with numerous innovations and transformations in the artistic forms and means of both the traditional Peking opera music and Western music."

CAST

YANG TZU-JUNG   leader of a PLA scout platoon
SHAO CHIEN-PO   a PLA regimental chief of staff [Commander 203]
SUN TA-TEH   assistant leader of a PLA scout platoon
PAI JU   girl nurse
KAO PO   a guard
TUNG CHUNG-SUNG   soldier
LI HUNG-YI   soldier
LUAN CHAO-CHIA   soldier
OTHER SOLDIERS

LI YUNG-CHI railway worker
MOTHER his mother
HUNTER CHANG
CHANG PAO Chang's daughter
MRS. LI Li Yung-chi's wife
CHANG TA-SHAN railway worker
OTHER VILLAGERS

EAGLE bandit chieftain of Tiger Mountain, leader of Kuomintang's
"Fifth Peace Preservation Brigade"
LUAN PING liaison adjutant under Horse Cudgel Hsu—bandit chieftain
of Breast Mountain
BIG POCKMARK chief of staff to Eagle
FLATNOSE chief adjutant to Eagle
CAPTAIN a bandit leader
OTHER BANDITS

SCENE ONE Advancing in Victory

Winter, 1946. A snowy forest in the Peony River area, in northeast
China.

[*A small detachment of the PLA in full battle kit, a red flag at their
head, is advancing swiftly.*]

CHAO-CHIA We've come to a fork in the road, 203.
SHAO Halt the march!
CHAO-CHIA Form ranks!

[*The men form ranks;* KAO PO *hands* SHAO *a map.*]

SHAO [*looks at map, examines terrain*] Chao-chia.
CHAO-CHIA Here.
SHAO We'll rest here.
CHAO-CHIA Right. Li Hung-yi, stand guard.

[*Li exits.*]

CHAO-CHIA [*turns and calls*] Supply chief. We'll rest here.

[*A voice responds. Horses neigh. The men stamp their feet to warm
up, and knock the snow from their clothes.*]

SHAO Are you tired?

SOLDIERS   No.

SHAO   Good. Comrades Yang Tzu-jung and Sun Ta-teh are scouting up ahead. We've arranged to meet them here. That Eagle has really hidden himself deep in the mountains. We've been marching through the snow for days, but there's still no sign of him. We must be prepared for a long struggle.

SOLDIERS   Right.

SHAO   Comrades, the regimental Party committee picked us thirty-six men and sent us as a small detachment into this snowy forest to carry out Chairman Mao's directive "Build Stable Base Areas in the Northeast." In other words our job is to rouse the masses in the Peony River area, wipe out the bandits, strengthen the rear, and coordinate with our field armies in smashing the U.S.-backed Kuomintang attacks. It's a task of great strategic importance. We must do as Chairman Mao teaches us: "Be resolute, fear no sacrifice, and surmount every difficulty to win victory."

SOLDIERS   We'll definitely fulfill our mission.

LI [*enters*]   Report. Comrades Yang and Sun are back.

[*The two enter and salute.*]

YANG   Report.

SHAO   You scouts have had a tiring job.

YANG   We went out in disguise, according to orders, but it took a long time before we could find any of the local people. Finally we rescued a boy—a mute—who had fallen into a ravine. Thanks to his father's directions, we discovered a little hamlet called Black Dragon at the end of a small-gauge railway used for hauling timber. Our investigations there put us on the trail of the Eagle.

SHAO   Excellent.

YANG   [*sings*]

> This section is infested with bandits,
> They call themselves "First Regiment of the Fifth
>   Peace Preservation Brigade."
> Every station on the line they've plundered,
> Last night they pillaged Black Dragon.
> The little hamlet is charred and dead,
> Another victim of the Eagle's crimes.
> From there the bandits went to Chiapi Valley,
> And probably have returned to Tiger Mountain.

SHAO   We're on the Eagle's trail, comrades. We must follow up. Chao-chia, we'll spend the night in Black Dragon. Comrade Yang.

YANG   Here.

SHAO   We need more information. Take Comrades Sun, Tung, and Li [*The three men step forward as their names are mentioned.*] and do some more scouting. Don't let a single clue to the bandits escape you.

YANG   Right. We're off. [*He departs with the other three scouts.*]

SHAO   Comrades! [*Sings*]

> Our responsibility to the people is heavy,
> We must support the front and strengthen the rear;
> No matter how dangerous the mountains and cliffs,
> We're determined to bring the sunshine in.

[*The lights darken. Curtain*]

SCENE TWO   Pillage of Chiapi Valley

Dusk. The edge of the village Chiapi Valley.

[EAGLE, BIG POCKMARK, FLATNOSE, *and other bandits are gazing toward the village.*]

BIG POCKMARK   We've picked up a lot of loot on the way back to our stronghold, Excellency. This village is more or less right on our doorstep. We ought to leave it alone this time.

EAGLE   Who cares? Chief of staff, go and grab me some of those paupers. We'll put them to work building more fortifications on Tiger Mountain. Men or women—take them all.

BIG POCKMARK   Yes, sir.

[*He leaves with the bandit gang.* FLATNOSE *starts to go too, but* EAGLE *stops him.*]

EAGLE   How many days is it since Tuft Cheek went off to find Luan Ping?

FLATNOSE   Exactly ten. I'm getting worried.

EAGLE   What for? I hear Chiang Kai-shek has already arrived in Shen-yang and is taking personal charge of the fighting. He'll be launching a general offensive toward northern Manchuria very soon.

FLATNOSE   Can we really look forward to such a day?

EAGLE   Don't you remember what Commissioner Hou said at the con-

ference in Peony River City? The Americans are pretending to be
working for peace talks between the Kuomintang and the Communists, but actually they're transporting soldiers north for Chiang Kai-
shek. They want to wipe out all the communist troops north and
south of the Great Wall in three months. Our time has come.

FLATNOSE Fine. We'll be able to work off our anger at last.

EAGLE The first thing we'll do when we get back to Tiger Mountain is
expand our forces.

FLATNOSE If Tuft Cheek can find Luan Ping and get his hands on
Horse Cudgel Hsu's Contacts Map, the whole Peony River area will
belong to us.

EAGLE I hear Commissioner Hou is looking all over for that map. We
mustn't let him get it.

FLATNOSE Don't worry, Excellency. Tuft Cheek and Luan Ping are
sworn brothers. It won't fly away. When the Kuomintang army returns, you'll be made general of all northern Manchuria.

EAGLE Ha! Ha! Ha! [*Sings*]

> Though three times the regime has changed,
> I'm still the master of Tiger Mountain.

FLATNOSE First it was Marshal Chang, then the Manchukuo of the
Japanese, then the Kuomintang of Chiang Kai-shek, but none of
them could do without you.

EAGLE Aha! [*Sings*]

> Chiang and the Yanks have launched a civil war,
> I'm going to take over the whole northeast.

[*He swaggers off with* FLATNOSE *in the direction of the village where
flames glow and crying and shouting are heard.*]

[LI YUNG-CHI *enters carrying a hunting rifle and some game.*]

YUNG-CHI [*sings*]

> Flames leap to the sky and people shout,
> Mothers call for their sons, children for their mothers;
> Again the bandits murder and plunder,
> I'll have it out with them though I die.

[*Bandits enter pulling young men and women whose arms they have
tied.* YUNG-CHI *fights with the bandits while the young people are
beaten by the bandits and dragged off.*]

[YUNG-CHI's *wife is pulled on, followed by* MOTHER *who is holding the baby. A bandit captain snatches the infant from the old woman and throws it over the cliff.* YUNG-CHI *attacks bandits furiously. His left arm is hurt in the struggle.*]

[EAGLE *enters and shoots at* YUNG-CHI. YUNG-CHI's *wife flings herself to cover him and falls dead. Exit* EAGLE *and the other bandits.*]

YUNG-CHI [*heartbroken and enraged*] Baby's ma . . . Baby's ma. . . .
MOTHER [*tragically*] Baby's ma. . . .
YUNG-CHI [*sings*]

> Disaster, like a bolt from the blue,
> Burns like fire in my breast;
> My wife, lying in a pool of blood,
> My baby, dead at the foot of the cliff.
> I swear that I shall get revenge—Eagle!
> I'll hack you to pieces to repay this debt.

[*He starts to run after* EAGLE. *Bandits swarm on, overcome him, and tie him up.*]

MOTHER Yung-chi!

[YUNG-CHI *struggles wildly.*]

[*Curtain*]

SCENE THREE   Asking About Past Bitterness

Afternoon. A remote mountain valley. High mountains can be seen in the distance. Sunlight filters through the trees. In a small log cabin in the foreground bowls and chopsticks lie in disarray on a table.

[CHANG PAO, *disguised as a boy, is clearing the table.* HUNTER CHANG *stands outside, looking around, then he goes back inside, quickly.*]

PAO That man and woman were very rude, Pa. They ate the bit of venison we'd just got.
CHANG We can't stay here, Pao. We've got to leave.
PAO Why?
CHANG Do you know who they were?
PAO He said he was in the PLA.
CHANG Huh! Eight years ago, when the bandits dragged me away, I

met him in their lair on Tiger Mountain. His name is Tuft Cheek. He's a bandit.

PAO Oh!

CHANG He doesn't remember me, but I remember him, all right. Wrap up our pelts, quick. We're going to your uncle Ta-shan's, in Chiapi Valley.

PAO Right. [*Gets some belongings together.*]

CHANG Those two fur traders who came through here a few days ago, said the Communists have reached Shantung Province already—our old home; they're helping the poor to take power. I wonder if it's true.

PAO They're good men, those two, Pa. They wouldn't lie. If they hadn't carried me out of that ravine, I would have frozen to death.

CHANG Right. We must ask more about it.

[CHANG *ties the furs into a bundle, and* PAO *gets the pelts out. Shadows appear on the window.*]

PAO Somebody's coming, Pa.

[CHANG *covers* PAO's *mouth with his hand.*]

CHANG Hush!

[*They listen cautiously.* YANG, SUN, TUNG, *and* LI *enter, muffled in hoods and capes which hide the red star on their caps. They look carefully around.*]

YANG [*sings*]

> With the help of the local people
> We've been following a suspicious pair,
> But here in the mountains we've lost the trail—

[*Gazes around.*]

Isn't this where Hunter Chang lives, Old Sun?

SUN Yes. We came here together last time.

YANG Right. [*Sings.*]

> We'll revisit the hunter to solve our problem.

You and Li scout on ahead, Comrade Sun. Report back here if you discover anything.

SUN and LI Right. [*Exit.*]

YANG Tung, stand guard.

TUNG Right. [*Exits.*]

YANG [*walks up to the cabin*] Anybody home?

[*The hunter comes out tensely.*]

CHANG [*examines him*] Who do you want?

YANG Don't you recognize an old neighbor? I'm the fur trader who was here a few days ago.

CHANG Fur trader?

[PAO *comes out.* CHANG *tries to stop her but he's too late.*]

YANG Your father doesn't remember me, little brother, but I'm sure you do. Wasn't I the one who brought you home that day?

[PAO *wants to speak, but stops, nods.*]

YANG [*has observed and guessed the truth but doesn't let on*] A clever child.

CHANG [*quickly*] He's a mute.

YANG Ah, I see.

CHANG [*observes* YANG *carefully, recognizing him*] Ah, you're Master Yang.

YANG Yes.

CHANG Please come inside. [*They all go in.*] Have a seat.

[*They sit down.*]

YANG [*pointing at* PAO] No ill effects from that fall?

CHANG Nothing serious. [*Quickly changes the subject.*] You said we're both from the same province and that you're a fur trader. But today you seem to be a soldier. What are you, after all?

YANG I'm not a trader. [*Throws back his hood and reveals his cap with its red star.*] A member of the Chinese People's Liberation Army.

CHANG [*still skeptical*] You're also in the PLA?

YANG Yes. Have you seen any of our men before?

CHANG [*guardedly*] No . . . never.

YANG We didn't have a chance to talk much, last time. I really am from Shantung Province, like yourself. Things are a lot better than when you left to come north of the Great Wall.

CHANG That's fine. But what are you fellows doing all the way up here?

YANG Fighting bandits.

CHANG They are very strong.

YANG We've got a big force not far behind. Let me tell you—our PLA has won several big victories in the northeast. The whole Peony River sector has been liberated. We've smashed most of the bandits. Only Eagle and his gang are left. They've buried themselves deep in this mountain forest, but we're going to finish them off too, and soon.

CHANG Wonderful.

YANG Eagle has wreaked havoc in this district. You two must have suffered great wrongs.

CHANG [*bitterly*] We do indeed.

YANG Tell me about it.

CHANG [*not wanting to mention the painful past*] It happened eight years ago, why talk about it?

PAO [*bursts out*] Pa—

CHANG [*startled*] Pao, how could you—

YANG [*sympathetically*] It's all right, child. The Communist Party and Chairman Mao will right your wrongs. Speak.

PAO I will, Uncle, I will. [*Sings.*]

> Disaster struck one snowy night eight years ago,
> Eagle killed my grandma and took off my ma and pa;
> Uncle Ta-shan raised me in Chiapi Valley, my pa came back,
> But my ma threw herself off a cliff and died;
> Afraid I'd fall into those devils' hands,
> Pa dressed me as a boy and said I was mute;
> We hunted in the mountains during the day,
> At night we thought of grandma and ma;
> We looked at the stars and looked at the moon
> And longed for the time when the sun would come,
> When we would be able to speak out freely,
> When I could dress as a girl again,
> When we could collect our debt of blood,
> If I only had wings I'd take my gun
> And fly to the summit and slaughter those wolves.

[CHANG *listens in misery.*]

YANG [*furious, sings*]

> Pao's tales of the bandits' crimes
> Rouse me to the utmost rage;
> Oppressed people everywhere suffer alike,
> They want vengeance, blood for their blood;

Destroy the Eagle and liberate the people.
Rising as masters, they'll see the sun;
Work with their savior, the Communist Party,
And bring a new life to our land,
Good days will come to this area too,
Just like our old home in Shantung.

CHANG [*with emotion*]   You've said what's in my heart, Old Yang. [*Sits down by* YANG.] But beating the Eagle won't be easy. Though the regime has changed hands three times, he flees to his Tiger Mountain every time he smells any danger. That stronghold is protected by nine groups of twenty-seven bunkers. There, he can attack, he can defend, and he can slip away. Nobody can touch him.

YANG   It's a tough problem, all right. They say it's impossible to fight your way to the top.

CHANG   That's right. There's only one direct path, and it's very steep. "One man can hold it against ten thousand," as the old saying goes. And it's very carefully watched. They've got guard posts at every stage. How can you fight your way up?

YANG   How did you manage to escape when the bandits held you a prisoner?

CHANG   There's a dangerous trail down the back of the mountain. It's full of cliffs and dense brush. No one dares to use that trail, so it's unguarded. Eight years ago, that's where I came down. If I hadn't been lucky enough to grab the branch of a tree, I'd have been dashed to pieces.

YANG   You've given us some very useful information. As long as we all stand together, there's no mountain top we can't conquer.

CHANG   Right. I'll be glad when you take this one. You mustn't blame me for being suspicious. A man and woman were here a while ago. The man plainly was a bandit, but he also said he was in the PLA.

PAO   My pa saw him eight years ago on Tiger Mountain. His name is Tuft Cheek.

YANG   Tuft Cheek, eh? What did he talk about?

CHANG   He called the woman sister-in-law. He said her husband Luan Ping was his sworn brother.

YANG [*bursts out*]   Luan Ping?

CHANG   The woman seemed to be Luan Ping's wife. Tuft Cheek had a big argument with the woman. He wanted her to give him some map or other.

PAO A Contacts Map.

CHANG That's right.

YANG Contacts Map?

[TUNG *enters and patrols outside cabin.*]

TUNG [*calls*] Platoon Leader.

[YANG *opens door.*]

TUNG Sun and Li have come back.

[SUN *and* LI *enter. They go into cabin.*]

SUN [*greets* CHANG] How are you, neighbor?

LI In the forest northeast of here we found a bloody glove and the body of a woman. [*Gives glove to* YANG.]

SUN We searched all around, but the snow had already blotted out any footprints. We couldn't tell where the murderer had gone.

YANG Have you seen this glove before, Old Chang?

CHANG [*examines glove*] Yes. It belongs to Tuft Cheek.

YANG He must have killed her and stolen the Contacts Map. But what does this have to do with Luan Ping?

TUNG [*pulls* YANG *aside*] Wasn't that bandit you caught in Nine River Confluence called Luan Ping?

YANG Right. That's the man. This murder is a complicated business, comrades, and Luan Ping is mixed up in it. Tung, I'm going after the murderer with Sun and Li. You go back to 203 and report. Tell him I suggest we interrogate Luan Ping and dig out the story of the Contacts Map.

TUNG Right. [*Trots out.*]

YANG This is urgent, neighbor. We've no time to chat. Here's a bit of food for you and Pao. [*Hands his ration bag to* CHANG. SUN *and the others hand theirs to* PAO.]

PAO [*moved*] Uncle. . . .

YANG It isn't safe for you two here. Better go into hiding. When our troops arrive things will be different. Goodbye for now.

CHANG Where are you going?

YANG After Tuft Cheek.

CHANG Wait. He's sure to be heading for Tiger Mountain. That trail has always been hard to follow, and in this snowstorm a stranger could never find it. Pao and I will show you the way.

YANG Thank you, Old Chang.

[*Curtain*]

SCENE FOUR Drawing Up A Plan

Morning. Black Dragon Village. A cabin in which the detachment is billeted. Outside the wind roars and heavy snow drifts.

[SHAO *faces a map, meditates, and looks out through the window.*]

SHAO [*sings*]

Wind howls through the wooded valley,
Snow mantles the mountains with silver;
What a magnificent scene of the north!
How can we let ravening beasts
Lay waste again this beautiful land?
The Central Committee points the way,
Revolutionary flames cannot be quenched.
Bearing the hopes of the people, the PLA fight north and south
And plant red banners all over our country.
Though the Yanks and Chiang collude,
Prating of peace, they move in forces to attack;
Fighting openly and stabbing in the dark, they resort to a
    hundred tricks,
Our just hatred cannot be quelled,
One against ten, we'll still wipe them out.
We fighters grew up under Mao Tse-tung's banner,
Thirty-six red hearts turn toward the sun.
Streak through the snowstorm over the mountains,
Break through brambles, grow ever stronger.
Tempered in the revolution's crucible,
We're toughened and hardened into steel.
Eagle is only a U.S.-Chiang flunky,
With them together he will be buried.
It matters not how he may struggle,
His days on Tiger Mountain are numbered.

[YANG *enters.*]

YANG Report.
SHAO Come in.

[YANG *comes into room.*]

SHAO You've been having a hard time. Did you catch the murderer?
YANG We got him. We found this letter and this map concealed in his

clothes. [*Hands them over.*] The trails in this region are very faint. Luckily, Hunter Chang acted as our guide. The murderer pretended to be one of our PLA scouts, but the hunter exposed him, and under our questioning he admitted that he's a Tiger Mountain bandit named Tuft Cheek.

SHAO   Good. That hunter has been a great help. Long ago Chairman Mao told us: "The revolutionary war is a war of the masses; it can be waged only by mobilizing the masses and relying on them." Without the masses we can't move a step.

YANG   How true. Hunter Chang says there are two trails up the mountain. I've sketched them out, according to his description. [*Hands* SHAO *a sketch.*] Tuft Cheek admits to the trail going up the face of the mountain. He says there are no fortifications along it and that it's easy to climb—obviously a lie. He didn't say a word about the other trail.

SHAO   I see. What have you done about the hunter and his daughter?

YANG   We left them our grain rations. They're planning to move to Chiapi Valley when our forces push forward.

SHAO   Good. [*Looks at map and letter.*] Luan Ping never said anything about this map.

YANG   Right. Tuft Cheek says it shows the location of three hundred secret contact centers throughout the northeast controlled from Breast Mountain. It's a very important problem.

SHAO   Kao Po has brought Luan Ping here. Let's question him and see whether we can't get the story of the Contacts Map.

YANG   Right. I'll get Luan Ping.

SHAO   He's your old adversary. You'd better do the questioning.

YANG   Right.

[SHAO *goes into next room.*]

YANG   [*to the soldier on guard*]   Young Chang, tell Kao Po to bring Luan Ping in.

[KAO PO *enters with* LUAN PING. LUAN PING *is startled to see* YANG, *but comes over to greet him.* YANG *waves him to a chair.* LUAN *sits down.*]

YANG   How are you getting on with your confession?

LUAN   I want to come clean. I'm writing down everything I know.

YANG   There's something you haven't mentioned yet.

LUAN   There is?

YANG   An important object.

LUAN I don't own a thing in the world except the clothes on my back, officer.

YANG What about that map?

LUAN Map?

YANG The Contacts Map.

LUAN [*startled*] Oh.

YANG Do you want to earn lenient treatment, or are you determined to be an enemy of the people?

LUAN [*pretending to be calm*] Slowly, let me think. [*Strikes a thoughtful pose.*] Ah, yes, yes, I remember now. They say Horse Cudgel Hsu had a map of secret contacts.

YANG Why have you been holding back information?

LUAN Don't misunderstand, officer. Horse Cudgel Hsu considered that map precious. I've never even seen it.

YANG Luan Ping, you ought to understand our policy.

LUAN I do, I do. Leniency to confessors; severity to resisters.

YANG I'm asking you—what was your job on Breast Mountain?

LUAN You know that. I was a liaison adjutant.

YANG Huh! A liaison officer who doesn't know about secret liaison stations, who never saw the Contacts Map—a likely story. It's plain you don't want to tell the truth. Kao Po, take him away.

KAO PO March.

LUAN [*agitatedly*] I'm a dog for trying to fool you, officer. I'll tell you the whole story. There is a map showing Horse Cudgel Hsu's secret contacts all over the northeast, three hundred of them. That map is now in my wife's hands. Let me go, and I'll find her and get the map and give it to you. I want to earn lenient treatment.

YANG Beside those three hundred places, where else did you have contacts?

LUAN Tiger Mountain. But for a long time Eagle has been trying to get control of northern Manchuria, and he and Horse Cudgel Hsu were only friends on the surface, so I had very little dealings with him. Last year, Eagle invited me to a Hundred Chickens Feast to celebrate his birthday, but I didn't go.

YANG [*listens with attention to his confessions and decides to end the questioning*] You'd better think it over. I want a detailed report on all your contact points. Take him away.

KAO PO March. [*He escorts* LUAN *out.*]

[SHAO *enters from other room.*]

YANG He's a crafty devil.

SHAO [*humorously*] The craftiest fox can't escape the skilled hunter. Anyhow, his story about the Contacts Map is the same as Tuft Cheek's.

YANG And he let slip a mention of the Hundred Chickens Feast. In that letter, Eagle is again inviting him to the one this year. There's something funny here.

SHAO I agree.

SUN [*enters*] Report.

SHAO Come in.

[SUN *comes into the room.*]

SHAO What's up, Comrade Sun?

SUN We've been here several days already, 203. The comrades have written requests for a battle assignment.

SHAO Are you at the head of this movement?

SUN Well. . . .

SHAO [*laughs*] I can understand how the comrades feel. The situation is this. Other troops of ours have sealed off all the roads to the fording point at the Peony River. Eagle can't get away. Our main army is already driving south. In order to secure its rear, we must wipe out this gang of bandits.

SUN That's why we're so eager for action.

SHAO Eagle is a wily bird, comrade. Haven't we discussed it several times? If we sent a large force after him, it would be like trying to hit a flea with your fist. The bandits have a sophisticated defense system on Tiger Mountain—so a direct assault like the one on Breast Mountain wouldn't be any good. Since the task is urgent, we haven't the time to lure them down the mountain and destroy them piece by piece. Ours is a special mission. We must remember what Chairman Mao tells us—strategically we should despise our enemy, but tactically we should take him seriously. Call another meeting of the comrades and talk it over again, in the light of the latest developments.

SUN Right. [*Exits.*]

[YANG *starts to leave.*]

SHAO What's your idea on how we should take Tiger Mountain, Old Yang?

YANG I haven't thought it out yet.

SHAO You never take the lid off the pot till the heat's just right.

YANG I want to question Tuft Cheek again and find out more about that Hundred Chickens Feast.
SHAO Go ahead. I'll be waiting to hear your proposal.
YANG Right. [*Exits.*]
SHAO [*sings*]

> We've learned much about the enemy in the past few days,
> We've analyzed carefully and pondered over our plan;
> Eagle has a system of bunkers and tunnels,
> So the right course is guile rather than force.
> Select a clever comrade to slip into the enemy's heart,
> Then strike together from without and within;
> Who should we choose for this critical task?

[*Thinks.*]

> Yang has all of the qualifications.
> Born of a hired-hand peasant father,
> From childhood he suffered in poverty;
> The landlord oppressed their family so cruelly,
> His pa hung himself, his ma died of epilepsy.
> Burning with hatred, Yang found his salvation
> In the Communist Party and took the revolutionary road;
> He joined the army vowing to uproot exploitation,
> A veteran in battle, he's been decorated many times.
> Single-handed, he blew up an enemy fort,
> He burned down an enemy ammunition dump;
> He's brought back intelligence from enemy territory,
> Killed traitors and rescued comrades from prisons.
> He's clashed several times with the bandits out here,
> Caught Tuft Cheek and Luan Ping as well as Hu Piao;
> I'm sure if I send him on this dangerous mission.
> With a heart red as fire,
> A will strong as steel,
> He'll defeat the Eagle.

[SUN *enters.*]

SUN 203.
SHAO How did your meeting go?
SUN We analyzed the situation and decided that guile is the only answer. We shouldn't try force. The best way would be to get a comrade into the enemy stronghold—

SHAO You're absolutely right.

[YANG *enters and waves his hand in a bandit greeting, as* SHAO *scrutinizes him.* SUN *looks on in surprise.*]

YANG [*acting the role*] Hu Piao is here to present the map.
SHAO Hu Piao? Have you thought it over carefully, Old Yang?

[YANG *nods and smiles.*]

SHAO Sit down, you two, let's talk this over. [*All sit.*] Tell me, quick, what's your idea?
YANG The best way to take Tiger Mountain, 203, it seems to me, is by guile.
SHAO Right.
YANG The Hundred Chickens Feast is a good opportunity.
SHAO Do you know what it's all about?
YANG I do. The last day of the last month of every lunar year is the Eagle's birthday. He gives himself a feast of chickens extorted from a hundred different families. That's what they call the Hundred Chickens Feast. I suggest we send a comrade up there in disguise to find out how the tunnels and bunkers are laid out. Then when the bandits are all drunk at the Hundred Chickens Feast in the Tiger Hall—
SHAO The detachment will attack and take them before they know what's happening!
YANG Right. I'm a veteran scout. Give the mission to me.
SUN Our comrades also propose Old Yang.
SHAO Exactly what I was thinking myself. Then our hearts beat as one. [*Laughs.*] Comrade Sun [*giving him the Contacts Map*], make a copy of this while I talk things over with him.
SUN Right. [*Exits.*]
SHAO So you want to disguise yourself as a bandit and get into the stronghold on Tiger Mountain. What makes you think you can carry it off?
YANG I've four things in my favor.
SHAO What are they? Let's hear.
YANG First, I've learned their bandit double-talk thoroughly and I know all about what the situation was on Breast Mountain, so I'm fully prepared.
SHAO Second?
YANG Horse Cudgel Hsu and his Breast Mountain gang have just been

defeated. His adjutant Hu Piao is in our hands and Eagle has never seen him. So it's safe for me to take his name.

SHAO Good.

YANG Third, if I present Eagle with the Contacts Map as a gift, he's sure to believe me.

SHAO Right.

YANG The fourth condition is the most important, namely—

SHAO The heart of a revolutionary soldier dedicated to the Party and the people.

YANG You understand me completely, 203.

SHAO This is no ordinary task, Old Yang.

YANG Comrade Shao. [*Sings*]

> A Communist always heeds the Party's call,
> He takes the heaviest burden on himself;
> I want only to smash the chains of a thousand years
> And open a freshet of endless happiness for the people.
> Well I know that there's danger ahead,
> But I'm all the more set on driving forward;
> No matter how thickly troubled clouds may gather,
> Revolutionary wisdom is bound to win.
> Like the Foolish Old Man who removed the mountains,
> I shall break through every obstacle;
> The flames that blaze in my red heart shall forge
> A sharp blade to slaughter evil.

SHAO I believe in you entirely, Old Yang. You can take Horse Cudgel Hsu's black-maned steed and ride northeast along the trail Hunter Chang has pointed out—

YANG And wind my way up the mountain.

SHAO The detachment will go to Chiapi Valley and mobilize the masses, practice skiing, and prepare for battle. We'll wait for word from you.

YANG I'll put a message for you in the pine grove southwest of Tiger Mountain. The tree will be marked in the agreed manner.

SHAO I'll send Sun on the twenty-sixth to pick it up.

YANG I guarantee it will be there on time.

SHAO Good. The detachment will set out as soon as we've heard from you. We'll strike from within and without and destroy Eagle and his gang.

YANG Our plan is complete then, 203. That's how we'll do it.

SHAO   Be bold but cautious, Old Yang. [*Sings.*]

> I'm confident you can fulfill this important task,
> Every move counts, this is of great significance;
> We'll call a Party committee meeting to approve the plan,
> With collective wisdom we'll defeat the enemy.

YANG   Right.

[*The lights slowly dim. Curtain*]

SCENE FIVE   In the Mountains

A few days after the previous scene. A snowy forest in the foothills of Tiger Mountain.

YANG [*sings offstage*]

> Boldly I press through the snowy forest. . . .

[*In disguise, he spurs his horse onward against the wind.*]

> Determined, the mountains I staunchly face.

[*Dismounts.*]

> We must plant red flags all over the land,
> Undaunted by dangers however great;
> I wish I could order the snow to melt,
> And welcome in spring to change the world of men.
> The Party gives me wisdom and courage,
> Risks and hardships are as naught;
> To wipe out the bandits I must dress as a bandit first,
> And slip into their stronghold like a knife.
> I'll bury the Eagle in these hills, I swear,
> Shake the heights with my will.
> With my courage the valleys fill,
> At the Hundred Chickens Feast my comrades and I
> Will make a shambles of the bandits' lair.

[*A tiger roars.*]

YANG   A tiger!

[*He shoots. The tiger howls and falls dead. The horse whinnies. Other shots are heard.* YANG *gazes alertly in the direction of the sound.*]

YANG   Ah, shooting. That means the bandits have come down the mountain. [*Calmly.*] I've just killed one tiger, and now a whole pack is coming. They're all due for the same fate.

[BIG POCKMARK *shouts:* "Halt!" *and advances with a gang of bandits.* YANG *walks forward coolly and gives a bandit salute.*]

BIG POCKMARK   What road do you travel? What's the price? *

[YANG, *head high, does not reply.*]

A BANDIT [*seeing the tiger* YANG *has killed, but not knowing it is dead*] Help! A tiger! [*Bandits hastily retreat.*]

YANG [*laughs*]   Brave, aren't you? That tiger is dead.

A BANDIT [*examines the beast cautiously*]   A beautiful shot. Right through the head.

BIG POCKMARK   Did you kill it?

YANG   It got in the way of my bullet.

BIG POCKMARK   Where's your gun?

YANG   Don't be scared. [*Tosses his pistol to one of the bandits.*]

BIG POCKMARK   Quite a man. Which gang are you from? What are you doing here?

YANG   I suppose you fellows are from Tiger Mountain?

BIG POCKMARK   That's obvious. [*Realizes he has made a slip.*] Where are you from?

YANG   That's not for you to ask. I want to see Brigadier Tsui in person. I've important business with him.

BIG POCKMARK   How is it you don't know the rules of the mountains? You're not one of the brotherhood. You're a fake.

YANG   If I were a fake, would I dare come barging into Tiger Mountain?

BIG POCKMARK   Moha? Moha? [Did you go it alone before?]

[YANG *does not reply.*]

A BANDIT   Speak up.

YANG [*haughtily*]   I'm not saying anything till I see Brigadier Tsui.

BIG POCKMARK   All right, then, let's go. [*Sticks his pistol in his belt.*]

[YANG *points at the tiger and the horse, then strides off.*]

BIG POCKMARK   Carry the tiger. Lead the horse.

[*The bandits comply.*]

[*Curtain*]

* Bandit double-talk for "Who are you?" "Where are you from?"

SCENE SIX   The Bandits' Lair

Immediately after the previous scene. A muffled gong strikes as the curtain rises. The interior of Tiger Hall, brightly lit by many lamps.

[EAGLE *sits on an armchair covered by tiger skins, his lieutenants—the "Eight Invincibles," stand on either side in a disorderly fashion. Other bandits stand on the left rear side of the hall.* EAGLE *signals to* BIG POCKMARK *to summon the newcomer.*]

BIG POCKMARK [*calls*]   Bring him in.
BANDITS   Bring him in!

[YANG *enters, head high.*]

YANG [*sings*]

> Though I've come alone to the dragon's den,
> Millions of class brothers are by my side;
> Let the Eagle spew flames ten thousand leagues high,
> For the people I'll battle fearlessly against this monster.

[*Advances and gives a bandit salute.*]

EAGLE [*suddenly*]   The lord of the heavens covers the earthly tiger.*
YANG   Precious pagoda represses the river sprite.†
INVINCIBLES   Moha? Moha?
YANG   Speak exactly at the stroke of noon. No one has a home.‡
EAGLE   Why is your face so red?
YANG   My spirits are flourishing.
EAGLE   Why so yellow again?
YANG   I smeared it with wax to ward off the cold.

[EAGLE *shoots out an oil lamp with his automatic.* YANG *takes a pistol from* BIG POCKMARK. *With one shot he knocks out two oil lamps. The bandits whisper among themselves.*]

EAGLE   According to you, you're one of Brigadier Hsu's men?
YANG   I am his cavalry adjutant, Hu Piao.
EAGLE   Hu Piao? Since you are Brigadier Hsu's man, let me ask you—when did you join his ranks?
YANG   When he became chief of police.

---

* How dare you come and offend your god?
† If I have done so, cast me from the cliff or drown me in the river.
‡ I was on the mountain of Horse Cudgel Hsu.

EAGLE   What possessions does he prize the most?

YANG   There are two.

EAGLE   What are they?

YANG   A fast horse and a sharp sword.

EAGLE   What does his horse look like?

YANG   It has a curly coat and a black mane.

EAGLE   What kind of sword has he?

YANG   A Japanese officer's saber.

EAGLE   Who gave it to him?

YANG   The Japanese Imperial Army.

EAGLE   Where was it presented?

YANG   In the Five Prosperities Pavilion in the city of Peony River.

EAGLE   [*pauses*]   If you really are Brigadier Hsu's cavalry adjutant, why did I see only Luan Ping and not you at the last meeting called by Commissioner Hou?

YANG   I didn't rate very high with Brigadier Hsu. How could I compare with a big shot like Luan Ping? He went to all the important functions.

EAGLE   Why have you come to Tiger Mountain?

YANG   I want to join Your Excellency and rise in the world. This is the first time I've crossed your threshold, but none of you big brothers seem to trust me. Aren't you being a bit ungallant?

EAGLE   We have to think of our stronghold's safety.

[*He signals, and one of the Invincibles brings* YANG *a bowl of wine, while another hands him a pipe and tobacco.* YANG *accepts them ceremoniously in the bandit manner.*]

EAGLE   If you want to join me you still have to present a gift even though you are at the end of your tether.

YANG   I've brought you Brigadier Hsu's prize horse and a fierce tiger I happened to kill at the foot of the mountain—thanks to the power your nearness gave me.

INVINCIBLES   Fine presents for Your Excellency's fiftieth birthday.

[*They laugh.* EAGLE *is very pleased.*]

EAGLE   When did the Breast Mountain stronghold fall, Hu Piao?

YANG   The third day of the twelfth lunar month.

EAGLE   What took you so long to get here?

YANG   It hasn't been easy. When Breast Mountain was taken, I fled from Candlestick Ledge and hid out in Pear Valley.

EAGLE   Pear Valley?

YANG   In the home of Luan Ping's uncle.

EAGLE   Did you see Luan Ping?

YANG   Yes.

EAGLE   And Tuft Cheek?

YANG   Tuft Cheek? No.

EAGLE   He's been gone over two weeks. What can be keeping him? You've come, Hu Piao, but why isn't Luan Ping with you?

YANG   Ah, don't ask.

EAGLE   What do you mean?

YANG   Well. . . .

[EAGLE *signals and all the bandits except the Invincibles leave.*]

EAGLE   Now, what's wrong with Luan Ping?

YANG [*swings his fist in a distressed gesture*]   It's a long story. [*Sings.*]

>   Just talking about him enrages me—

EAGLE   What did he do?

YANG [*sings*]

>   He cares nothing for our code of honor.

EAGLE   But he's one of our most trusted members. How could he go back on our code?

YANG [*sings*]

>   We fled together when Breast Mountain fell,
>   I urged him to come with me and give service to the Tiger Mountain.

[*Invincibles look at each other with satisfaction.*]

EAGLE   Is he coming?

YANG [*sings*]

>   Every man has a right to make up his own mind,
>   But he shouldn't have—
>   He shouldn't have said such awful things.

EAGLE   What did he say?

YANG   He said. . . .

EAGLE [*impatiently*]   Out with it, Old Hu, be quick.

YANG [*sings*]

> Eagle takes his orders from Commissioner Hou.

EAGLE [*leaps to his feet*]   What! I take orders from him!
INVINCIBLES   Rubbish. That dirty dog.
YANG   That wasn't all he said.
INVINCIBLES   What else?
YANG [*sings*]

> The Eight Invincibles are a pack of worthless rats.

INVINCIBLES [*enraged*]   What! That son of a bitch.
YANG [*sings*]

> He said he's a phoenix who wants a high branch to perch on,
> That Commissioner Hou is a big tree and his roots are deep.

INVINCIBLES   To hell with him.
YANG [*sings*]

> He showed me a map—

EAGLE   A map?
YANG [*sings*]

> He was intending to take it to Commissioner Hou to earn a
> promotion.

EAGLE   Was it the Contacts Map?
YANG   Yes, the secret Contacts Map.
EAGLE [*worried*]   Then he's given it to Commissioner Hou?
YANG   Don't get upset. [*Sings*]

> Pleased with himself, he grinned all over,
> And laid out drinks for the two of us;
> I filled him eight bowls, one after the other,
> I got him so drunk he couldn't see.

I thought to myself—If I'm going to do it, I should go all the way,
and do it now.
INVINCIBLES   That's right. Swipe it from him.
YANG   So, taking my chance while he was deadly drunken, I—
EAGLE   Killed the dog!
YANG   I couldn't do that. We've been pals for years.
EAGLE [*changing his tone*]   Of course, of course. Friendship is impor-
tant. Go on, Old Hu, go on.

YANG   He had his plans, but I had ideas of my own.

EAGLE   What did you do?

YANG   I—[*Sings.*]

> I changed tunics with him while he was drunk,
> Then jumped on the black-maned horse, and through
> The snowstorm galloped directly to Tiger Mountain.

EAGLE   You mean you've got the map?

YANG   [*laughs lightly, sings*]

> Please accept, oh, Brigadier,

[*Holds up the map.*]

> The map I present to you here.

[EAGLE *takes the map and examines it avidly while the Invincibles crowd around.*]

INVINCIBLES   You're a marvel, Old Hu, a hero.

EAGLE   [*laughs wildly, sings*]

> The map I've thought of day and night,
> Today is in my hands;
> This makes me master of the whole secret network
> In all of the Peony River region;
> What you have done, Hu Piao, dear friend,
> Is of unusual merit.

Bravo, Old Hu!

YANG   With the map in our possession, the Peony River region is ours.

EAGLE   Right. Well said. When our Kuomintang army returns, I'll be a commanding general. The rest of you will head brigades and divisions.

INVINCIBLES   We rely on your beneficence, Excellency. [*Laugh wildly.*]

[YANG *laughs coldly.*]

EAGLE   Because of what you've done for Tiger Mountain, Old Hu, I proclaim you the Ninth Invincible.

YANG   Thank you, Excellency.

EAGLE   That's not all. [*Pauses.*] As part of the Kuomintang army, we have grades and ranks. I appoint you full colonel and deputy regimental commander in the Fifth Peace Preservation Brigade of the Eastern Heilungkiang Region.

YANG [*gives a bandit salute*] Your Excellency is too kind. [*To Invincibles.*] I shall rely on you brothers for guidance.
INVINCIBLES You shouldn't be so modest.
BIG POCKMARK Bring wine!

[*A bandit enters and fills the bowls.*]

BIG POCKMARK Drink, everyone. Drink to congratulate Old Ninth.
INVINCIBLES Congratulations, Old Ninth.
EAGLE He deserves high reward for delivering the Contacts Map.
YANG [*sings*]

> Let me take a hearty drink to celebrate the merit today,
> I shall never rest until my bold task is completed.
> The day is yet to come for me to show my skill,
> I'm willing to shed my blood to write the history.

[*Smiles triumphantly, drains his cup.*]

[*Lights dim. Curtain*]

SCENE SEVEN Mobilizing the Masses

Chiapi Valley. A house with two rooms, home of Li Yung-chi. Walls show signs of having been charred. Noon. A snowstorm is raging.

[YUNG-CHI's mother *stands beside the stove. She removes the lid from the cooking pot and finds it empty. She shakes her head and sighs. As the wind roars outside, she totters to the table.*]

MOTHER [*sings*]

> Bone-biting snow blows through the walls,
> My clothes are thin, my grain is gone;
> Neither my son nor my daughter-in-law can hear me,
> Deep is my hatred for the crimes against us.

[CHANG TA-SHAN *enters.*]

TA-SHAN Aunt.
MOTHER It's Ta-shan! [*Opens door.*]

[TA-SHAN *comes into the house.*]

TA-SHAN Are you feeling any better today?
MOTHER I was dizzier than ever when I got up this morning.

TA-SHAN You're worried and hungry—that's what's wrong with you. We've still got some sweet potato roots. At least they'll take the edge off your hunger.

MOTHER I'm always such a nuisance to you and your wife. I'm really sorry.

TA-SHAN When Yung-chi's here, he looks after you. When he's away, you can rely on us neighbors. [TA-SHAN *sets water to boil on the stove.*]

[MOTHER *takes potato roots into next room.* YUNG-CHI *enters. Pushes open door and comes into house.*]

TA-SHAN [*surprised*] Yung-chi!

YUNG-CHI Ta-shan!

[MOTHER *emerges from side room.*]

YUNG-CHI Ma!

MOTHER Son! [*Sings.*]

> Can I be dreaming that you've returned?
> It pains me to see you so bruised and battered;
> I cried myself ill when they took you away.

YUNG-CHI [*sings*]

> In the bandits' lair, I thought of you day and night.

MOTHER [*sings*]

> I haven't been well but
> Our neighbors have looked after me.

YUNG-CHI [*sings*]

> I'm very grateful.

TA-SHAN [*sings*]

> It was only right.

MOTHER [*sings*]

> How did you escape from the tiger's den?

YUNG-CHI [*sings*]

> I jumped down a cliff and scaled the mountains.

MOTHER [*sings*]

> I'm overjoyed to see you but I grieve
> For my daughter-in-law and grandson.

YUNG-CHI [*sings*]

> The many crimes to be avenged are all
> Engraved upon my heart.
> Today I've preserved my life,
> Some day I'll kill my foe with might.

[*Voices offstage cry:* "Soldiers are entering the village!"]

TA-SHAN Another raid by Eagle?

YUNG-CHI Are they after me?

TA-SHAN Hide, quick. I'll go out and take a look. [*Exits.*]

MOTHER What shall we do!

YUNG-CHI If it's me they're after, I'll fight them to the death.

MOTHER I don't know what I'd do if anything should happen to you, son. Hide yourself.

YUNG-CHI Hide? Where? It's better to fight it out. At least I can take one or two of them with me.

MOTHER [*pleads*] Yung-chi, you mustn't.

[TUNG *and* LI *enter.*]

LI Let's visit this family.

TUNG [*knocks on the door*] Anybody home?

YUNG-CHI Yes. We're not all dead yet.

MOTHER Yung-chi.

TUNG Neighbor, old mother, open the door.

[YUNG-CHI *wrenches the door open.* LI *and* TUNG *enter, accompanied by a cold gust of wind.* TUNG *closes the door behind him.* MOTHER *is alarmed. She moves closer to* YUNG-CHI *protectingly.*]

LI Don't be afraid, old mother. We're only. . . .

YUNG-CHI Come to the point.

TUNG You've got us wrong, neighbor. We're the Chinese People's Liberation Army.

YUNG-CHI Liberation Army? [*Looks them over.*] This "army" and that "army," I've seen plenty. Who knows what you really are! Speak out, whatever you want. If it's money, we haven't got any. If it's grain, your gang has already robbed us clean. If it's our life—

LI   We PLA are the people's soldiers. We protect the people.
YUNG-CHI   That's what you say.
MOTHER   Yung-chi! [*She wavers, dizzy.*]
LI   Are you ill? We'll send for our medic.
YUNG-CHI   Who are trying to fool? [*Supports his mother into next room.*]

[TUNG *and* LI *look at each other, go out, close door.* SHAO *and* KAO PO *enter.*]

SHAO   How are you doing?
TUNG   We've called on several families, but they're all the same. The man in this house is particularly bitter.
LI   The old mother there is sick.
SHAO   Call our medic. Tell her to bring some grain.
LI   Right. [*Exits.*]
TUNG   It's certainly tough getting close to these people.
SHAO   Impatient again, Young Tung? They don't understand us. They've probably been fooled before. Don't you remember—Tuft Cheek pretended to be one of our scouts. Once they understand, their hatred will change into strength.
TUNG   I know that, 203, it's only. . . .
SHAO   We must be concerned about the troubles of the masses. If we don't mobilize them, we won't be able to get a firm foothold and wipe out the Eagle. On the other hand, unless we destroy the bandits, the masses won't be really aroused.
TUNG   I realize that.
SHAO   Tell our men to explain our Party's policy patiently. We must strictly carry out the Three Main Disciplines and Eight Points for Attention. We've got to mobilize this place by the example of our own behavior.
TUNG   Right. [*Turns to leave.*]
SHAO   By the way, find out if Hunter Chang has returned.
TUNG   Right. [*Exits.*]

[PAI JU *enters.*]

PAI   I've brought the grain, 203. [*Hands him a sack.*] Where's the patient?
SHAO   In the house. Let's take a look at her, Comrade Pai Ju.
PAI   Right. [*Knocks at door.*] Hello, neighbor.
SHAO   Our medic is here, neighbor. Open the door.

[YUNG-CHI *rushes into outer room, a dagger in his hand. His mother follows, trying to stop him.*]

MOTHER Yung-chi, you mustn't. . . .
YUNG-CHI What do I fear? I can fight it out with them with this. [*Stabs dagger into table.*]
MOTHER [*very upset*] Yung-chi, I beg you. [*Faints.*]
YUNG-CHI [*supporting her*] Ma. Ma.

[SHAO *forces open the door. Goes in with* PAI JU *and* KAO PO. *Protecting his mother,* YUNG-CHI *glares at them.*]

SHAO Look after her, Pai Ju, quick.

[PAI JU *slips off her overcoat and wraps it around* MOTHER, *then helps her into inner room, followed by* KAO PO *and* YUNG-CHI. SHAO *pours some grain into pot and sets it to boil.* YUNG-CHI *comes out for some water.* SHAO *goes into inner room.*]

YUNG-CHI [*discovering pot of gruel*] The PLA? [*Sings.*]

These soldiers worry about the people and cure
Their ailments; they're considerate and kind.
But soldiers and bandits have always been one,
And oppressed us with equal cruelty.
This certainly is very strange.

Can the saviors we've longed for have really arrived?

[MOTHER *calls from inner room:* "Water."]

[YUNG-CHI *fills a bowl with gruel.* KAO PO *emerges and takes it in.* SHAO *comes out.*]

SHAO Your mother has revived, neighbor. It's not serious. Don't worry.
YUNG-CHI Oh.
SHAO What's your name? What do you do?
YUNG-CHI I'm Li Yung-chi. I used to be a railway worker.
SHAO A worker? Fine. So we're no strangers then. How long has your family been living here?
YUNG-CHI For two generations already.
SHAO How many of you are there?

[YUNG-CHI *looks upset. Sighs.*]

SHAO [*takes up the sack*] I hear you have nothing to eat. Here's a little grain. [YUNG-CHI *doesn't accept it.* SHAO *puts it on the table. Sees dagger.*] You don't need this against us, neighbor. We're all one family.

YUNG-CHI [*looks him over carefully*] Whose troops are you, anyhow? What are you doing here in our mountain forests?

SHAO [*sings*]

> We're the sons of workers and peasants, come
> To destroy the reactionaries and change the world.
> We've fought all over China in the last few decades,
> With the Party and Chairman Mao leading the way,
> A red star on our army caps, two red flags
> Of the revolution on our collars.
> Where the red flag goes dark clouds disperse,
> Liberated people overthrow the landlords,
> The PLA shares the people's hardships,
> We've come to sweep clean Tiger Mountain.

YUNG-CHI [*moved, sings*]

> Our eyes are nearly worn out, looking for you, and today
> You've come, to fight the bandits and save the poor.
> Our own army, I should have known you, I'm ashamed
> To have mistaken a friend for an enemy.
> For thirty years we've been enslaved, soothing our wounds,
> Suppressing our rage, struggling in a bottomless pit.
> The people of Chiapi Valley hate the bandits
> Of Tiger Mountain, they've suffered without end.
> Who would have believed an iron tree could blossom,
> That we should at last live to see this day.
> I'll go with the Party to drive out those beasts,
> Whatever the danger, be it fire or water,
> When Tiger Mountain is being swept clean and free,
> I, Yung-chi, in the front ranks will be.

[SHAO *grasps* YUNG-CHI'S *hand.*]

[*His mother comes out, supported by* PAI JU *and* KAO PO.]

MOTHER This girl cured me, Yung-chi.

YUNG-CHI They've brought us some grain, too.

[MOTHER *is moved to tears.* SHAO *helps her to a seat.* LI *enters.*]

LI These neighbors have come to see you, 203.

[*Villagers swarm in, headed by* TUNG *and* TA-SHAN, *together with* HUNTER CHANG *and his daughter* PAO.]

TUNG [*to* CHANG]   This is our detachment leader.

SHAO [*comes forward and shakes the hunter's hand*]   So you're Chang the hunter. Have you come from the valley?

CHANG   We couldn't stay in the valley. We've moved in with Uncle Ta-shan, here.

SHAO [*pats* PAO *on the shoulder*]   Good girl.

CHANG   So you've guessed.

YUNG-CHI [*greets him*]   Brother Chang.

CHANG [*hails him and his mother*]   Ah, Yung-chi, and you, Aunt. We've our liberators here at last.

TA-SHAN   Commander, we're all burning with one desire—to attack Tiger Mountain.

SHAO   Our PLA is winning big victories at the front, neighbors. The Peony River area has been liberated. Eagle has no place to flee.

TA-SHAN   Let's destroy his nest. Give us guns, commander.

VILLAGERS   Yes. Please, give us guns, commander.

YUNG-CHI   If we had guns, there isn't a man in Chiapi Valley who couldn't bring down two or three of those bandits.

SHAO   We'll definitely give you weapons. [*Touches their ragged clothing.*] But none of you have any warm winter clothes and every family is short of grain. How can you go after the bandits in the deep mountain forests?

VILLAGERS   What can we do?

SHAO   There are plenty of medicinal herbs in Chiapi Valley and lots of timber. If we get the little train running again, we can ship them out and buy clothing and grain in return.

CHANG   That's right. We have a saying in these parts: "When the train whistle blows, the grain here flows. When the locomotive runs, we've clothing in tons."

A VILLAGER   That's only what everybody wished for. But what usually happened was "When the locomotive thunders, Eagle comes down and plunders. We got poorer and the Kuomintang got richer."

YUNG-CHI   But we've got the PLA with us now. We're not afraid of ten Eagles.

SHAO   Right. We're here now, and you can organize a militia. We'll get the little train running again and you'll have food and clothing. When we fight Eagle, you'll be all the stronger.

YUNG-CHI   When can we start repairing the railway?

SHAO   What about now? We'll work with you.

TA-SHAN   It's heavy labor, commander.

TUNG   Who do you think we are—little gentlemen? We're all from poor families. When we've guns in our hands, we fight; when we've tools in our hands, we work.

YUNG-CHI   We really are all one family, commander. [*Sings.*]

> We mountaineers mean what we say,
> Our words are straight, our hearts are true,
> To seize a dragon we'll go with you under the sea,
> To catch a tiger we'll follow you up the heights.
> With the thunders of spring the earth will shake!

Then Eagle—beware.

VILLAGERS [*sing*]

> Your days are numbered.

[*The stage darkens. Curtain*]

SCENE EIGHT   Sending Out Information

Dawn. A clearing on Tiger Mountain. A fork in the trail, its right branch leading to the only road down the mountain. Forts are visible in the rear distance. Yang's dwelling is to the rear left. Path in left foreground leads to Tiger Hall.

[*As curtain rises,* EAGLE *and* BIG POCKMARK *are walking on from left.*]

EAGLE   Is this where Old Ninth usually does his traditional shadow boxing?

BIG POCKMARK   Yes.

EAGLE   Where else has he been?

BIG POCKMARK   He's made a tour of the forts on our five peaks.

EAGLE   What! You even let him inspect our nine groups of twenty-seven bunkers?

BIG POCKMARK   He's one of us, isn't he? Why not show him how strong we are?

[EAGLE *gives a dissatisfied grunt.*]

BIG POCKMARK   Old Ninth is as loyal as he's tough and clever. Why don't you trust him?

EAGLE   I don't like the look of things. There's a lot of activity down below, and Tuft Cheek still hasn't returned. Why should Hu Piao show
up at a time like this? We've got to be careful.

[FLATNOSE *enters from right.*]

FLATNOSE   We've prepared everything as you've ordered, Excellency.
EAGLE   Good. No matter whether he's true or false, put him to the test,
the way I told you last night.
BIG POCKMARK   Hu Piao isn't a man to be trifled with, Excellency. Be-
sides, he's loyal to you. If you bungle it and he finds out, it'll be bad.
FLATNOSE   You never met him before he came here, brother. We don't
know really what's in his heart.
EAGLE   That's right. None of us ever saw Hu Piao before. Adjutant,
proceed according to plan.
FLATNOSE   Yes, sir. [*Exits.*]

[EAGLE, BIG POCKMARK, *seeing* YANG *approaching, leave quickly.*]

YANG [*sings, offstage*]

It's hard, operating in the heart of the enemy;

[*Enters.*]

But when I look off into the distance and think of my
Comrades-in-arms and the people, awaiting my signal
To attack these wolves, my spirits soar.
The Party has placed limitless hope on me,
The comrades in the Party committee, by their
Exhortations and advice, have warmed
My heart with their kindness and concern.
I must never forget to be bold yet cautious,
And succeed through courage, but mostly through guile.
Each word of the Party is victory's guarantee,
Tiger Mountain is heavily fortified
Mao Tse-tung's thought is eternally glorious.
With forts above and tunnels below,
Our leader's order to use guile is right,
A direct attack would mean heavy losses.
After seven days here I know the layout well,
I have the secret report concealed upon my person.
Now at daybreak, pretending to take a stroll, I'll send it out. . . .

[*Notices something.*]

Why have the guards suddenly been increased?
Something's up.

But this message—[*Sings.*]

> If I don't get it out,
> I'll be ruining our attack plan and
> Letting down the people and the Party.
> New Year's Eve is fast approaching
> I mustn't hesitate, I must push on,
> Though the grass be knives and the trees
> Be swords, and get to the foot of the slope.
> What though the mountain be tall? I'll melt
> The ice and snow with the sun that is in my heart.

[*Thinks.*]

Today is the twenty-sixth. I've got to get this message out. [*Offstage voices: "Hurry up." "I'm coming as fast as I can."*]

[YANG *removes his coat and pretends to be practicing traditional shadow boxing. Two guards walk by. They hail him and exeunt.* YANG *ends his performance. A burst of gunfire is heard.*]

YANG   Shooting!

[*Shouts in the distance: "Charge!" "Kill!" Nearer voices cry: "The communist forces are coming!"*]

[*The firing increases.*]

YANG   What? Can my comrades be here? Impossible. 203 wouldn't have come without receiving my message. [*The shooting becomes more intensive, and the sound of shouting draws nearer.*]

YANG   The sound of the firing isn't right. Ah, another test. I'll reply to their trick with one of my own and get this message off. [*Call toward the left.*] Brothers. [*Four bandits enter.*] The Reds are here. Get down there and fight.

[*The bandits rush off to right.* EAGLE *and* BIG POCKMARK *enter stealthily.* FLATNOSE *comes forward to greet them.*]

EAGLE   Not so fast, Old Ninth.
YANG [*shouts to bandits offstage*]   Stay where you are.

FLATNOSE [*in same direction*] Cease firing.

[*Bandits shout acknowledgment of order.*]

YANG What's up?

EAGLE It's a practice maneuver I've ordered.

YANG A good thing you stopped me. If I fired this clip I'd have killed a few of them.

[EAGLE *laughs.*]

YANG Why didn't you tell me you were arranging this maneuver, Excellency?

EAGLE Don't let it bother you, Old Ninth. I didn't tell anybody about it. If you don't believe me, ask him.

FLATNOSE It's true. I thought the Reds were coming, myself.

YANG [*chuckles*] I wish they would. I'm just waiting for them.

EAGLE You're quite a man, Old Ninth. [*Laughs.*]

[*Bandit captain, offstage "March!" Enters, escorting another bandit.*]

CAPTAIN This guy bumped into the wall outside, Excellency.

EAGLE What!

BIG POCKMARK How did it happen?

BANDIT [*trembling*] I went down, under orders, with a few of the boys. Far off, we saw the little train running again. But before we got to Chiapi Valley, we ran into some Red soldiers.

EAGLE Chiapi Valley, eh? [*Thinks.*] How many of them were there?

BANDIT A lot. Hundreds.

EAGLE [*suspiciously*] And you're the only one who got away?

FLATNOSE Nine out of ten you were captured by the Reds and they let you go.

BANDIT No, no.

EAGLE [*draws his gun and points it at bandit*] You son of a bitch.

YANG [*intervenes*] Why get excited, Excellency? If he really had been a prisoner of the Reds, he wouldn't dare come back.

BIG POCKMARK That's right. Everyone knows how Your Excellency hates any man who lets the Reds capture him.

[EAGLE *grunts.*]

YANG [*to bandit*] Get out of here. Can't you see you're making His Excellency angry?

BANDIT   Yes, sir.

BIG POCKMARK   Beat it.

BANDIT [*softly, as he goes out*]   That Old Ninth is a good fellow.

BIG POCKMARK [*to* CAPTAIN]   Give the order—tighten all defenses.

CAPTAIN   Yes, sir. [*Exits.*]

EAGLE   Hurting my prestige again. I won't stand for that.

BIG POCKMARK   It's only a few days till New Year's Eve, Excellency. I'll send some men down on a raid. That will restore our prestige and be something to celebrate at the Hundred Chickens Feast.

EAGLE   Not a bad idea, but those Reds can't be trifled with. It's not safe to venture into Chiapi Valley. But since the train has started running we can attack the train outside the village.

BIG POCKMARK   Very well. [*Exits.*]

YANG [*his plan thought out*]   I'm afraid the Reds are there for the purpose of attacking us, Excellency. Of course we've nothing to worry about with the defenses we've got on Tiger Mountain. But we shouldn't just sit here and wait for them to come after us.

EAGLE   What do you think we should do?

YANG   Whoever strikes the first blow has the advantage, as the old saying goes. We ought to practice charging, and get our soldiers into top shape. Then, after the Hundred Chickens Feast, we'll roll down into Chiapi Valley.

EAGLE [*pleased*]   You're a clever fellow. [*Sings.*]

> You're brave and clever, really sharp,
> Of all my men, you are the best,
> And loyal to me, absolutely—

Take command, Old Ninth. Put the men through some practice charges.

YANG   Right.

EAGLE [*sings*]

> Steadily, I'll raise your rank,
> This I guarantee.

[*Laughs. Exits with* FLATNOSE.]

YANG   That dumb cluck. [*Sings.*]

> A fool and cheat, who thinks he's intelligent,
> Gives me my chance with his "clever" plan.
> While we're "charging" I'll send off my message—

And add a line about the Eagle's plan to raid Chiapi Valley and wreck the train. [*Sings.*]

Pick it up, Comrade Sun, I'm counting on you.

[*Curtain*]

SCENE NINE   Surprise Attack

Morning, a few days before New Year's Eve. As the curtain rises the whistle of the little train is heard. The scene is the clearing outside Yung-chi's house.

[*A girl, offstage, cheers:* "There goes the little train again. Come and look!" *Smiling villagers, with sacks of grain on their backs, watch as the train pulls out, and they exit joyfully.* YUNG-CHI's *mother puts down her sack of grain.*]

MOTHER [*sings*]

> Soldiers and people are one family,
> Happiness reigns in our mountain village.
> A good snow falls, everyone smiles,
> Sharing food and clothing, we celebrate emancipation.

[SHAO *enters.*]

SHAO   Have you got enough to eat and use for this time of the year?
MOTHER   Plenty. Who would have dreamed that Chiapi Valley could have such a good New Year? If you PLA boys hadn't come, I don't know what we'd have done.
SHAO   The best is yet to come.
MOTHER   We owe it all to the Communist Party and Chairman Mao.
SHAO   I'll carry the grain in for you.
MOTHER   I can manage.

[SHAO *puts the sack of grain on his back.* YUNG-CHI *enters.*]

YUNG-CHI   Commander.

[MOTHER *snatches the sack from* SHAO *and takes it into house.*]

SHAO   Comrade Yung-chi.
YUNG-CHI   The bandit prisoners Luan Ping and Tuft Cheek have been

led away and our PLA reinforcements have arrived. Does that mean we're ready to attack Tiger Mountain?

SHAO Just about. Eagle's fall is only a question of days.

YUNG-CHI How we've been longing for it.

SHAO Is your militia prepared?

YUNG-CHI Yes. We've divided into two groups, as you've suggested. One will stay here to guard the village, the other will march with the detachment. You must let me be your guide.

SHAO We'll be depending on you, militia leader. You know these mountain trails well. A lot depends on you.

YUNG-CHI We're only doing what we should. All our militia want to go and destroy Eagle. Pao is making an awful fuss. She refuses to stay with the guard unit. We can't do a thing with her.

SHAO That girl has a lot of drive. Defending the village is also important, Comrade Yung-chi. You have another talk with her.

YUNG-CHI Right. [*Exits.*]

[SHAO *paces to and fro, thinking.* LI *and* TUNG *enter.*]

TUNG New Year's Eve is nearly here, 203, but Sun still hasn't come back with the message. Are we supposed to just hang around, waiting?

SHAO What do you think we should do?

TUNG We've all learned how to ski and can move quite fast. We've Yung-chi to guide us. . . .

LI And we've been sent reinforcements and more ammunition. . . .

TUNG So, if you ask me, even if we don't get the message, we ought to set out immediately. We can win anyhow.

SHAO Comrades. [*Sings.*]

> Eagle can't escape his doom,
> You must be patient when problems arise.
> Return to quarters and wait for orders. . . .

TUNG Right. [*Exits with* LI.]

SHAO [*sings*]

> Although I've urged patience
> I'm impatient myself.
> Time is fleeting and the appointed day is nearing.
> But there's no sign of Sun.
> If anything's gone wrong . . .

I've another idea. We mustn't miss
Our chance at the Hundred Chickens Feast.
Yung-chi says there's a dangerous
Trail up the back of the mountain,
With courage we'll climb up and
Charge into Tiger Hall.

[YUNG-CHI *and* HUNTER CHANG *enter.*]

YUNG-CHI Everything's ready, commander. Are we starting right away?

SHAO Wait a little, Comrade Yung-chi. If we take that back trail, are you sure we can reach the top in a day and a night?

YUNG-CHI It's eighty *li* longer that way, but the bandits have no defenses there. And now that all the comrades can ski with great speed, I guarantee we can do it in a day and a night.

CHANG That route is full of bluffs and cliffs. It's rough going.

SHAO No matter how rough it is, it can't stop the PLA.

[CHANG *is about to reply when* PAO *and* PAI JU *enter.*]

PAO I applied long ago to go with the detachment to attack Tiger Mountain, uncle. Today, you're setting out. Why are you leaving me behind?

SHAO The militia also have to protect the village.

PAO I hate that Eagle. I've got to kill him with my own hands. You must let me go!

SHAO So this is a complaint against me. It's only because you're too young, Pao.

PAO What do you mean—young? I'm sixteen. See, I'm not much shorter than her. [*Indicates* PAI JU.] Sister, talk to him, please. . . .

PAI JU Pao has class consciousness, 203, she skis well, she's a good shot, and she can help me look after the wounded. Let her go.

SHAO Ah, so you two are in league.

CHANG Let her come along, commander.

SHAO What do you say, Yung-chi?

YUNG-CHI All right.

SHAO Very well, then. Since your militia leader approves, you can go and get ready.

PAO You've agreed. [*Jumps for joy. Exits with* HUNTER CHANG.]

[CHAO-CHIA *enters.*]

CHAO-CHIA Sun is back, 203.

[SUN *enters.*]

SHAO [*hurries forward*] Comrade Sun.
SUN Report. Here is the message. [*Hands it over.*]
SHAO You're back at last. You must be tired. Get some rest.

[*Exit* CHAO-CHIA, SUN, PAI JU, *and* YUNG-CHI.]

SHAO [*eagerly reads message*] ". . . A steep trail up the back of the mountain leads directly to Tiger Hall. Enemy defences are weak there. . . . Burning pine torches will be the signal. . . ." [*Excitedly*] Old Yang, you're a hero. [YUNG-CHI *enters.*]
SHAO Does that trail up the back of the mountain go directly to Tiger Hall, Comrade Yung-chi?
YUNG-CHI Yes, directly.
SHAO We're depending on you to take us there.
YUNG-CHI Don't worry, commander. When I escaped from Tiger Mountain I took that trail. I know it well.
SHAO Good. Assemble your militia. Get ready to go.
YUNG-CHI Right. [*Shouts in all directions.*] Militia, assemble. Militia, assemble. [*Exits.*]
SHAO [*discovers writing on back of message*] ". . . The bandits are going to raid Chiapi Valley in a few days and wreck the train. . . ." [*Startled.*] What!

[KAO PO *calls "203" and enters running, followed by soldiers,* TA-SHAN, HUNTER CHANG, YUNG-CHI's *mother and villagers.*]

KAO PO Reporting to 203. When the train reached Two Branch River, the bridge was down. We got out to repair it and were attacked by bandits. We drove them off, but the train was blown up.
SHAO What about those two prisoners?
KAO PO Tuft Cheek was killed in the blast.
SHAO And Luan Ping?
KAO PO He escaped while we were chasing the bandits.
SHAO He escaped? If he runs up to Tiger Mountain, that'll be dangerous for Comrade Yang, and it may ruin our plan. Chao-chia, assemble the detachment.
CHAO-CHIA Right. [*Exits.*]
SHAO Comrade Ta-shan, I give the job of repairing the train to you and Comrade Chang.

TA-SHAN Right.

[*Soldiers and militiamen enter.*]

SHAO Comrades. [*Sings.*]

> Our plan mustn't go wrong,
> Every second counts. Let's fly forward,
> Fully armed, to Tiger Mountain
> And wipe out the foe.

[SHAO *and soldiers say goodbye to villagers.* SHAO *mounts a rock and waves his arm.*]

SHAO Forward, march.

[*Soldiers and militia set out quickly.*]

[*Dark change*]

[*A snowstorm. Two or three soldiers move forward as an advance guard.*]

[*To the tune of "March of the Chinese People's Liberation Army,"* YUNG-CHI *leads the soldiers and the militia along a trail. It is heavy going through the snow, but they push on indomitably.*]

[*At the foot of a cliff, they remove their skis and start climbing.*]

[*Boldly, they scale height after height, then again ski confidently through the snowstorm.*]

[*The lights slowly dim. Curtain*]

SCENE TEN The Hundred Chickens Feast

New Year's Eve. In Tiger Hall on Tiger Mountain. Eagle is seated on his "throne." His Eight Invincibles stand beside him.

[*As curtain rises a bandit is reporting to* EAGLE.]

BANDIT He says he's Luan Ping, adjutant on Breast Mountain.
EAGLE Luan Ping?
INVINCIBLES So he's come. We won't let him off.
EAGLE Bring him in.
BANDIT Bring the guy in.

[*Two bandits enter with* LUAN PING.]

LUAN Your Excellency.
EAGLE What brings you here, adjutant?
LUAN I've come to—to wish you a long life.
EAGLE Pretty brazen, aren't you?
LUAN But, Excellency—
EAGLE Answer me. Where have you been?
LUAN I . . . I. . . .
INVINCIBLES Speak!
LUAN I. . . .
INVINCIBLES Out with it!
LUAN I . . . I've come from Commissioner Hou.
EAGLE [*laughs coldly*] So you've been with Commissioner Hou. Sum-
mon Old Ninth.
BIG POCKMARK [*to a bandit*] Call Old Ninth!
BANDIT Old Ninth, you are asked to go in.

[YANG *enters.*]

YANG [*sings*]

> I'm exultant.
> The Hundred Chickens Feast is ready.
> Lighting the torches will be the signal for the bandits' end.

Everything is in readiness for the feast, Excellency.

[*A silence falls on the assembled bandits.*]

EAGLE Look who's here, Old Ninth.
YANG [*startled at the sight of* LUAN, *but controls himself immediately.
Decides to take the initiative*] Why, Brother Luan. It's been a long
time.

[LUAN'S *jaw drops.*]

YANG Hu Piao got here before you, brother. How did you make out
with Commissioner Hou? I'll bet he gave you a high post. Congratulations.
INVINCIBLES [*mockingly*] What are you now—a colonel? [*They laugh.*]

[LUAN *is bewildered.*]

EAGLE That's right. What kind of post did he give you? Why bother
coming to me?

LUAN [*understands. Looks at* YANG *and smiles wickedly*]   Hu Piao, my
   eye. You're mistaken if you think—
YANG [*sternly*]   You're the one who's mistaken. As a friend I advised
   you to join His Excellency, but you tried to drag me off to Commis-
   sioner Hou. You can't say I wasn't a true friend. [*Menacingly.*] An-
   swer His Excellency. Be quick. What post did the commissioner give
   you? What official business brings you here?
LUAN [*tries to get away from* YANG]   Excellency, listen to me—
YANG   Don't be so long-winded. Today is His Excellency's fiftieth birth-
   day. He's no time for your chatter.
LUAN   Excellency. . . .
EAGLE   Come to the point. I want to know why you've come.
LUAN   To join Your Excellency's forces.
YANG   Then why did you ask an appointment from Hou?

[LUAN *gets confused, hesitates.*]

[*The hall is silent.* EAGLE *and the others glare at him.*]

YANG   Why has the commissioner sent you here? The truth, now!
INVINCIBLES   Right. Why have you come?
LUAN   I haven't been sent by Commissioner Hou.
BIG POCKMARK   He certainly changes his tune fast. Quite a bird.

[*The bandits laugh uproariously.*]

LUAN   What are you laughing about? You've been hoaxed. He isn't Hu
   Piao. He's a communist army man!

[*Invincibles draw their guns and point them at* YANG.]

YANG [*tenses, then relaxes, laughs*]   Good. So I'm a communist army
   man, since you say so. Now tell His Excellency and his Eight Invin-
   cibles more details about this communist army man.
EAGLE   Yes. You say he isn't Hu Piao. How did you come to know a
   communist army man?
LUAN   He . . . he . . . he. . . .
YANG   All this fellow can do is stammer and contradict himself. He's
   up to some trick, Excellency.
BIG POCKMARK   I'll bet he was caught by the Reds, and then released
   and sent here.
LUAN   No . . . no. . . .
YANG   Did the Reds let you go? Or did they send you here?
LUAN   I . . . I. . . .

FLATNOSE The Reds sent you, didn't they?
INVINCIBLES Speak, speak.

[LUAN *stares, tongue-tied.*]

YANG Our defenses on Tiger Mountain are absolutely watertight, and the Reds can't get in. But now this fellow has come. There's something fishy about this.
LUAN [*hastily*] There isn't. I swear!
YANG It doesn't matter what you say. [*Sings*]

> Inconsistent, sinister fellow,
> His evasiveness surely conceals tricks.
> To our fortress he came, leaving his tracks
> In the snow for the Reds to follow.

Captain—
CAPTAIN [*comes forward*] Here.
YANG [*sings*]

> Strengthen the guard and keep a close watch,
> Let no one off duty without my order.

EAGLE Right. Without Old Ninth's order, no one is to leave his post.
CAPTAIN Yes, sir. [*Exits.*]

[*Invincibles nod approvingly.*]

EAGLE [*comes down from his seat*] You treacherous dog. First you try to get Old Ninth to go with you to Commissioner Hou. Now you come here, sowing discord among us, and scheming to lead the Reds in after you. This is too much.
LUAN He's not Hu Piao, Excellency. He's a communist army man. [*Kneels.*]

[*Bandits gaze at him contemptuously.*]

YANG [*menacingly*] What a snake you are, Luan, trying to turn His Excellency against me. I'm sorry I didn't kill you in Pear Valley.
INVINCIBLES That's right.
YANG Excellency, I've never let myself be pushed around by little men. Because, for your sake, I offended this mad dog, he attacks me viciously. If you believe that I'm a communist army man, then finish me off, at once. If you believe that I'm Hu Piao, then permit me to leave this mountain. It's either him or me; one of us has to die. You

decide, Excellency. [*Removes his officer of the day sash and tosses it at* EAGLE's *feet.*]

BANDITS You mustn't leave, Old Ninth, you mustn't leave.

INVINCIBLES Stay with us, Old Ninth.

EAGLE [*hesitates, then breaks out irritably*] Don't be childish. It's not worth getting yourself worked up over this mad dog. [*Picks up the sash.*] Wear it, wear it. I will treat you right.

[BIG POCKMARK *takes the sash from him and puts it on* YANG.]

LUAN [*realizes the situation is against him, pleads*] Excellency. . . .

EAGLE [*brushes him aside*] Humph! [*Returns to his seat.*]

LUAN [*prostrates himself before* YANG] Brother Hu Piao! [YANG *ignores him.*]

LUAN [*slaps his own face*] I'm trash, I'm not even human.

YANG [*not looking at* LUAN, *shouts to the assembled bandits*] The hour has come. Let everyone congratulate His Excellency on his birthday.

[*Bandits noisily assent.*]

BIG POCKMARK You're fifty today, Excellency. You mustn't let this cur spoil the event.

FLATNOSE It will be bad luck for Tiger Mountain if you don't blot out this evil star, Excellency.

BANDITS Right. He must be killed.

LUAN Old Invincibles, Brother Hu Piao, Excellency, spare me.

[*With a peal of blustering laughter,* EAGLE *steps down from his seat and menacingly confronts* LUAN, *who grovels before him.*]

EAGLE If I don't kill you, I'll be spoiling my fiftieth birthday and letting Old Ninth down. Destroy this evil star, drive away the bad luck, kill this ill-omened owl, and I'll live well and long. Ha! Ha! Ha! . . .

LUAN Excellency, spare me. . . .

FLATNOSE Take him away.

YANG I'll do it. [*Seizes* LUAN, *who is paralyzed with fright.*] [*Sings.*]

> You've murdered and slaughtered
> For dozens of years. To avenge
> The people, in the name of our country,
> I sentence you to death.

[*Drags him out. A shot is heard.* YANG *re-enters.*]

YANG Everything is ready for the celebration. Allow us to offer our respects, Excellency.

EAGLE You're officer of the day, Old Ninth. You officiate.

YANG Light the lamps in the hall, brothers. Burn torches outside. Let's offer our best wishes for His Excellency's birthday.

[*Bandit captain enters and repeats the order.*]

INVINCIBLES Best wishes to you, Excellency.

[*Invincibles and other bandits bow to* EAGLE.]

YANG Brothers, let's celebrate together, masters and disciples. Let everyone eat and drink his fill. Get good and drunk.

BANDITS Right. We'll get good and drunk.

YANG Please be seated at the table, Excellency.

EAGLE After you, brothers.

YANG It's your fiftieth birthday, Excellency. You must be seated first.

[EAGLE *laughs complacently. Leaves for adjoining cave room. Bandits file in after him and begin feasting.*]

YANG Call in the brothers on guard and let them drink their fill.

CAPTAIN Yes, sir. [*Exits.*]

[*Bandits can be heard playing rowdy drinking games in adjoining cave room.*]

YANG [*surveys the scene, sings*]

> New Year's Eve and the mountain is
> A blaze of light—my signal to our troops.
> The Hundred Chickens Feast has started as planned,
> The bandits are drunk and befuddled.
> I hope my comrades will come quickly
> And smash this den of stubborn enemies.
> How time drags, what makes our men so slow?
> I long to go out and have a look—
> But I must keep calm at this critical moment
> And block this secret tunnel.

[*Points at spot below* EAGLE's *throne.*]

[EAGLE, BIG POCKMARK, *and others enter, staggering drunk.*]

EAGLE Why don't you join the feast, Old Ninth? Although you're new here, you've done a lot of work for our mountain fortress. Everyone wants to drink to your health.

YANG Today's your fiftieth birthday. It's your health we should be drinking to. Fill His Excellency's cup. [*A bandit pours wine for* EAGLE.]

EAGLE [*very drunk*] I've really had too much, Old Ninth.

YANG It's your birthday, Excellency. You must drink up.

EAGLE All right, all right. I'll have this one more.

YANG And now three more for the chief of staff to drink up.

BIG POCKMARK Right.

[*Everyone drinks.*]

[*Shots are heard. Bandits throw down their cups. One of the Invincibles, wounded, enters, running.*]

INVINCIBLE [*shouts*] The Reds have sealed off the entrance to Tiger Hall with a machine gun.

EAGLE Fight your way out, brothers.

BANDITS Charge! Charge!

[*PLA men, offstage yell:* "Surrender your guns and live."]

EAGLE Into the tunnel with me, Old Ninth, quick. [*Pushes over throne, but* YANG *shoves him aside.*]

YANG Nobody move!

[*PLA men charge in shouting:* "Surrender your guns and live."]

EAGLE What! Who are you?

YANG A member of the Chinese People's Liberation Army.

EAGLE Ah!

[EAGLE *draws his gun.* YANG *knocks it out of his hand.* EAGLE *runs off. Bandits follow.*]

YANG There's a secret tunnel here, comrades. Nab Eagle and rescue the captured villagers. [*Runs to pursue* EAGLE.]

[*PLA men follow.*]

[SUN *fights with an Invincible. Kills him with a thrust of his bayonet.* BIG POCKMARK *enters.* SUN *stabs and wounds him.* BIG POCKMARK *flees, with* SUN *in pursuit.*]

[CHAO-CHIA *chases in after another Invincible. They fight.*]

PAO *pursues a bandit. They wrestle. She subdues him. She and* CHAO-CHIA *lead him off.*]

[YUNG-CHI, PAI JU, *soldiers and militia, with villagers the bandits had been holding captive, walk across stage and exit.*]

[*Bandit captain enters, running.* YUNG-CHI *shoots him dead.*]

[EAGLE, *followed by two bandits, enters, fleeing wildly.* YANG *pursues them. Shoots the two bandits dead. He and* EAGLE *lock in struggle.*]

[TUNG *and soldiers chase on* FLATNOSE *and bandits. They fight.*]

[YANG *grabs a gun and kills several bandits.*]

[SUN, YUNG-CHI, PAI JU, KAO PO, *and militia come running on. They capture all the bandits.* YUNG-CHI, *raging, wants to hit* EAGLE. SUN *holds him back.*]

[*Liberated captives enter and embrace their militia neighbors.*]

[DETACHMENT COMMANDER SHAO *enters.*]

SHAO [*pumps* YANG's *hand, very moved*] Old Yang! [*Introduces* YUNG-CHI *to him.*]

[*The two warmly shake hands.*]

[*Curtain*]

The
Red
Lantern

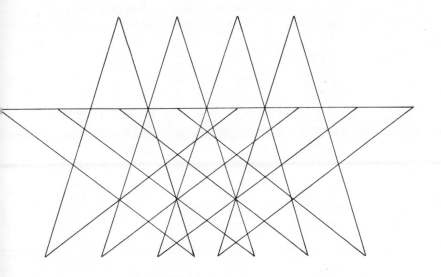

The Battle of the Piano

*The highlight of the Peking cultural season in the summer of 1968
was Chairman Mao Tse-tung's attendance of a performance of*
The Red Lantern, *which the official announcement pointedly
identified as a "Peking opera sung to piano accompaniment, newly
created during the great proletarian cultural revolution." Official
photograph showed that Mao climbed up to the stage after the
show, on July 1, where he stood with one of the male performers to
his left. Next stood Lin Piao, then Vice Chairman of the Communist Party; to his left, one of the female stars of the show, and next
to her, Mao's wife, Chiang Ching, for whom the evening must have
been a moment of particular triumph. Others on the stage included
Premier Chou En-lai.*

*The official announcement of the event stated: "Our great teacher
and great leader Chairman Mao and his close comrade-in-arms
Vice Chairman Lin Piao in the evening on July 1 attended a
musical performance sponsored by the Cultural Revolution Group
under the Central Committee of the Communist Party in celebration of the 47th anniversary of the founding of the Party." When
Mao and Lin appeared in the Great Hall of the People, the announcement continued, "all present stood up and, holding high
their copies of the red-covered* Quotations from Chairman Mao
Tse-tung, *cheered long and enthusiastically: 'Long live the great,
glorious and correct Communist Party of China! Long live the invincible thought of Mao Tse-tung! Long live our great leader
Chairman Mao! A long, long life to Chairman Mao!' In high
spirits, Chairman Mao waved and clapped again and again in
greeting."*

The announcement also said: "The singing of Peking opera The

Red Lantern, *with piano accompaniment jointly performed by revolutionary literary and art fighters of the Central Philharmonic Society and the China Peking Opera Troupe was recently created under the brilliant guidance of the great leader Chairman Mao's proletarian line for literature and art, by implementing Chairman Mao's principle, 'Make foreign things serve China and weed through the old to bring forth the new,' and in accordance with instructions from Comrade Chiang Ching."*

Rarely has the piano created such controversy, or achieved such prominence, as it did in Peking up to and during this performance of The Red Lantern. *Quotations from Mao were mobilized to justify the use of this Western instrument to convey the Chairman's ideas. His appeal to "make foreign things serve China" was repeated over and over again. On the surface it seemed a contradiction that the elimination of Western methods and themes from the Chinese cultural scene should be accompanied by the introduction—one is tempted to say, imposition—of an instrument as clearly European as the piano. Yet, starkly and almost defiantly, the black silhouette of a piano was printed, standing by itself, on the red cover to the music of* The Red Lantern. *In the photographs selected to publicize the opera, the piano was featured as prominently as the human performers.*

Actually, of course, no instrument now used before major audiences is truly alien to another culture. The piano, grandchild of the clavichord and the spinet, cousin to the harp and harpsichord, is a distant relative of the stringed instruments in Chinese tradition. Its vigorous sound, as compared with instruments of more delicate tonality, may have attracted Chiang Ching's attention— and there can be no doubt that it was Mao's wife who personally fought vigorously, against sustained opposition, for the adoption of the piano as a favorite musical weapon. The Peking Review *wrote on July 5, 1968, that "the singing of the Peking opera,* The Red Lantern, *with piano accompaniment, a proletarian art of a new type, has been created under the personal guidance and care of Comrade Chiang Ching." The article recalled that as early as 1964 Mao's wife had "instructed that the piano should be used to accompany Peking operas with contemporary revolutionary themes." It added that "the handful of counter-revolutionary revisionists" had "blocked this important instruction and kept it from the revolutionary artists." After noting that "this crime" had been "completely smashed," the article continued:*

"Inspired by the excellent situation in which victories have been achieved one after another in the great proletarian cultural revolution, the revolutionary literary and art fighters have displayed dauntless revolutionary initiative, broken with fetishes and displayed the spirit of daring to think, to act, to make revolution. Starting with the beginning of 1967 and after repeated experiments, they finally succeeded in composing piano accompaniments for the main parts sung by Li Yu-ho, the hero, and Li Tieh-mei, the young heroine, in the Peking opera The Red Lantern. *As a result, the piano, the Western musical instrument, takes a place on the Peking opera stage for the first time in history."*

The periodical then summed up what may well be the core of the argument advanced by Chiang Ching in favor of Western musical instruments generally and the piano in particular:

"The Peking opera The Red Lantern *with piano accompaniment retains the basic characteristics of singing in Peking opera; at the same time, it brings into full play the characteristics of the piano —its wide range, great power and varied means of expression. Thus the lofty and heroic images of Li Yu-ho and Li Tieh-mei are even better depicted. This successful trial in making foreign things serve China is a new creation in proletarian revolutionary literature and art. It has opened up a new road for Western musical instruments and symphonies and for musical accompaniments to Chinese operas."*

Changes in The Red Lantern *have been continuous. Adapted from a Shanghai opera into a Peking opera, it was prominently included in the First Festival of Peking Operas on Contemporary Themes, a repertory held in Peking in 1964. Its basic plot deals with a railway switchman, Li Yu-ho, who acts as the courier for a secret code to the Chinese guerrillas during the war against Japan. He falls into Japanese army hands and is tortured by Hatoyama, a Japanese captain, but he does not reveal the code. Hatoyama then tries his ruthless wiles on the railwayman's adopted mother, Granny Li, and his adopted daughter, Li Tieh-mei, but he fails again. Li is executed by the Japanese, as is Granny Li. But Tieh-mei is released and eventually brings the code to the guerrillas.*

The opera was rewritten after the 1968 performance, and the final version, released in May 1970, is offered on the following pages. Libretto and music have been changed to polarize the characters and to eliminate elements of plot that might have distracted from its main message. These changes have been well summarized by Colin Mackerras in his paper, "Chinese Opera after the Cultural Revolution (1970-72)," which appeared in China Quarterly, *July-September 1973. Mackerras noted that "the central point of the accusations against the early versions of the story lay in the portrayal of the hero." He further wrote:*

"The original Peking opera version had watered down Li Yu-ho's communist ideals, made him share prominence with Granny Li and Tieh-mei, and emphasized his family relationship with the two women. The new version stresses his heroism much more strongly, shows his warm feelings for the masses much more sharply and reduces the roles of Granny Li and Tieh-mei to those of giving play to the heroism of the central character. It is always Yu-ho who holds the initiative and not the subordinate characters; certainly never Hatoyama, as was sometimes the case in the earlier version. The main point is to emphasize the heroism of the main character and to show his consciousness of class struggle

and attachment to Chairman Mao and the Party. In other words, the 1970 script not merely plays out a good story, which was the sum total of the version performed at the 1964 festival, it defines Li Yu-ho's ideological commitment, thus explaining the cause of his triumph."

Mackerras noted that "revisions have also been made in the characterization of the villains." The early version had pictured Captain Hatoyama as "elegant, even capable of gentleness, and other Japanese and collaborators as clownish," while the new opera "portrays their brutality much more sharply." The author also writes that the earlier version of The Red Lantern had, according to official Peking claims, "overstated the horrors of war," and had "allowed the heroes to subordinate armed conflict to secret work." According to Hung Chi (No. 5, 1970), the basic task was to avoid both a pacifistic note and a picture of the war equivalent to "strolling in a garden of flowers."

Colin Mackerras found "the most striking difference" between the two versions in their music." He wrote:

"The earlier version uses instrumentation, melodic structure and vocal techniques which are strikingly similar to the music of the traditional Peking opera. The dialogue sections are mostly more realistic than in a classical drama, but even these show very strong traces of the stylized 'recitative' common in the old operas. The new version, on the other hand, sounds very different from a traditional Peking opera. The orchestra contains both western and Chinese musical instruments in which the former generally dominate, although the classical gongs and cymbals are still much in evidence. Sung sections where only the Chinese instruments can be heard are very few; no more than a line or so here and there. The overall impression is a more powerful dramatic impact, but it is ironic that the Chinese should feel the need to appeal to the West for techniques to strengthen the heroics of their own theatre.

"The fact that the four main roles are the same in the recordings of both versions emphasizes the very great differences in their portrayal of characters. In the earlier version all the characters adhere relatively closely to the slightly colorless characterization of the traditional opera, but in the new they sing with far greater passion. In her monologue on seeing her father for the last time Tieh-mei sounds, in the older version, not unlike the typical 'feudal' woman of the classical opera, slightly simpering and behaving as though she lacked the courage to overthrow the oppressors. In the new she is much more forthright, courageous and full of hatred for the enemy."

Changes in the dialogue are minor, but significant in that they were made at all. In the older version, Tieh-mei's father expresses his regret, when he is dying, that he has not left her any money. Such material concern is eliminated from the later version. Mackerras observed that the music during the execution scene was changed from "a solemn procession with the Chinese double-reeded so-na *dominating," to a full-orchestra rendition of the* Internationale, *the traditional Communist hymnlike marching song. Colin Mackerras, who is a Senior Research Fellow at the Australian National University and author of* The Rise of the Peking Opera, 1770-1870, *comes to this conclusion: "The overall effect of the newer version is certainly more heroic, and my personal impressions generally bear out the claims and theories put forward for it in the Chinese press. Although one's value judgment of the revisions will depend largely on how one assesses the relative merits of traditional and westernized Chinese opera, to my ear at least, the new* Red Lantern *is more exciting and the music better adapted to the theme of the drama."*

According to Mao's wife, the new versions of Chinese operas and dramas are not only designed for domestic audiences, but are also addressed to an overseas public, notably in the so-called Third World countries of Asia, Africa, and Latin America. It may well be that the merging of Western and Eastern techniques, together with polarized characterizations, make these productions more easily accepted before international audiences. Whether the break with Chinese traditions in music, instruments, and style is final, or whether further gradations in these artistic compromises will be required, only future developments in the volatile Chinese culture scene are likely to reveal.

C H A R A C T E R S

LI YU-HO   switchman and Communist Party member
TIEH-MEI   his daughter
GRANNY   Tieh-mei's grandmother
OLD CHOU   worker and Communist Party member
AUNT LIU   Li's neighbor
KUEI-LAN   her daughter
THE LIAISON MAN OF THE COMMUNIST PARTY
THE KNIFE GRINDER   a guerrilla
GUERRILLA COMMANDER LIU
THE GRUEL SELLER
THE CIGARETTE VENDOR
GUERRILLAS, TOWNSPEOPLE, ETC.

HATOYAMA   chief of the Japanese military police
HOU HSIEN-PU   his Chinese lieutenant
A JAPANESE SERGEANT
INSPECTOR WANG   a renegade
THE PEDLAR   a spy for the Japanese
THE COBBLER   a spy for the Japanese
JAPANESE GENDARMES, THUGS, ETC.

SCENE 1   The Liaison Man Is Rescued

A late autumn night in 1939 during the War of Resistance Against Japan. A siding near Lungtan Station in northeast China. It is dark and the wind is howling. Four Japanese gendarmes march past on a tour of inspection. There is a slope nearby, with hills in the distance. A train passes on the other side of the slope.

[*Enter* LI YU-HO, *quietly, with a signal lantern.*]

LI

        Red lantern in hand, I look round;
        The Party is sending a man here from the north;
        The time fixed is half past ten. [*Looks at his watch.*]
        The next train should bring him.

[*Enter* TIEH-MEI *with a basket.*]

TIEH-MEI Dad!

LI Well, Tieh-mei, how was business today?

TIEH-MEI [*angrily*] The gendarmes and their thugs kept searching people and made them too jittery to buy anything.

LI Those gangsters!

TIEH-MEI Do be careful, Dad.

LI Don't worry. Go home and tell Granny that an uncle is coming. Ask her to have a meal ready.

TIEH-MEI Right.

LI Come over here. [*Wraps his own scarf round her neck.*]

TIEH-MEI Dad, I'm not cold.

LI No, you have it.

TIEH-MEI Where's he from, this uncle?

LI [*kindly*] Children shouldn't bother their heads about such things.

TIEH-MEI [*to herself*] I'll go and ask Granny. Take good care of yourself, Dad. I'm off now. [*Exit.*]

LI Our girl is doing all right.

        She can peddle goods, collect cinders,
        Carry water and chop wood.
        A poor man's child soon learns to cope
        With all tasks at home and outside.
        Different trees bear different fruit,
        Different seeds grow different flowers.

[*Enter* INSPECTOR WANG.]

WANG Who's that?

LI It's Li.

WANG The Japanese are keeping a close watch today, Old Li. They must be up to something.

[*Enter two Japanese soldiers.* WANG *and* LI *step apart. Exeunt the Japanese.*]

WANG [*taking out a cigarette*]   Got a light?

LI   Here. [*He goes over to light his cigarette, bending close to* WANG.] Things are tense, Old Wang. We must take special care. Let's get in touch once every ten days from now on. I'll let you know where to meet.

WANG   Right.

[*A whistle sounds in the distance and a train roars past. When it nears the station the* LIAISON MAN *jumps off. The Japanese police on the train fire two shots.* LI *and* WANG *step back.*]

[*The* LIAISON MAN, *wounded in the chest, staggers in and falls by the track.* LI *and* WANG *rush over to him.*]

LI [*helping him up*]   Are you hurt?

LIAISON [*regaining consciousness, looks around*]   What's this place?

LI   The fifty-first siding, Lungtan Station. You. . . . [*With an effort the* LIAISON MAN *raises his left hand in a blue glove. Then he faints.*]

LI [*to himself*]   The left hand gloved. [*To* WANG.] He's our man.

[*Not far off Japanese yell and whistles are blown.*]

WANG   Get him away, quick. I'll cover you.

LI [*carrying off the man on his back*]   Be careful, Old Wang. [*Exit.*]

[*The shouts and whistles come nearer.*]

[WANG *draws his pistol and fires two shots in the direction opposite to that taken by* LI. *Pounding footsteps can be heard and angry yells. To fox the enemy,* WANG *clenches his teeth and shoots himself in the arm. As he falls to the ground in come the Japanese sergeant,* HOU HSIEN-PU, *and several gendarmes.*]

SERGEANT [*to* WANG]   Where's the man from that train?

WANG [*pointing toward the opposite direction and groaning*]   Over there.

SERGEANT [*in alarm*]   Down! [*All the Japanese flop to the ground.*]

SCENE 2   The Secret Code

The same evening. The road where Li's house stands. The house, in the center of the stage, has a door on the right and by the door a window. In the middle of the room is a square table with a lamp on it. Behind is a *kang.** The wind howls. The room is dark. Granny strikes a match and lights the lamp. Wind rustles the window paper.

GRANNY

> Fishermen brave the wind and waves,
> Hunters fear neither tigers nor wolves;
> The darkest night must end at last
> In the bright blaze of revolution.

[GRANNY *draws back the curtain and looks out. Shaking her head she mutters,* "Still not back." *She goes to the table and takes up her needlework. Enter* TIEH-MEI *with a basket.*]

TIEH-MEI   Granny.

GRANNY   You must be cold, child.

TIEH-MEI   I'm not. Granny, Dad told me to let you know there's an uncle coming. He wants you to get a meal ready. [*Puts down the basket.*]

GRANNY   Oh, just coming, are they? I've rice and dishes ready.

TIEH-MEI   Why do I have so many uncles, Granny?

GRANNY   Your father has so many sisters, of course you have lots of uncles.

TIEH-MEI   Which one is coming today?

GRANNY   Why ask? You'll know when he arrives.

TIEH-MEI   Even if you won't tell me, Granny, I know.

GRANNY   What do you know?

TIEH-MEI   Listen.

> I've more uncles than I can count;
> They only come when there's important business.
> Though we call them relatives, we have never met,
> Yet they're closer to us than our own family.
> Both you and dad call them your own folk;
> Well, I can guess the secret—
> They're all men like my dad,
> Men with fine, loyal hearts.

GRANNY [*smiling*]   You smart girl.

[*Sound of a police siren. Enter* LI *with the wounded man on his back. He pushes open the door and staggers in.* GRANNY *and* TIEH-MEI *hurry to help the* LIAISON MAN *to a chair.*]

* A brick bed which can be heated.

TIEH-MEI [*frightened*]   Oh!
LI [*to* TIEH-MEI]   Watch the street.

[*The girl goes to the window.* GRANNY *brings a towel.* LI *cleans the man's wound and gives him a drink of water.*]

LIAISON   Can you tell me if there's a switchman here named Li?
LI   That's me.

[*The* LIAISON MAN's *eye lights on* GRANNY *and he hesitates.*]

LI   It's all right. You can speak.
LIAISON [*using the password*]   I sell wooden combs.
LI   Any made of peachwood?
LIAISON [*eagerly*]   Yes, for cash down.
LI [*with a pleased glance at* GRANNY]   Fine.

[GRANNY *lights the small square lantern to show the* LIAISON MAN *that one side is pasted with red paper.*]

LIAISON [*not seeing the right lantern, struggles to get up*]   I must . . . go.
LI [*holding high the other lantern*]   Look, comrade!
LIAISON [*grasping* LI's *hand*]   Comrade, I've found you at last.

[*He faints.*]

[TIEH-MEI *is puzzled by this business with the lantern.*]

LI   Comrade. . . .
GRANNY   Comrade, comrade. . . .

[*The* LIAISON MAN *comes to.*]

LIAISON   Comrade Li, I'm . . . the liaison man . . . sent . . . from the north. [*With difficulty he tears open the lining of his padded jacket, produces the code and hands it to* LI.] This is . . . a secret code. [*Panting.*] Send it . . . quickly . . . to the guerrillas in the north hills. [*Gasping for breath.*] Tomorrow afternoon, the gruel stall in the junk market. . . .
LI   Yes, comrade. What about the junk market?
LIAISON   A knife grinder will get in touch with you there.
LI   So a knife grinder will get in touch with me.
LIAISON   Same password as before.
LI   The same, yes.
LIAISON   The task must be carried out. . . . [*He dies.*]

[TIEH-MEI *cries.* GRANNY *quickly stops her.* LI *takes off his cap and looks at the code in his hands. All three bow their heads before the dead man.*]

LI   I swear to carry out the task.

[*The siren of the police car wails.* GRANNY *hastily blows out the light.*]

SCENE 3   A Commotion at the Gruel Stall

The next afternoon. The gruel stall in the junk market. To the right of the shabby booth is a rickety table at which three men, A, B and C are eating gruel. At the foot of the pillar on the left squats a woman selling cigarettes. As the curtain rises the market hums with noise.

[*Enter* LI *with his lantern in one hand and a canteen in the other.*]

LI

> Come to find our man in the junk market
> I have hidden the code in my canteen;
> No obstacles can stop me,
> I must send it up to the hills.

[*He enters the booth and greets the people there.*]

A bowl of gruel, please, mum. [*Hangs his lantern on the right-hand pillar.*] How is business?
GRUEL SELLER   So-so. [*She serves him.*]

[C *finishes his gruel and pays for it.*]

GRUEL SELLER   Another bowl, brother?
C   No more, thanks.
GRUEL SELLER   Is one bowl enough for you?
C   Enough? It's all I can afford. We work all day but don't earn enough to buy gruel. It's a hell of a life. [*Exit.*]

[*Enter another man,* D.]

D   A bowl of gruel, please.

[*The woman serves him.*]

D [*drinking the gruel*]   What a smell this has got! The rice is moldy.
A   It's government rice. What can we do?

[*With a sigh* D *takes the bowl to the left pillar to drink. He then squats down and buys a cigarette.*]

B Hey, what's this in the gruel? Nearly broke one of my teeth.
A It's full of stones.
GRUEL SELLER You'd better put up with it.
B The swine just don't treat us as human.
A Keep quiet, or you'll find yourself in trouble.
B [*sighing*] How are we to live?
LI

> Our people are fuming with discontent,
> Trampled by iron hoofs they seethe with fury
> And wait for the first rumble of spring thunder.
> China's brave sons will never bow their heads;
> May our guerrillas come soon from the north hills!

[*Enter the* KNIFE GRINDER *with a carrying pole.*]

KNIFE GRINDER

> Glancing around in search of my man,
> I see the red lantern hanging high to greet me.
> (Raising his gloved left hand to his ear he cries.)
> Any knives or scissors to grind?

LI

> The knife grinder has his eye on my red lantern
> And he raised his hand to accost me.
> I shall casually give him the password.

[*Before* LI *can speak the siren wails and Japanese gendarmes charge in.*]

GENDARMES Don't move. This is a search.

[*The knife grinder deliberately drops his tools to divert the attention of the Japanese.*]

LI Good man.

> He draws their fire in order to cover me.

[*He empties his bowl of gruel into his canteen and asks for another helping. The gendarmes finish searching the* KNIFE GRINDER, *wave him angrily away, and turn toward* LI. *He offers them his canteen and lantern but they push them aside.* LI *puts them on the table and lets himself be searched.*]

GENDARME A [*having searched him*]   Clear out.

[LI *picks up his canteen and lantern and goes out.*]

SCENE 4   Wang Turns Renegade

The following afternoon in Hatoyama's gloomy office. On his desk are a medal, a medical report and a telephone. Beside the desk stands a screen.

[*Enter* HOU HSIEN-PU *with* WANG'S *file.*]

HOU

> The man from the train fired a shot
> And wounded Inspector Wang's arm;
> The damage done is not serious
> But Hatoyama is making much of it.
> No doubt he has his reasons.

[*The telephone rings.* HOU *takes the call.*]

HOU   Yes? [*Standing to attention*] Yes, sir. [*He puts the receiver down.*] A call for you, Captain Hatoyama. [*Enter* HATOYAMA *from behind the screen.*]

HATOYAMA   Where from?

HOU   From the commander.

HATOYAMA   You should have said so. [*Takes the phone.*] Hatoyama speaking. What? Got away? Eh? Hmm. . . . Don't worry, sir, I promise to get the code. Yes, sir. What? An order from the Kwantung Army Headquarters. [*He stands to attention.*] The deadline for clearing this up. . . . Yes, sir. [*Rings off, muttering to himself.*] Those Reds are the devil. Headquarters discovered some clues in the north, but now they've covered their tracks again. The Communists are the very devil.

HOU   Report! Here is the dossier on Inspector Wang. [*Presents the file.*]

HATOYAMA   Good. [*He takes it and looks through it casually.*]

SERGEANT [*off*]   Report!

HATOYAMA   Come in.

[*Enter the* SERGEANT.]

HATOYAMA Find him?

SERGEANT We searched all the hotels, bathhouses, theaters, and gambling dens but found no trace of the man from the train. We arrested a few suspects. Would you like to see them, sir?

HATOYAMA What's the use of arresting suspects? This is urgent. Headquarters have just notified us that this man from the train is a liaison officer for the Communists in the north. He has a very important secret code with him.

HOU and SERGEANT [*standing at attention*] Yes, sir.

HATOYAMA This code has been sent from the Reds' headquarters in the north to the guerrillas in the north hills, who are waiting for this to get in touch with them. If this code reaches the guerrillas it will be like fitting several thousand tigers with wings, and that would be most detrimental to our empire.

HOU and SERGEANT [*standing at attention*] Most detrimental. Yes, sir.

HATOYAMA How could you let such an important Red slip through your fingers?

[*The* SERGEANT *and* HOU *look at each other.*]

HATOYAMA Fools!

HOU and SERGEANT Yes, sir.

HATOYAMA How about Inspector Wang?

HOU He was shot in the left arm, but the bone. . . .

HATOYAMA That's not what I was asking. Tell me his background.

HOU Very good, sir. His name is Wang Hung-chang, otherwise known as Wang Lien-chu. His grandfather used to sell opium, his father kept a tavern, and he was one of the first graduates from the Manchukuo police school. He has one wife, one son, and one father.

HATOYAMA So he comes from a good family. This time he did his best. Bring him here.

HOU Yes, sir. [*Calling.*] Inspector Wang.

[*Enter* WANG *with one arm in a sling. He salutes* HATOYAMA.]

WANG Captain.

HATOYAMA Well, young man.

You have paid for your courage, young fellow,
Stopping the enemy's bullet with your body
And fearlessly defending our great empire.
On behalf of headquarters I give you this medal, third class.

WANG [*surprised and pleased*] Ah!

> My ill luck has changed to good,
> Hatoyama does not suspect me.

[*Turns to* HATOYAMA.]

> Thank you, sir, for your goodness,
> This is too great an honor.

HATOYAMA Young man,

> Provided you serve the empire loyally
> You have every chance to rise high;
> One who repents can leave the sea of troubles,
> The choice is up to you.

WANG I don't follow, sir.

HATOYAMA You should understand. You are not an actor, so why try to fool me? I'm afraid I can't compliment you on your performance.

WANG Sir. . . .

HATOYAMA I don't suppose you have followed my career. Let me tell you that when you were still a baby I was already a surgeon of some reputation. Though you fired that shot accurately enough, you forgot one thing. How could the man from the train get within three centimeters of your arm to fire?

WANG I'm sorry you should think such a thing, sir.

HATOYAMA [*chuckling*] Sorry. I'm sure you are. Sorry that I wasn't taken in by your trick. You can't fox me so easily, young fellow. So now, out with the truth. Who was your accomplice?

WANG Accomplice?

HATOYAMA Does that word surprise you? It's obvious enough. That man who jumped off the train was badly wounded. Without an accomplice to help him and another to cover their escape, could he have grown wings and flown away?

WANG Sir, you can investigate what happened. I was shot and fell to the ground. How could I know where that man went?

HATOYAMA You knew all right. Why else should you shoot yourself? Don't try to outsmart me, young fellow. Tell me the truth. Who's in the underground Communist Party? Who were your accomplices? Where is the liaison man hiding? Who's got the secret code now? Make a clean breast of things, and I have plenty of medals and rewards ready for you.

WANG You're making my brain whirl, sir.

HATOYAMA [*laughing derisively*] In that case we shall have to sober you up. Hou Hsien-pu!

HOU Yes, sir.

HATOYAMA Take this young man out and help to sober him.

HOU Very good, sir. Guards!

[*Enter two gendarmes.*]

WANG I've done nothing, sir. Nothing wrong.

HATOYAMA Take him away.

WANG Don't punish an innocent man, sir.

[HATOYAMA *jerks his head in dismissal.*]

HOU Come on.

[*The guards march* WANG *out, followed by* HOU.]

HATOYAMA [*smiling cynically after them*]

> Iron hoofs trample the whole northeast,
> Human skulls are used for goblets;
> The crack of whips, the sound of sobs
> And drumming on bones make music.
> No matter how tough the fellow,

[*His singing is punctuated by the sound of blows and cries.*]

> He must break down under torture.

[*Enter* HOU.]

HOU If you please, sir, he has confessed.

HATOYAMA Who was his accomplice?

HOU Li Yu-ho, the switchman of the No. 51 siding.

HATOYAMA Li Yu-ho! [*He takes off his glasses.*] Well, well. . . .

SCENE 5 The Family's Revolutionary History

The next afternoon. Li's house. Granny is sewing and worrying about Li.

GRANNY

> Already dusk, but my son is still not back.

[*In the distance sound shouts and the wails of the siren.* TIEH-MEI *rushes fearfully in with her basket and locks the door.*]

TIEH-MEI   It looks bad, Granny.

GRANNY   What's happening?

TIEH-MEI   Granny,

> The streets are in confusion
> With sentries at every crossroad;
> They are searching and arresting men right and left,
> It's even worse at the station.
> I ran home because I'm worried about Dad.

GRANNY   Don't worry, child.

> Your dad is brave and wary,
> He knows the way to deal with the Japanese. [*She tries to calm herself.*]

[*Enter* LI *with the red lantern and canteen.*]

LI [*knocking at the door*]   Mother.

TIEH-MEI   It's Dad. [*She quickly opens the door.*] Dad.

LI   Yes. . . . Mother.

GRANNY   So you're back, Son. You had me really worried.

LI   It was a near thing, Mother. [*He walks toward the pillar by the bed and signs to her to take the canteen.*] Let me have the thing in that, quick.

GRANNY [*signing to* TIEH-MEI *to watch the street while she opens the canteen*]   There's nothing here but gruel.

LI   It's underneath, Mother.

[*She empties out the gruel, produces the wrapped code and hands it to* LI.]

GRANNY   What is this?

[TIEH-MEI, *standing guard by the window, keeps an eye on her father.*]

LI [*hiding the code in a crack in the pillar by the bed*]   Mother,

> I'd just met the knife grinder by the gruel stall
> When a police car came and the Japanese started a search;
> He drew their fire to protect me,
> And I got a chance to outwit them;

They didn't find the code hidden under the gruel,
I smiled calmly while they searched.

TIEH-MEI   Trust both of you, Dad. But what are we to do with this?
LI   Don't worry. We'll think of some way to send it, Tieh-mei. [*He makes her sit down opposite him and speaks gravely.*] You've seen everything. I can't keep this from you any longer. This is something more important than our own lives. We must keep it a secret even if it costs us our heads.

[GRANNY *lights the paraffin lamp.*]

TIEH-MEI [*naively yet earnestly*]   I understand.
LI   Hah, I suppose you think you're the smartest girl in the world.
TIEH-MEI [*pouting*]   Dad!
GRANNY   Now you two.
LI [*consulting his watch*]   It's getting late. I must go out.
GRANNY   Don't be too late.
LI   I won't. [*He gets up to go.*]
TIEH-MEI   Wait till you've had supper, Dad.
LI   I'll eat when I come back.
TIEH-MEI [*giving him the scarf*]   Take this, Dad. [*She wraps the scarf round his neck.*] Come back early.
LI   I will. [*Exit.*]

[GRANNY *polishes the lantern with care.*]

TIEH-MEI [*struck by an idea*]   Polishing the red lantern again, Granny?
GRANNY [*deciding to tell her the truth*]   Tieh-mei, the time has come to tell you something. Sit down and listen to the story of the red lantern.
TIEH-MEI   Yes.
GRANNY   We've had this lantern for thirty years. For thirty years it has lighted the way for us poor people, for workers. Your grandad carried this lantern, and now your dad carries it. It's bound up with all that happened last night and today, which you saw for yourself. I tell you, this red lantern is our family treasure.
TIEH-MEI   Our family treasure?
GRANNY   It's dark, time to get supper. [*She puts the lantern carefully down and goes to the kitchen.*]

[TIEH-MEI *picks up the lantern to examine it carefully and then puts it gently down. She pensively turns up the paraffin lamp.*]

> Granny has told me the story of the red lantern,
> Only a few words, yet how much it means.
> I have seen my father's courage,
> My uncles' willingness to die for it.
> What are they working for?
> To save China, save the poor, and defeat the Japanese invaders.
> I know they are in the right,
> They are examples for the rest of us.
> You are seventeen, Tieh-mei, no longer a child,
> You should lend your father a hand.
> If his load weighs a thousand pounds,
> You should carry eight hundred.

[*Enter* GRANNY. *She calls* TIEH-MEI, *who does not hear.*]

GRANNY What were you thinking about, child?

TIEH-MEI Nothing.

GRANNY The food will soon be ready. When your dad comes, we'll start.

TIEH-MEI Right.

[*The child next door cries.*]

GRANNY Listen, is that Lung-erh crying next door?

TIEH-MEI [*looking toward the curtain over the kang*] Yes, it is.

GRANNY Poor child, he's hungry I'll be bound. Have we any of that corn flour left?

TIEH-MEI Not much.

[*The child cries again.*]

TIEH-MEI [*eager to help*] There's a little, Granny. Shall I take them a bowl? [*She gets the flour.*]

GRANNY Yes, do.

[*Enter* KUEI-LAN.]

KUEI-LAN [*knocking at the door*] Aunty Li.

TIEH-MEI It's Sister Kuei-lan. [*Opens the door.*] I was just going to call on you, sister.

GRANNY Is Lung-erh any better?

KUEI-LAN Yes, but . . . we've nothing at home to eat.

TIEH-MEI   Sister Kuei-lan, this is for you. [*Gives her the bowl of flour.*]
KUEI-LAN [*hesitating to accept it*]   Well. . . .
GRANNY   Take it. I heard Lung-erh crying and thought you probably
   had nothing for him. Tieh-mei was just going to take this over.
TIEH-MEI [*to* KUEI-LAN]   Go on, take it.
KUEI-LAN [*accepting the bowl*]   I don't know what to say, Aunty.
   You're too good to us.
GRANNY   Well, with the wall between us we're two families. If we
   pulled the wall down we'd be one family, wouldn't we?
TIEH-MEI   We are one family even with the wall.
GRANNY   That's true.

[*The child next door cries again.*]

[*Enter* AUNT LIU *and opens the door.*]

AUNT LIU   Kuei-lan, the child is crying. [*Sees the bowl in her hand.*]
   How can we accept it? You haven't got much yourselves.
GRANNY   Never mind. In times like these we must help each other and
   make do as best we can. You'd better go and fix a meal for the child.
AUNT LIU   I don't know how to thank you. [*She starts out with* KUEI-
   LAN.]
GRANNY   It's nothing. [*She sees them to the door.*]
TIEH-MEI [*closing the door*]   Granny, look at Kuei-lan's family. Her
   husband out of work and the little boy ill. How are they going to
   manage?
GRANNY   We'll do our best to help them.
TIEH-MEI   Yes.

[*An enemy agent posing as a pedlar comes to the door and knocks
lightly three times.*]

PEDLAR   Is Old Li in?
TIEH-MEI   Someone wants Dad.
GRANNY   Open the door.
TIEH-MEI   Right. [*Opens the door.*]
GRANNY   You want. . . .

[*Enter the* PEDLAR. *He looks around and closes the door behind him.*]

PEDLAR [*raising his gloved left hand*]   I sell wooden combs.
GRANNY [*observing him carefully*]   Have you any peachwood combs?
PEDLAR   Yes, for cash down.

TIEH-MEI [*eagerly*]   Wait! [*She turns to pick up the red lantern.*]

[GRANNY *coughs.* TIEH-MEI *stops.* GRANNY *strikes a match and lights the small square lantern while* TIEH-MEI, *understanding, catches her breath.*]

PEDLAR [*raises the curtain and looks out as if on his guard. Then he eyes the small lantern*]   Thank goodness, I've found you at last.
TIEH-MEI [*realizing that this is a trick, angrily*]   You. . . .
GRANNY [*throwing her a warning glance*]   Well, let me see your combs.
PEDLAR [*pretending to be in earnest*]   This is no time for jokes, old lady. I've come for the code. That's important to the communist cause. The revolution depends on it. Every minute is more precious than gold to the revolution. Give it to me quickly, without any more delay.
TIEH-MEI [*vehemently*]   What nonsense are you talking? Get out.
PEDLAR   Now then. . . .
TIEH-MEI   Get out quickly! [*She pushes him out and closes the door with a bang.*] Granny!

[*Two plainclothesmen enter, making signs to each other, and stand outside the door.*]

TIEH-MEI   He nearly fooled me, Granny. Where did that mangy dog come from?
GRANNY   Child, this is a bad business.

> Never mind that mangy dog,
> A poisonous snake will be following behind;
> It's clear that someone
> Has talked.

TIEH-MEI   We must send the secret code away at once.
GRANNY   It's too late. They'll have laid a trap.
TIEH-MEI   Ah! [*Runs to the window and looks out.*] Granny. [*She comes back to her.*] There's a man by the telegraph pole watching our door.
GRANNY   Things are really bad. Hurry up and paste the sign on the window.
TIEH-MEI   What sign?
GRANNY   The paper butterfly* I told you to cut out.

* In north China many families decorate their windows with colored papercuts.

TIEH-MEI It's in the box of patterns.

GRANNY Get it out then.

TIEH-MEI Right. [*Hurries behind the bed curtain and fetches the paper.*] How shall I paste it, Granny?

GRANNY Open the door to keep the window dark before you start. I'll sweep the ground outside so that they can't see you.

[TIEH-MEI *opens the door and* GRANNY *gets a broom. Before she can go out* LI *enters and walks in.*]

TIEH-MEI [*startled*] Why, Dad. [*The paper butterfly falls to the ground. The old woman drops her broom.*]

LI [*seeing the paper butterfly on the ground*] Has something happened, Mother? [*Closes the door.*]

GRANNY There are agents outside.

[*They fall silent.* GRANNY *is thinking hard.* TIEH-MEI *waits for her father to speak.* LI *paces thoughtfully up and down.*]

LI Mother, they may be coming to arrest me. I went to look for Old Chou just now but couldn't find him. If you need any help, get in touch with Old Chou at No. 36 West Bank. You must be careful.

GRANNY I know. Don't worry.

[*Enter* HOU HSIEN-PU.]

HOU [*knocking*] Is Mr. Li at home?

TIEH-MEI Dad.

LI Tieh-mei, open the door.

[LI *calmly sits down.* HOU *enters the room beaming.* GRANNY *makes a show of sweeping the floor.* TIEH-MEI *takes this chance to paste up the paper sign.*]

HOU Are you Mr. Li?

LI Yes, sir. Take a seat.

HOU [*with an awkward laugh presents an invitation card*] Mr. Li, Mr. Hatoyama is celebrating his birthday today. He wants you to go and have a cup of wine with him.

[GRANNY *and* TIEH-MEI *are startled.*]

LI [*calmly*] What, is Mr. Hatoyama inviting me to a feast?

HOU Just to be friendly.

LI He wants to make friends with me?

HOU   You'll understand when you see him. Come along.

LI   All right. Mother, [*gravely*] I'm going now.

GRANNY   Wait. Tieh-mei, bring some wine.

TIEH-MEI   Yes. [*She fetches wine from the table.*]

HOU   There'll be plenty for him to drink at the feast, old lady.

GRANNY [*with a contemptuous glance*]   Pah.

> The poor prefer their own wine,
> Each drop of it warms the heart.

You like wine, Son, but I don't usually encourage you to drink. To-day I want you to drink up this bowl. [*She passes him the wine.*]

LI [*taking the bowl*]   Right. With this to put heart into me I can cope with whatever's coming. Watch me drink, Mother.

GRANNY   I'm watching you.

LI [*looking at her as if to reassure her with his strength. He grasps the bowl hard and drains it in one breath. His cheeks are flushed, his eyes gleam*]   Thank you, Mother.

> I drink your wine at parting
> And it fills me with courage and strength.
> The Japanese is offering me a feast,
> Well, I can manage even a thousand cups.
> This is stormy, treacherous weather,
> Be ready for squalls.

TIEH-MEI   Dad. [*Clasps him and sobs.*]

LI   Tieh-mei.

> Keep your weather eye open outside,
> Don't forget our unsettled accounts;
> Keep watch for wild dogs at the door,
> And listen for the magpie's lucky cry.*
> You must help at home
> And share your granny's troubles.

TIEH-MEI   Dad. [*Clasps him and sobs.*]

GRANNY   Don't cry, Tieh-mei. Our family has this rule: when one of us leaves, nobody must cry.

LI   Always do as Granny says, Tieh-mei. Don't cry.

---

* In Chinese folklore the magpie is a lucky bird, bringing good news.

TIEH-MEI [*wiping her tears*]   I won't.
GRANNY   Open the door, child, and let your father go to the feast.
LI   Mother, look after yourself.

[*Grasping* LI's *hands,* GRANNY *gazes at him while* TIEH-MEI *opens the door. A gust of wind.* LI *strides out into the wind. Huddled up in his coat,* HOU *follows.* TIEH-MEI *runs after them with the scarf.*]

TIEH-MEI   Dad!

[*Four enemy thugs bar her way.*]

THUG A   Go back. [*He forces her back through the door. Then he enters and tells* GRANNY.] We're making a search.

[*The thugs give the place a professional going over.* TIEH-MEI *nestles up to* GRANNY *as they turn everything upside down. They discover an almanac and toss it away but fail to find anything incriminating.*]

THUG A   Come on. [*He signs to the others to leave. Exeunt.*]
TIEH-MEI [*closes the door, draws the curtain and looks at the chaos in the room*]   Granny! [*She falls into her arms and sobs.*]
GRANNY [*weeping despite herself*]   All right, cry, child. Have a good cry.
TIEH-MEI   Granny, will Dad ever come back?
GRANNY [*restraining her own tears. She knows there is little hope of his returning but does not want to say so. She takes up* LI's *scarf and strokes it*]   Tears won't help him, child. [*Looks at her.*] Tieh-mei, the time has come to tell you about our family.
TIEH-MEI   Yes, Granny?
GRANNY   Sit down. I'll tell you.
TIEH-MEI   Yes. [*Sits down on a stool.*]
GRANNY   Tell me: Is your dad good?
TIEH-MEI   There's no one better in the whole wide world.
GRANNY   Well . . . he's not your real father.
TIEH-MEI [*incredulously*]   Ah! What do you mean, Granny?
GRANNY   Neither am I your real granny.
TIEH-MEI [*startled*]   What's come over you, Granny? Have you taken leave of your senses?
GRANNY   No, child. We don't belong to one family. Your surname is Chen, mine is Li, and your dad's is Chang.
TIEH-MEI [*blankly*]   Oh.

GRANNY

For seventeen storm-tossed years I held my peace,
Eager to speak but afraid you were not ready for the truth.

TIEH-MEI   You can tell me, Granny. I won't cry.

GRANNY

Your father can hardly escape
And they may imprison me too;
Then the work for the revolution will fall to you.
When I tell you the truth, Tieh-mei,
Don't break down but take it bravely,
Like a girl of iron.

TIEH-MEI   Tell me. I won't cry.

GRANNY   It's a long story. When my husband was a maintenance man in Kiangan, he had two apprentices. One was your real father, Chen Chih-hsing.

TIEH-MEI   My father, Chen Chih-hsing.

GRANNY   The other was your present dad, Chang Yu-ho.

TIEH-MEI   Chang Yu-ho.

GRANNY   The country was torn by the fighting between warlords. [Standing up.] But then the Chinese Communist Party was born to lead the Chinese people's revolution. In February 1923, workers of the Peking-Hankow Railway set up a trade union in Chengchow. One of the warlords, Wu Pei-fu, was a stooge of the foreign invaders. When he tried to suppress the union it called on all the workers on the line to strike. More than ten thousand men in Kiangan demonstrated. That was another cold, dark night. I was so worried about your grandfather that I couldn't rest or sleep. I was mending clothes by the lamp when I heard someone knocking at the door, calling, "Aunty, Aunty, quickly open the door." I opened the door, and he came in.

TIEH-MEI   Who was it?

GRANNY   Your dad.

TIEH-MEI   [surprised]   My dad?

GRANNY   Yes, your present dad. Dripping with blood and all gashed with wounds, in his left hand he held this red lantern. . . .

TIEH-MEI   Ah, the red lantern.

GRANNY   In his right arm he held a baby.

TIEH-MEI   A baby?

GRANNY A mite less than one year old.

TIEH-MEI That baby. . . .

GRANNY That baby was none other. . . .

TIEH-MEI Than who?

GRANNY Than you.

TIEH-MEI Me. . . .

GRANNY [*quickly*] Hugging you tight to his chest, with tears in his eyes your dad stood before me and said, "Aunty, Aunty. . . ."

[TIEH-MEI *gazes expectantly at her.*]

GRANNY For some minutes he just stared at me and couldn't go on. In a panic, I begged him to speak. He said, "They've murdered . . . my master, my brother, and his wife. This is Brother Chen's child, a child of the revolution. I must bring her up to carry on our work." He said, "Aunty, from now on I am your son and this child is your granddaughter." Then I took you in my arms.

TIEH-MEI Granny! [*She buries her head in the old woman's lap.*]

[GRANNY *holds and comforts her.*]

GRANNY Ah! You mustn't cry. Take a grip on yourself and listen.

> In the strike those devils murdered your father and mother,
> Li Yu-ho went east and west for the revolution;
> He swore to follow in their steps, keep the red lantern burning;
> He staunched his wounds, buried the dead, and went back to the fight.
> Now the Japanese brigands are burning, killing, and looting,
> Before our eyes your dad was taken away;
> Remember this debt of blood and tears,
> Be brave and make up your mind to settle scores,
> A debt of blood must be paid for with enemy blood.

TIEH-MEI

> Granny tells a stirring tale of the revolution,
> They brought me up in wind and rain and storm,
> How much I owe you, Granny, for all these years!
> My mind is made up now, I see my way clear;
> Blood must be shed for our blood,

I must carry on the task my father began.
Here I raise the red lantern, let its light shine far.
My father is as dauntless as the pine,
The Communist Party fears nothing under the sun,
- I shall follow it and never, never waver.
The red lantern's light
Shines on my father fighting those wild beasts.
Generation shall fight on after generation,
Never leaving the field until the victory is won.

[GRANNY *and* TIEH-MEI *hold high the red lantern, which throws a radiant light over the stage.*]

SCENE 6　Hatoyama Is Defied

That evening. Hatoyama's house. A sumptuous feast is spread. Through the lattice screen glittering lights can be seen. Soft music. Girls dance behind the screen.

[*Enter* HOU *with* LI YU-HO.]

HOU　Please wait a minute. [*He starts off to report* LI's *attitude to* HATOYAMA.]

LI　As you like. [*He stands there looking round, lighting his pipe, disgusted by the surroundings.*]

HOU [*off*]　Captain Hatoyama.

HATOYAMA [*hurrying in*]　Ah, my old friend, it's good to see you again. Have you been keeping well?

LI　How are you, Mr. Hatoyama?

HATOYAMA　So we meet again after all this time. Do you remember when we were both working on the railway in Harbin?

LI [*drily*]　You were a celebrated Japanese doctor while I was a poor Chinese worker. We were like two trains running on different tracks, not traveling in the same direction.

HATOYAMA　Well, brother, there's not all that difference between a surgeon and a worker. We're old friends, not strangers, right?

LI　In that case can I hope for good treatment from you?

HATOYAMA　That's why I asked you over for a chat. Do sit down, please. [*They sit down.*] Today is my birthday, friend, a time to celebrate. Suppose we just talk of friendship and leave politics out of it?

LI　I'm a switchman. I don't understand politics. You can say whatever you like.

HATOYAMA   Fine, I like your frankness. Come on. [*Pours wine.*] Just a cup of wine for friendship's sake. Now, drink up. [*Raises the cup.*]

LI   You are too polite, Mr. Hatoyama. Sorry, but I've given up drinking. [*He pushes the cup away.*]

HATOYAMA   Well, friend. [*Taking up his own cup.*] If you won't oblige me, I can't force you. [*He drinks and then starts his offensive.*] Why take things so seriously? There's an old Chinese saying, "Life is over in a flash like a dream. We should drink and sing, for who knows how soon life will end?"

LI   Yes, listening to songs and watching dances is living like an immortal. I wish you long life, Mr. Hatoyama, and all prosperity.

HATOYAMA   [*frustrated, lamely*]   Thank you, thank you.

LI   [*eyeing him contemptuously*]   You are too ceremonious. [*He laughs.*]

HATOYAMA   [*with a hollow laugh*]   My friend, I am a believer in Buddhism. A Buddhist sutra tells us, "Boundless the sea of sorrow, yet a man who will turn back can reach the shore."

LI   [*jokingly*]   For myself, I don't believe in Buddhism but I've heard the saying, "The evil is strong, but the good is ten times stronger."

HATOYAMA   Good. [*On the defensive.*] Well said. In fact we can sum up all human beliefs in two words.

LI   What are they?

HATOYAMA   "For me."

LI   "For you," eh?

HATOYAMA   No. "Each for himself."

LI   "Each for himself." [*He laughs.*]

HATOYAMA   [*earnestly*]   Old friend, you know the saying, "Heaven destroys men who won't look out for themselves."

LI   Oh? Heaven destroys men who won't look out for themselves?

HATOYAMA   That's the secret of life.

LI   So life has a secret.

HATOYAMA   Everything has a secret.

LI   I'm afraid it's too difficult for a blockhead like me to grasp. [*He laughs.*]

HATOYAMA   [*to himself*]   What a stubborn fool!

> His heart is hard to fathom;
> He parries my thrusts
> With no thought of his own safety,
> Impervious to both praise and flattery.

I must be patient.
With my experience and tact
I'll get hold of that secret code.

Let's stop this shadow-boxing, friend. I want your help.

LI [*with an air of surprise*]   What do you mean? How can a poor switchman help you?

HATOYAMA [*unable to keep his temper*]   Quit joking. Hand it over.

LI   What is it you want?

HATOYAMA [*coldly and distinctly*]   The secret code.

LI   What's that? All I can do is work switches. I've never used any such thing as a code.

HATOYAMA [*rising abruptly*]   If you choose to do things the hard way instead of the easy way, friend, don't blame me if we get rough.

LI   Do as you like.

HATOYAMA   All right. [*Beats his plate with a chopstick.*]

[*Enter* INSPECTOR WANG *in army uniform wearing his medal.*]

HATOYAMA   My old friend, look, who is this?

LI [*shocked by the sight of* WANG]   Ah!

WANG   Brother. . . .

LI   Shut up!

WANG   Don't be too pigheaded, brother.

LI   You shameless renegade!

Only a coward would bend his knees in surrender,
A cur afraid of death and clinging to life.
How often did I warn you
Against enemy threats and bribes?
You swore you would gladly die for the revolution;
How could you sell out and help the Japanese?
They are treating you like a dog,
Yet you count disgrace an honor.
Come here and look me in the eyes,
Shame on you, you sneaking slave.

[HATOYAMA *waves* WANG *away and he slinks out.*]

HATOYAMA   Steady on, my friend. I didn't want to play my trump card but you forced me to.

LI [*laughing derisively*]   I expected as much. Your trump card is nothing but a mangy dog with a broken back. You'll get no satisfaction out of me.

HATOYAMA I can give you some satisfaction. Let's hear your terms.

LI Terms?

HATOYAMA Here's your chance to strike a good bargain.

LI Bargain?

HATOYAMA Yes, bargain. I understand you Communists very well, you have your beliefs. But beliefs can be bought or sold. The main thing is to make a profit.

LI That's frank enough. It follows that there's nothing you wouldn't sell if you could make a profit. [*He laughs.*]

HATOYAMA [*furious*] You. . . . [*Fuming.*] You go too far, friend. You must know my job. I'm the one who issues passes to Hell.

LI You don't seem to know my job. I'm the one who takes your pass and destroys your Hell.

HATOYAMA You know, my leg-screws are hungry for human flesh.

LI I tried out that silly gadget of yours long ago.

HATOYAMA [*impressed by* LI's *spirit, makes a show of sympathy*] Take my advice and recant before your bones are broken.

LI I'd sooner have my bones broken than recant.

HATOYAMA Our police are rough. They think nothing of killing people.

LI We Communists are tough. We look on death as nothing.

HATOYAMA Even if you are made of iron, I'll force you to speak.

LI Even if you have hills of swords and a forest of knives, you'll get nothing out of me, Hatoyama.

> The Japanese militarists are wolves
> Hiding their savagery under a smile;
> You kill our people and invade our land
> In the name of "Coprosperity in East Asia."
> The Communists lead the people's revolution;
> We have hundreds of millions of heroes in the resistance;
> For you to rely on renegades
> Is like fishing for the moon in the lake.

HATOYAMA Sergeant!

[*Enter the* SERGEANT *and two gendarmes.*]

HATOYAMA I'll let you taste the leg-screws.

LI I need to take the weight off my feet.

SERGEANT Get moving.

[*The gendarmes grasp* LI's *arms.*]

LI   I can do without your help. [*He throws them off and calmly picks up his cap, blows the dust off it, shakes it, and walks out with dignity.*]

[*The* SERGEANT *and gendarmes follow* LI *out.*]

HATOYAMA [*pacing to and fro, very put out, scratches his head and mutters*] Quite mad, these Reds.

My eyes are dim, my head is ready to burst;
My blood pressure has risen, my hands are cold;
The Reds are flesh and blood like us,
What makes them tougher than steel?
He refuses to say where the code is hidden, curse him!
What shall I do if I can't get hold of it?

[*The telephone rings.*]

HATOYAMA [*taking the call*] Hatoyama here. Yes, sir, we are still searching for the code. Quite so, sir. Certainly, certainly. Yes, sir. I'll stake my life on it. [*He replaces the receiver and shouts.*] Here. How are you doing?

[*Enter the* SERGEANT.]

SERGEANT   We have tried all the tortures, but Li Yu-ho would rather die than speak.
HATOYAMA   Rather die than speak?
SERGEANT   Let me take some men to search his house, sir.
HATOYAMA   That's no use. Judging by my experience, ten thousand men can't find something which a Communist has hidden. Fetch him in.
SERGEANT   Bring Li Yu-ho here!

[*Two gendarmes push* LI *in. Blood-stained and battered, he stands there defiantly.*]

LI

You cur with the heart of a wolf.

HATOYAMA   The code! Give me the code!
LI   Hatoyama!

You have tried every torture to break me;
Though my body is mangled I clench my teeth,
I shall never bow my head. [*He laughs.*]

SCENE 7 The Code Finds a New Hiding-Place

One morning several days later. Li's house. By the telegraph pole not far from the door is an enemy agent disguised as a cobbler. While pretending to mend shoes he watches the house.

TIEH-MEI [*just out of bed and emerging from behind the curtain*]

Ever since Dad was arrested—

GRANNY We've been worrying and cannot rest.

[*The* KNIFE GRINDER *offstages cries,* "Any knives or scissors to grind?"]

TIEH-MEI Granny, listen.

[*Enter the* KNIFE GRINDER.]

KNIFE GRINDER Any knives or scissors to grind?

[GRANNY *pulls* TIEH-MEI *to the window and they look out.*]

[*The* KNIFE GRINDER *comes up to the window and sees the butterfly sign. He hesitates, then nods, and starts shouting again.*]

COBBLER There's no business for you in this poor part of town. Why do your hawking here?
KNIFE GRINDER [*in a loud voice*] You stick to your business, and I'll stick to mine. We knife grinders have to call out. If you make me keep quiet, how am I to find customers?
COBBLER You clear out if you don't want to run into trouble.
KNIFE GRINDER All right, all right. I get it. I'll try my luck somewhere else. [*As he leaves he raises his left hand to his ear and yells.*] Any knives or scissors to grind? [*Exit.*]
COBBLER Still hawking, blast him.
GRANNY [*pulling* TIEH-MEI *close*] That knife grinder probably came to make contact with us. He went away after seeing the sign on the window.
TIEH-MEI I'll run after him quickly with the code and lantern and see whether he's our man or not. I'll get the code.

GRANNY It won't do, child, not with those agents outside. You can't go.

TIEH-MEI What shall we do, then?

> I want to run after the knife grinder,
> But I can't leave the house and am worried.
> I wish I could grow wings and fly like a bird.

[*Sees the curtain.*]

TIEH-MEI Granny, I have an idea.

GRANNY What is it?

TIEH-MEI Granny.

> I know a way out.

Look. [*Points to the kang.*] There's only a wall between this and the Lius' *kang.* I can make a hole and slip through.

GRANNY [*pleased*] That's a good idea. Go ahead.

[TIEH-MEI *disappears behind the curtain.* GRANNY *starts chopping cabbage to hide the noise she makes.*]

TIEH-MEI [*coming back*] It's done, Granny.

GRANNY [*takes the code from the crack in the pillar and gives it her with the red lantern. Solemnly*] Make sure he's the right man, Tieh-mei. He must get the password correct. Be very careful.

TIEH-MEI I will. [*She disappears behind the curtain.*]

COBBLER [*calling outside*] Open the door.

GRANNY Who's that?

COBBLER It's me. The cobbler.

GRANNY Wait, I'll open the door. [*Opens the door.*]

COBBLER [*sees the knife in her hand*] What are you doing?

GRANNY Tomorrow is my son's birthday. We are going to have some vegetable rolls.

COBBLER Ah, vegetable rolls.

GRANNY What do you want?

COBBLER I want to borrow a light.

GRANNY [*indicating the matchbox on the table*] Help yourself.

COBBLER How many of you are there, old lady?

GRANNY You've been squatting outside our door the last few days, you should know all about us. One has gone, there are two of us left.

COBBLER Where's the girl?

GRANNY She's not well.

COBBLER   Not well? Where is she?

GRANNY   She's lying down in bed.

COBBLER   Lying down, eh? [*He walks toward the kang.*]

GRANNY [*stopping him*]   Keep away. Don't frighten the child.

COBBLER [*sniggering*]   If she's ill, old lady, why isn't she whimpering?

GRANNY   My granddaughter never whimpers when she's ill.

COBBLER   That means she isn't ill. But perhaps *you* feel sick at heart?

GRANNY   Seems to me you're the one who is sick.

COBBLER   Me sick? How?

GRANNY   There's a canker gnawing at your bones—they're moldering.

COBBLER   That's nothing that a little sun won't cure.

GRANNY   You're too rotten to face the sun.

COBBLER   Men's bones have got to rot some day, so let them be rotten. Tell your girl to sit up for a bit, old lady. It's no good lying down all the time. [*He tries to lift the curtain.*]

GRANNY   What d'you think you're doing? Asking all these foolish questions, throwing your weight about in other people's houses, and insulting women. What's the idea? Clear off. Get out!

COBBLER   All right, just wait. [*He stalks out angrily and beckons.*]

[*Enter two enemy agents. They whisper together and the agents open the door.*]

GRANNY   Who are you?

AGENTS   We are checking up. How many people live here?

GRANNY   Three.

AGENTS   Where is your son?

GRANNY   You should know where my son is now.

AGENTS   Where's your granddaughter?

GRANNY   She's ill.

AGENTS   Where is she?

GRANNY   She is in bed.

AGENTS   Let's take a look. [*Go to lift the curtain.*]

VOICE FROM BEHIND THE CURTAIN   "Granny. Who's there?"

GRANNY   Police checking up.

[*The agents grunt, shrug, and go out.* GRANNY *closes the door behind them.*]

AGENTS [*to the* COBBLER]   What a fuss over nothing. She was on the *kang* all the time.

COBBLER   All right. That old bitch tried to make a fool of me. [*Exeunt.*]

GRANNY   When did you come back, Tieh-mei? [*She lifts the curtain and* KUEI-LAN *sits up.*]

GRANNY   So it's you, Kuei-lan.

KUEI-LAN [*getting off the kang to catch hold of* GRANNY]   Granny Li.

> After Tieh-mei slipped away from our house
> My mother sent me to tell you.
> When I heard those spies questioning you
> I pretended to be Tieh-mei lying ill in bed.
> When Tieh-mei comes, she can come through our house,
> With me helping, you don't have to worry.

GRANNY   You've saved us. We shall never forget what you've done.

TIEH-MEI [*emerging from behind the curtain*]   Granny, Sister Kuei-lan.

GRANNY   So you're back at last.

KUEI-LAN   Your granny was worried about you.

GRANNY   If not for Kuei-lan we'd have been in serious trouble.

TIEH-MEI   Thank you, Sister Kuei-lan. What would we have done without you?

KUEI-LAN   It was nothing. Why thank me for such a little thing? It's good that you're back. I must be going now.

TIEH-MEI   Won't you stay a while?

[KUEI-LAN *points at the door and they understand. She steps behind the curtain and leaves.*]

GRANNY   You go and tidy up the *kang.*

TIEH-MEI   Yes.

[TIEH-MEI *straightens the bedding and pulls the curtain back.*]

GRANNY   Did you find the knife grinder?

TIEH-MEI [*in a low voice*]   I searched several streets but couldn't find him. Then I looked for Uncle Chou but he wasn't at home. So I hurried back for fear those spies might discover that I was out.

GRANNY   Where is the code?

TIEH-MEI   I left it outside.

GRANNY [*disturbed*]   But why?

TIEH-MEI   I thought it would be safer outside, so I hid it under a pier of Short Bridge.

GRANNY [*relieved*]   You've done right, child. I shan't worry provided the code's in a safe place.

[*Enter* HATOYAMA *in a Chinese gown and hat with a walking stick.*

He is followed by HOU *carrying two boxes of cakes. They knock at the door.*]

GRANNY   Who's there?

HOU   Captain Hatoyama is paying you a visit.

GRANNY   [*grasping* TIEH-MEI] Child, if your granny is arrested now you must find Uncle Chou and give him the code, then go to the north hills.

TIEH-MEI   Granny! [*She cries.*]

GRANNY   Don't cry. Go and open the door.

[TIEH-MEI *opens the door.*]

HATOYAMA   [*entering with a show of sympathy*] How are you, madam? I am Li Yu-ho's old friend, but I have been too busy to call before. [*Signs to* HOU *to leave after he has put the cakes on the table.*] This is a trifling present.

GRANNY   So you are Mr. Hatoyama?

HATOYAMA   Yes, I'm Hatoyama, Haytoyama.

GRANNY   Will you let me tidy up a bit before I come with you?

HATOYAMA   Don't misunderstand. That's not what I came for. Please sit down.

[GRANNY *ignores him.* HATOYAMA *takes a seat.*]

HATOYAMA   You must be longing to see your son, madam.

GRANNY   Of course, a mother naturally thinks of her son.

HATOYAMA   You needn't worry. He'll come back very soon safe and sound.

GRANNY   So much the better.

HATOYAMA   This wasn't our doing. We had orders from above. As a matter of fact, we are looking after him very well.

GRANNY   Thank you.

HATOYAMA   We heard from Li, madam, that he left something with you.

GRANNY   Left what?

HATOYAMA   [*casually*] Some code.

GRANNY   I don't know what you mean. [*To* TIEH-MEI.] What does he mean, child?

HATOYAMA   A code. A book.

GRANNY   A book? My son can't read, Mr. Hatoyama. My granddaughter has never been to school and I can't tell one character from another. Our family has never bought books.

HATOYAMA   Since Li Yu-ho has told us about that book, old lady, why try to hide it?

GRANNY   If he told you, why not let him come and find it? Wouldn't that be simpler?

HATOYAMA [*to himself*]   She's a crafty old bitch. [*To* GRANNY.] Don't try to fool me, old lady. Let's make a bargain. You give me that book, and I'll send your son straight back. If he wants a job, the railway can make him a vice-section chief. If he wants money, he can have five thousand dollars.

GRANNY   Five thousand dollars and the job of a vice-section chief? What book can be worth that much?

HATOYAMA   You have to sell to someone who knows its value.

GRANNY   If that book means so much to you, I'll have a look for it. Wait a minute. Tieh-mei, help me find it.

HATOYAMA   Take your time. There's no hurry.

[GRANNY *takes* TIEH-MEI *behind the curtain.*]

HATOYAMA [*waiting expectantly, to himself*]   So after all money can work miracles.

[GRANNY *comes back with* TIEH-MEI *carrying a bundle.*]

HATOYAMA [*very pleased*]   You've found it, madam?

GRANNY   Yes. This is what my son brought back.

HATOYAMA   Right, that must be it. That's it.

GRANNY   You can have it. [*Gives him an almanac.*]

HATOYAMA [*furiously*]   Bah, an almanac. [*He wants to throw it away but thinks better of it, fuming.*] I'll take it back anyway. Ah. . . . You must be worried about your son. Suppose I take you to see him then you can find out about the book. We are bound to find it. There's no hurry.

GRANNY   That's very good of you. Thank you. [*To* TIEH-MEI.] Look after the house, child.

HATOYAMA   She had better come as well to see her father.

GRANNY [*startled*]   But she's only a child.

HATOYAMA [*beckoning*]   Come along.

TIEH-MEI   All right. I want to see my dad.

HATOYAMA   You'd like to help your father, wouldn't you?

TIEH-MEI   Yes.

HATOYAMA   Fine. Come on.

[*Enter* HOU *with several gendarmes.*]

HATOYAMA [*threateningly*]   Look after them well. [*He strides out. To the agent.*] Keep an eye on the house. [*Exit.*]

HOU [*to* GRANNY *and* TIEH-MEI *with a sinister smile*]   Come on, old lady. Come on, miss.

[*They leave the house together. The agents seal up the door.*]

TIEH-MEI [*upset to see the door sealed*]   Granny!

GRANNY [*putting one hand through* TIEH-MEI's *arm and wrapping the scarf round her neck*]   Come on.

[*A gust of wind.*]

SCENE 8   A Fight in the Face of Death

Night. The Japanese police headquarters, outside the prison. Enter Hatoyama, Hou Hsien-pu, and the sergeant.

HATOYAMA   It doesn't look as if we shall get anywhere with our inter-rogation. Hurry up and get the tape recorder ready. We'll hear what the old woman says when she meets her son. We may find out some-thing.

HOU and SERGEANT   Yes, sir.

HATOYAMA   Bring the old woman in.

HOU   Yes, sir. Fetch the old woman.

[*Two Japanese gendarmes bring* GRANNY *in.*]

HATOYAMA   Do you know this place, madam?

GRANNY   It's the police headquarters.

HATOYAMA [*pointing*]   And over there?

[GRANNY *glances in that direction.*]

HATOYAMA [*with a menacing smile*]   That's the gate to paradise, where your son will mount to heaven.

[GRANNY *shivers.*]

HATOYAMA   When a man has committed a crime, madam, and his mother refuses to save his life, don't you think she is rather cruel?

GRANNY   What do you mean, Mr. Hatoyama? You've arrested my son for no reason and thrown him into prison. Now you want to kill him. You are the ones that are committing a crime, you are the ones that are cruel. How can you shift the blame for his murder on to me?

HATOYAMA Have you thought what will come of talking like that, old lady?

GRANNY The lives of our family are in your hands. You can do whatever you like.

HATOYAMA [controlling himself] All right, go and see your son. [GRANNY starts off.] This is his last chance, old lady. I hope you will all decide to steer clear of trouble and be reunited as one family.

GRANNY I know what's right.

HATOYAMA Take her away.

[Exit HOU with GRANNY.]

HATOYAMA Here. Take Li to the execution grounds.

SERGEANT Bring Li Yu-ho.

[The scene changes. On the left is the path to the prison. In the center is a stone. In the rear on the left a slope leading to the execution grounds is backed by a high wall covered with barbed wire. It is dark. Offstage the Japanese gendarmes yell: "Fetch Li Yu-ho!" Chains clank.]

[Enter LI.]

LI

> At the jailers' bloodthirsty cry I leave my cell;
> Though my hands and feet are manacled and fettered
> They cannot chain my soaring spirit.
> Hatoyama has tortured me to get the code;
> My bones are broken, my flesh torn, but firm is my will.
> Walking boldly to the execution grounds
> I look up and see the red flag of revolution;
> The flames of resistance are spreading.
> Not for long will these invaders lord it over us,
> And once the storm is past fresh flowers will bloom;
> New China will shine like the morning sun,
> Red flags will flutter over all the country—
> I feel a surge of confidence at the thought.
> I have done very little for the Party,
> Worst of all, I failed to send the code to the hills;
> That renegade Wang's only contact was with me,
> The wretch can betray no one else;
> And my mother and daughter are as staunch as steel,

So Hatoyama may search heaven and earth,
But he will never find the secret code.

[*Enter* GRANNY *and looks round.*]

GRANNY [*seeing* LI, *cries*]   Yu-ho!
LI [*startled*]   Mother!
GRANNY   My son.
LI   Mother.

[GRANNY *runs over to put her arms around him.*]

GRANNY

Again I live through that day seventeen years ago,
And burn with hate for the foe of my class and country.
The cruel Japanese devils
Have beaten and tortured you, my son, my son!

LI   Don't grieve for me, Mother.
GRANNY

I shouldn't grieve to have such a fine son.

LI

Brought up in a hard school
I'll fight and never give ground;
Though they break every bone in my body,
Though they lock me up until I wear through my chains.
As long as our country is ravaged my heart must bleed;
We shall have no peace till the revolution triumphs.
However hard the road to revolution,
We must press on in the steps of the glorious dead.
My one regret if I die today
Is the debt I have left unpaid.
I long to soar like an eagle through the sky,
Borne on the wind above the mountain passes
To rescue our millions of suffering countrymen—
Then how gladly would I die for the revolution!

GRANNY

That unpaid debt is in good hands,
Cost what it may, we shall pay it.

[*Enter* HOU *with the guards.*]

HOU I'll say this for you: You certainly know how to keep your mouths shut and not give anything away. Come on, old woman. Captain Hatoyama wants you.

LI Mother. . . .

GRANNY Don't worry, Son. I know what he wants.

[*She goes out fearlessly, followed by the guards.*]

HOU Bring Tieh-mei here! [*Exit.*]

LI [*calling*] Tieh-mei!

TIEH-MEI [*running in*] Dad!

LI Tieh-mei.

TIEH-MEI Dad.

> I hoped day and night to see my dad again,
> Yet I hardly know you, so battered and drenched with blood!
> I wish I could break your chains,
> Dear Father. . . .

LI [*smiling*] Silly child.

TIEH-MEI [*sobbing*] If you have anything to say to me, Dad, tell me quickly.

LI Child,

> One thing I have wanted many times to tell you,
> It's been hidden in my heart for seventeen years. . . .

TIEH-MEI [*quickly stopping him*] Don't say it. You are my own true father.

> Don't say it, Father,
> I know the bitter tale of these seventeen years.
> You are so good, our country needs you;
> Why can't I die in your stead?
> Ah, Dad.

[*She kneels and clasps* LI's *knees, sobbing.*]

LI

> Nurse your hatred in your heart.
> Men say that family love outweighs all else,
> But class love is greater yet.
> Listen, child, your dad is a poor man,
> With no money at home to leave you;

All I have is a red lantern,
I entrust it to your safekeeping.

TIEH-MEI

You have left me a priceless treasure,
How can you speak of money?
You have left me your integrity
To help me stand firm as a rock;
You have left me your wisdom
To help me see clearly through the enemy's wiles;
You have left me your courage
To help me fight those brutes;
This red lantern is our heirloom,
A treasure so great
That a thousand carts and boats
Could not hold it all.
I give you my word I shall keep the lantern safe.

LI

As wave follows wave in the great Yangtse River,
Our red lantern will be passed from hand to hand.
If they let you go home,
Find friends to help settle that debt and I'll be content.

TIEH-MEI   I will, Father.
LI   Good child.

[*Enter* HOU.]

HOU [*to* TIEH-MEI]   What about the secret code, girl? [*She ignores him.*]
HOU   Why don't you speak?
TIEH-MEI   My dad and my grandmother have said all there is to say. I've nothing to add.
HOU   Even this child is so pigheaded, confound her! Here. Bring that old woman back.

[*Two guards bring in* GRANNY.]

HOU   Now your whole family is here. Think well. If you don't give us the code, not one of you will leave this place alive. [*Exit.*]

[LI *and* TIEH-MEI *help* GRANNY *to a stone to sit down.*]

LI   They've tortured you, Mother. The swine!

GRANNY   It doesn't matter if my old bones ache a little, my mind is at ease.

[TIEH-MEI *sobs with her head on* GRANNY's *lap. Enter the* SERGEANT. TIEH-MEI *looks up.*]

SERGANT   Captain Hatoyama gives you five more minutes to think it over. If you still won't give up the secret code, you will all be shot.

GRANNY [*indignantly*]   You brutes, won't you even let the child go?

SERGEANT   We'll spare no one.

[LI *and* GRANNY *look at* TIEH-MEI, *who meets their eyes and straightens up.*]

SERGEANT [*dragging* TIEH-MEI *away*]   Only five minutes left, girl. Give up the code and save your whole family. Speak!

[TIEH-MEI *shakes off his hand and walks back to stand between* GRANNY *and* LI.]

SERGEANT   Where is the code?

TIEH-MEI   I don't know.

SERGEANT [*looking at his watch*]   Firing squad!

LI   There's no need for such a commotion. This is nothing.

GRANNY   That's right, child, let's go together, the three of us.

LI   Tieh-mei, take Granny's other arm.

TIEH-MEI   Right.

[*Proudly they walk up the slope. Enter* HATOYAMA.]

HATOYAMA   Wait! I want to give you every chance. You can have another minute to think it over.

LI   Hatoyama, you can never kill all the Chinese people or Chinese Communists. I advise you to think *that* over.

HATOYAMA [*frustratedly to himself*]   These Reds are the very devil. Carry out your orders. [*Exit.*]

SERGEANT   Shoot them!

[*The three disappear from the slope followed by the* SERGEANT *and guards.*]

LI [*off*]   Down with Japanese imperialism! Long live the Chinese Communist Party!

[*Two shots are heard. Then two guards push* TIEH-MEI *back.*]

TIEH-MEI [*dragged down the slope in a daze, turns to call*] Dad!
  Granny!
HATOYAMA [*entering behind her, followed by* HOU] Where is the code
  book? Tell me quick.

[TIEH-MEI *says nothing but stares at him with loathing.*]

HATOYAMA Yes, let her go.
HOU What? Let her go? [*He looks at* HATOYAMA *in surprise.*]
HATOYAMA Yet, let her go.
HOU Very good, sir. [*He grabs* TIEH-MEI.] Get out, get out. [*He pushes
  her away. Exit* TIEH-MEI.] Why are you letting her off, sir?
HATOYAMA [*smiling coldly*] If I kill them all, how can I find the code?
  This is called using a long line to catch a big fish.

SCENE 9   The Neighbors Help

  Immediately after the last scene. Li's house. The door is sealed. The
room is unchanged but wears an air of desolation.

[TIEH-MEI *walks slowly in. She stares at the house, quickens her steps,
and pushing the door open, steps inside. She looks around, crying "Dad!
Granny!" then rests her head on the table and sobs. Slowly rising, she
sees the red lantern and picks it up.*]

TIEH-MEI Ah, red lantern, I've found you again but I shall never see
  Granny or Dad again. Granny, Dad, I know what you died for. I
  shall carry on your work. I've inherited the red lantern. That scoundrel Hatoyama has only let me go in the hope that I will lead them
  to the code. [*Pause.*] Never mind whether you arrest me or release
  me, you'll never get the code. [*She puts down the red lantern and
  smooths her hair.*]

> My heart is bursting with anger,
> I grind my teeth with rage;
> Hatoyama has tried every trick to get the code,
> He has killed my granny and dad.
> In desperation he threatened me,
> But I defy his threats,
> Nursing hatred in my heart;
> No cry shall escape me,
> No tears wet my cheeks,

But the sparks of my smoldering fury
Will blaze up in flames of anger
To consume this black reign of night.
Nothing can daunt me now:
Arrest, release, torture, imprisonment. . . .
I shall guard the code with my life.
Wait, Hatoyama! This is Tieh-mei's answer.

[*She polishes the red lantern and rearranges her pedlar's basket. Sadly.*] Granny, Dad, I'm leaving now. This isn't our home any more. Only the red lantern will be ours forever. I promise to take the code to the north hills. I promise to avenge you. Don't you worry. [*She puts on her scarf and picks up the lantern and basket.*]

[AUNT LIU *and* KUEI-LAN *have heard* TIEH-MEI's *sobbing and slipped in through the hole in the wall.*]

AUNT LIU   Tieh-mei!

TIEH-MEI   Aunty. Sister Kuei-lan.

AUNT LIU   Where are your dad and granny?

TIEH-MEI   Aunty. . . . [*She leans her head on* AUNT LIU's *shoulder and cries.*]

AUNT LIU   I see. It'll soon be their turn, the devils. There's a spy outside, Tieh-mei, so you mustn't leave by the door. You can slip out again from our house. Hurry up now and change clothes with Kuei-lan.

KUEI-LAN   Yes, quick. [*She takes off her jacket.*]

TIEH-MEI   No, Aunty, Sister, I mustn't bring you into this.

AUNT LIU [*helping* TIEH-MEI *to change*]   Tieh-mei,

None but the poor will help the poor,
Two bitter gourds grow on a single vine;
We must save you from the tiger's jaws,
And then you can press on.

TIEH-MEI   But what if something happens to you?

AUNT LIU   Tieh-mei, your people were good people. I may not understand much, but that I know. No matter how risky it is, I must see you safely away. [*She weeps.*]

TIEH-MEI   Aunty. [*Leans her head on* AUNT LIU's *shoulder.*]

KUEI-LAN   Go quickly. [*Gives her the red lantern.*]

TIEH-MEI   I shall never forget you, sister.

AUNT LIU   Hurry, child. [TIEH-MEI *slips behind the curtain.*] Be very careful, Kuei-lan. [AUNT LIU *in turn leaves from behind the curtain.*]

[KUEI-LAN *wraps* TIEH-MEI's *scarf round her head and steps out of the door with the basket. Enemy agent C comes up and follows her. Enter the* KNIFE GRINDER. *He is about to call out when he notices the agent trailing a girl who looks like* TIEH-MEI. *He follows them.*]

SCENE 10   The End of the Renegade

Immediately after the last scene. The street.

[*Enter* INSPECTOR WANG *with two agents. A third agent comes in from the other side.*]

AGENT C   Inspector, I've lost Tieh-mei.
WANG   What?
AGENT C   She got away.
WANG   You fool! [*Slaps his face.*] Well, she must be making for the north hills. Ring up Captain Hatoyama and ask him to send reinforcements to the road to the north hills. The rest of you come with me to catch her. I'll see that you don't escape me, Li Tieh-mei.

[*Blackout. The scene changes to the north suburb of Lungtan and the road to the hills. Enter* CHOU *with three guerrillas.*]

[*Enter* TIEH-MEI *with the lantern. She greets the men.*]

TIEH-MEI   Uncle Chou!
CHOU   Tieh-mei!
TIEH-MEI   At last I've found you. [*Cries.*] My granny and dad. . . .
CHOU   We know. [*Pause.*] Don't give way. Take a grip on yourself. Have you got the code with you?
TIEH-MEI   Yes, I took it from under Short Bridge where I'd hidden it.
CHOU   Good.

[*The* KNIFE GRINDER *hurries in.*]

KNIFE GRINDER   Old Chou. Ah, Tieh-mei, so you're here. How was it I missed you?
TIEH-MEI   It was thanks to the help of my neighbors, uncle. Kuei-lan disguised herself as me and led the agent off on the wrong track so that I could get the code and bring it here.
KNIFE GRINDER   So I was chasing the wrong girl.

CHOU They'll start suspecting Kuei-lan's family now. [*To one of the guerrillas.*] Old Feng, go and help them move away at once.
FENG Right. Just leave it to me. [*Exit.*]

[*The police car's siren is heard.*]

CHOU [*to the* KNIFE GRINDER] The enemy's coming, Old Chao. You deal with them while I take Tieh-mei to the north hills. [*Exit with* TIEH-MEI.]
KNIFE GRINDER All right.

[*Enter* INSPECTOR WANG *with four enemy agents.*]

[*The* KNIFE GRINDER *blocks* WANG's *way and* WANG *gives him a shove. The* KNIFE GRINDER *kicks the pistol out of* WANG's *hand and they start fighting.* WANG *and the agents are killed. The police siren wails in the distance.*]

SCENE 11 The Task Is Accomplished

Music throughout the scene. The north hills, which rise steep and sheer. The guerrillas have formed a line stretching behind the hills. Halfway up the slope is a big red flag and scouts there are keeping a lookout.

[LIU *and other guerrilla officers come down the slope. Enter the* KNIFE GRINDER. *He salutes* LIU *and points behind him.* CHOU *comes in with* TIEH-MEI. *A bugle blows.* TIEH-MEI *gives* LIU *the code. The curtain falls. It rises again after music.* LIU *and* TIEH-MEI *mount the slope.* TIEH-MEI *holds the red lantern aloft. The stage is flooded with crimson light as the curtain falls slowly.*]

[*Curtain*]

Azalea
Mountain

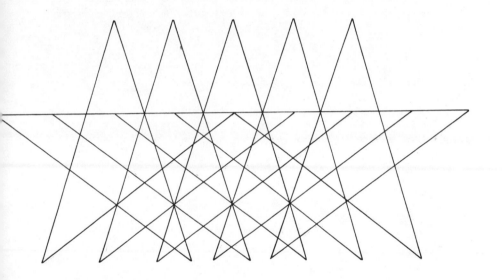

Deputy Chief Wen, an Allegory

The changes made in Peking plays during and immediately after the Cultural Revolution were explained as thrusts against deposed Communist Party Secretary Liu Shao-chi. By 1972, when Liu was replaced in the role of major antagonist by Lin Piao, who had been Chairman Mao's "closest comrade-in-arms" and official deputy since 1969, Lin, became a cultural target as well. The Chinese Communist Party organ Hung Chi *stated (No. 12, 1973) that Liu and Lin had been equally guilty in seeking to undermine Mao's policies and authority. The paper said: "After the bourgeois headquarters, with Liu Shao-chi as its ringleader, had been smashed, Lin Piao took over its counter-revolutionary undertakings and vainly tried to negate the great victories of the Cultural Revolution, thus becoming the ringleader of another bourgeois headquarters."*

During the years of Lin's prominence, the star of Chiang Ching, Mao's wife, temporarily lost its glitter. Although her efforts at changing the production and impact of plays, operas, ballets, and films were much in evidence, she was acting publicly under the "instructions" of Lin. Mao's deputy occupied a position which enabled him to "recommend" Chiang Ching's talents to the army and to benignly endorse, as it were, her propagandistic concepts. After his disgrace and death, Lin became the number one target of a campaign of denunciation. It is not surprising, therefore, that a key villain in one of the dramas produced under the direction of Mao's wife resembles the image of Lin, while the play's heorine may be compared to the role in which Chiang Ching saw herself.

This play, Azalea Mountain, *was first produced in the fall of 1973. The Peking correspondent of Agence France-Presse reported on*

October 29, 1973, that the play was receiving wide publicity in the Chinese capital. The correspondent, Serge Romensky, noted that Azalea Mountain *gave prominence to a woman, Ko Hsiang, who managed "to transform a disparate band of rebellious peasants into a disciplined combat unit that goes on to join the forces of 'Political Commissar Mao.'" The report added: "Before this happy ending, she is obligated to expose the traitor, Wen Chi-chiu, who is no other than the deputy chief of the group of peasants and a secret accomplice of Mr. 'Viper,' a local tyrant."*

Romensky viewed the play as "an allusion to Lin Piao—Chairman Mao's designated successor, but publicly denounced last August at the 10th party congress for attempting a coup d'état before dying in a plane crash in September 1971." At the same 'me, the Peking daily Renmin Ribao *commented on the play as ,ollows: "The class enemies all know that a fortress is most easily taken from inside. They use a thousand and one tricks to break up the revolutionary ranks. The presence of a traitor and renegade like Wen Chi-chiu is in itself neither unusual nor terrifying. What is really dangerous is to lose our revolutionary vigilance." Emphasis on "revolutionary vigilance" permeates today's Peking revolutionary dramas, and in this case, vigilance is specifically applied to the treacherous deputy chief.*

Political analysts in Hong Kong, quoted in the New York Times *(November 20, 1973), noted that the script of* Azalea Mountain, *although set in the year 1928, contained "many elements of Peking, 1971, when Lin Piao, once Chairman Mao's 'chosen successor,' had his disastrous fall from grace." These analysts observed that the deputy in the play is called "hidden traitor," which is "one of the epithets used for onetime Vice Chairman Lin." The illustrated magazine* China Pictorial *(No. 1, 1974) summarized the plot of the play as follows:*

"In the autumn of 1927 Chairman Mao led the Autumn Harvest Uprising, organized the first detachment of Workers' and Peas-

ants' Red Army and set up the first revolutionary base in the Chingkang Mountains. This was in keeping with his strategy for the Chinese revolution—building rural bases, surrounding the cities by the countryside, and ultimately seizing the cities. Based on this background, the opera Azalea Mountain *develops. It is the spring of 1928, at the beginning of the Second Revolutionary Civil War. Ko Hsiang, a Communist, has been sent by the Party to the Azalea Mountain to find a Peasants' Self-Defense Guards unit which rose in rebellion under the influence of the Autumn Harvest Uprising. She is arrested on the way. The self-defense unit, having suffered three defeats in a row, is eagerly seeking Communist Party leadership. They rescue Ko Hsiang on the execution ground. Ko Hsiang becomes the Party representative of the guards. She works hard to implement Chairman Mao's revolutionary line and the Party's policies and patiently teaches the leader Lei Kang and other guards to distinguish friend from foe and treat correctly exploited class brothers, ordinary merchants, and captives of the reactionary army. She mobilizes the masses and expands the people's militia. The self-defense guards correct their shortcomings and make a fresh start.*

"The counter-revolutionary armed force of the landlord tyrants attacks the self-defense unit. Snake [translated as "Viper" in the text on following pages], the leader, arrests Mother Tu and colludes with Wen Chi-chiu, a hidden traitor, in an attempt to lure the guards down the mountain into a trap. Ko Hsiang sees through the enemy's scheme but Lei Kang, blinded by a thirst for personal vengeance, turns a deaf ear to the advice and rushes down the mountain. He is captured and thrown into prison.

"Ko Hsiang remains cool and calm. Relying on the Party and the masses, she leads a night raid and rescues Lei Kang and Mother Tu. The self-defense guards join the Workers' and Peasants' Revolutionary Army and wipe out the enemy. They set out for the Chingkang Mountains and Comrade Mao Tse-tung."

The picture magazine added that the new opera was "one of several new vehicles created under the guidance of Chiang Ching, Member of the Political Bureau of the Chinese Communist Party, who is leading the reform and vitalization of Peking opera. It illustrates Chairman Mao's thesis that peasant armed uprisings cannot win victory unless they follow a revolutionary line and are led by a Communist Party." The magazine stated that "the libretto combines revolutionary realism with revolutionary romanticism and uses various artistic methods to emphasize the proletarian qualities of Ko Hsiang," while "the other characters all have their special traits and enhance, positively or by contrast, Ko Hsiang's leading role."

China Pictorial also said that "the music, while preserving many of the traditional Peking opera themes, also makes many improvements." It noted that "the style of singing breaks through the old strictures," a back stage chorus is introduced, and the spoken dialogue is rhymed in a "colloquial" manner which is "concise, rhythmic, expressive and lively." The dances, acrobatics, as well as the "dramatic poses and decor" are "carefully incorporated to suit the characters involved." The magazine ends its appraisal this way: "Azalea Mountain confirms the correctness of Chairman Mao's line in army building. It is a rousing addition to China's new theater."

There is a firm political point in emphasis on Mao's "line in army building." Following the disarray of the Cultural Revolution, the army, headed by Lin Piao, was the single force in the country that could act as a rallying point. Much was made, during this interim period, of the army's guiding role on all levels of society, ranging from factory operations to cultural affairs. Azalea Mountain dramatizes the Communist Party's prominence, its primacy over the army. The leadership role played by the party's woman representative can be interpreted as symbolizing, or at least paralleling, Chiang Ching's own position. That the China Pictorial account, echoing similar comments in other publications, noted that the play was one of those "created under the guidance" of Mao's wife, lends further support to the hypothesis that Azalea Mountain *may be read as an allegory on the rise and fall of leading Peking personalities.*

The Peking Review *of January 25, 1974, summarized the plot of* Azalea Mountain *in an article entitled "In Praise of the Proletarian Line in Army Building." It specified as "the fundamental reason why the armed peasants led by Lei Kang on Azalea Mountain did not repeat history's tragedies was that it had Party leadership in the person of Ko Hsiang and her firm implementation of Chairman Mao's line in army building."*

C H A R A C T E R S

KO-HSIANG   a woman of thirty, Party representative of the peasants' self-defense corps

LEI KANG   35-year-old leader of the self-defense corps

LI SHIH-CHIEN   a cadre of thirty in the self-defense corps, who joins the Party and becomes a member of the branch committee

GRANNY TU   a poor peasant of sixty, widow of a revolutionary killed by the reactionaries

TIEN TA-CHIANG   32-year-old hired hand who joins the self-defense corps and the Party

CHENG LAO-WAN   45-year-old fighter of the self-defense corps, who joins the Party

TU HSIAO-SHAN   Granny Tu's 15-year-old grandson who joins the self-defense corps

LO CHENG-HU   20-year-old fighter of the self-defense corps, who joins the Party

OTHER PARTISANS

SOLDIERS OF THE WORKERS' AND PEASANTS' REVOLUTIONARY ARMY

OTHER PEASANTS

WEN CHI-CHIU   renegade deputy leader of the self-defense corps

CHIU CHANG-KENG   formerly Wen's orderly in a warlord's army

THE VIPER   landlord and head of the local reactionary "civil guards"
CAPTAIN OF THE "CIVIL GUARDS"
CIVIL GUARDS

SCENE ONE   Darkness Before Dawn

Spring 1928, late at night.
Lion's Jaw on Azalea Mountain.

[*The curtain rises to show a precipitous mountain pass shrouded in darkness. The barking of dogs, rifle fire, and the sound of shouting approach from the distance. Men yell offstage: "Lei Kang's escaped! Catch him!" Some of the landlord's civil guards run in with lanterns and search. The* VIPER *enters followed by a guard with a lantern.*]

GUARD [*points at the cliff*]   Look!

[*A shadowy figure clinging to a vine swings over a chasm and disappears into the forest beyond.*]

VIPER [*fires his pistol*]   After him!

[*The* VIPER *and his men give chase.*]

[*Blackout.*]

[*The stage lights up again. It is the next morning. Distant mountain ranges can be glimpsed through the clouds. Close by yawns a chasm shaped like the jaws of a lion. Among the trees and undergrowth azaleas are coming into bloom, their red and white flowers brilliant and vigorous. In the left foreground is a flat rock. Further back on the right rises a large boulder.* LEI KANG *emerges from behind the boulder. He parts the grass and takes a good look round, then leaps out and strikes a pose. His feet are shackled and he walks with difficulty. Panting and wiping his brow, weak from hunger and thirst, he staggers toward the right and looks round, then stamps his foot in exasperation. He sees the rock and lurches over to it. Holding up his chain he whirls round, sits on the rock, and picks up a stone to smash his shackles. The stone crumbles, but his shackles remain intact. Hearing someone approaching, he springs to his feet.*]

[GRANNY TU *appears with firewood on her back and an ax in her hand. She and* LEI KANG *stare at each other. She approaches him slowly and holds out the ax. Surprised at first,* LEI KANG *takes it to smash his shack-*

les which he tosses behind the rock. GRANNY TU *puts down her firewood.*
LEI KANG *returns her the ax. She produces a sweet potato and offers it to him.*]

LEI KANG [*takes the sweet potato. Very touched*]
  Parched paddy soaked by sweet rain
  Remembers every drop.
GRANNY TU Ten thousand leaves grow from a single root:
  All the poor are one family.

  [LEI KANG *tucks the sweet potato inside his jacket.*]

LEI KANG Every drop of kindness must be repaid.
  Please tell me your name, ma'am.
GRANNY TU My name is Tu.
LEI KANG [*startled*] Your name is Tu? Who else do you have in your
  family?
GRANNY TU My son Tu Shan, driven from home by the landlord,
  Joined Lei Kang's band of insurgents;
  I've had no news of him since.
LEI KANG You are Tu Shan's mother?
GRANNY TU Yes. And you . . . ?
LEI KANG [*abashed*] I'm Lei Kang.
GRANNY TU [*taken aback*] Lei Kang?
  [*Urgently*] And Tu Shan?
LEI KANG [*in distress*] Your fine son,
  Our dearest brother . . .
  Has died a hero's death.

  [GRANNY TU *staggers and drops her ax, then takes a grip on herself
  and clenches her teeth.* LEI KANG *helps her over to sit down on the rock.*]

GRANNY TU [*sings*]

    Countless debts of blood and tears to be repaid!
    But his father's death still unavenged he dies. . . .

LEI KANG [*sings*]

    No martyr's blood is shed in vain;
    Each drop becomes a red azalea bloom.
    Do not grieve; I shall avenge you;
    You shall be my own dear mother.

  Mother! [*Kneels before her.*]

GRANNY TU [*with resolution*]   Child!
No ax can fell all the bamboo on the south mountain,
No fire can burn the root of the wild plantain. [*Makes* LEI KANG *rise.*]
When my husband fell there was still my son;
Now though my son is killed there is still my grandson.
His name is Hsiao-shan; I entrust him to you;
Toughen him, temper him to take revenge!

[GRANNY TU *picks up the ax as* LO CHENG-HU *runs in.*]

LO   Brother! [*Beckons to others offstage.*]

[*Enter* CHENG LAO-WAN, WEN CHI-CHIU, PARTISAN C, *and* CHIU CHANG-KENG.]

PARTISANS   Chief!
LEI KANG   Brothers! [*He goes toward them and takes* CHENG *and* WEN
    by the hands.]
This is Brother Tu Shan's mother
And my own dear mother.

[*The men greet her.*]

GRANNY TU [*caresses* LO CHENG-HU]   My children!

[PARTISAN C *goes off to keep a lookout.*]

CHENG [*to* LEI KANG]   Last night came word that you had escaped;
At once we sent search parties out.
At last we've found you, safe and sound!
LO   We feel joy and sorrow, both.
LEI KANG [*with feeling*]   Ah!
Our band of brothers, several dozen strong . . .
WEN   Has been routed, with so many killed and wounded!
LO   Brother!

[LEI KANG *sighs and strikes one fist against his palm.* LO *squats down
holding a sword.*]

[HSIAO-SHAN *offstage calls:* "Granny!"]

GRANNY TU   Hsiao-shan!
HSIAO-SHAN [*runs in*]   Granny, my dad. . . .

[GRANNY TU *stops him.* HSIAO-SHAN *clings to her knees and sobs.*]

LEI KANG [*fervently*]   His memory will live on

Evergreen as the pines on Azalea Mountain.

HSIAO-SHAN [*angrily*]   That bloody butcher the Viper. . . .

LEI KANG [*quickly*]   What has he done now?

HSIAO-SHAN   He's posted a notice, sent our criers with gongs,
And hung my father's head from a flagpole.
He says. . . .

LEI KANG   What does he say?

HSIAO-SHAN   "Anyone who joins the partisans
Will have his whole family wiped out."
They'll take reprisals: Kill all,
Burn all, loot all!

LEI KANG [*furious*]   Ah!
The rich must be sent to hell
Before the poor can win heaven.
Follow me, brothers! [*Snatches the sword from* LO.]

[*All are burning to fight.*]

GRANNY TU [*stops them*]   Wait.

LEI KANG [*halts*]   Mother!

GRANNY TU [*firmly*]   Give me that sword.

[LEI KANG *hesitates, but she insists. Reluctantly he passes the sword to her.*]

GRANNY TU [*gravely*]   Vines cling to the cliff,
Sheep follow the bellwether;
We must find some leader to guide us
And stop striking out at random. [*Sits on the rock.*]

LEI KANG [*with feeling*]   We heard that last September
The Communist Party
Led the poor in the Autumn Harvest Uprising
Which shook Kiangsi and Hunan.
Despotic landlords were humbled,
The poor stood up. [*Walks to rock, plants one foot on it, raises his fist
and strikes a pose.*]
But I failed to find the Communist Party,
All I could do
Was to follow their example
And rise in arms.
So I unfurled the banner of revolt
And assembled partisans on Azalea Mountain. . . .

Little did we think
That it would come to this. . . . [*Sighs and strikes his fist on his palm. Sings.*]

> Three times we rose in arms, three times were crushed,
> The blood of many fine brothers stained these mountains;
> In defeat we long to find the Communist Party,
> For wild geese to fly far must have a leader.
> Dark the night as we wait for the dawn.
> *Ah, Party, you are the lamp to light up our path.*
> But where can I find you? [*Gazes into the distance.*]

[*All gaze eagerly into the distance.* PARTISAN C *hurries in.*]

PARTISAN C   Here's Li Shih-chien, chief.

[LI *strides in.*]

LI [*walks up the boulder*]   Brother Lei Kang!
LEI KANG [*approaches him*]   Shih-chien!

[LI *leaps down from boulder and clasps* LEI KANG'S *arms.* PARTISAN C *goes off to keep watch.*]

CHENG   Why are you back so late?
LI   I went to Sankuan to scout round the town.
CHIU   You had us worried.
WEN   While you yourself had a good time.
LI   You can stop being worried,
   I've brought good news.
WEN   What is it?
LI   I've found the Communist Party. [*Leaps up the boulder.*]
ALL   Found the Party?
LI   Right.
CHENG   Where?
LI   So far and yet so near.
LEI KANG   What do you mean?
LI   Very near. [*Leaps down and strikes a pose.*]
ALL   Go on, tell us.
LI [*stands up*]   Listen then. [*Turns and sets one foot on the stone.*]
   The word's gone round in town
   That two Communists came to Azalea Mountain;
   They ran into the enemy,

Put up a fearless fight;
One was shot and killed,
The other wounded and captured.
Early tomorrow the prisoner will be paraded
Before the ancestral temple and executed.

LEI KANG Executed?

ALL What's to be done?

LI One must plunge deep into the sea
To find precious pearls! [*Points.*]

CHENG [*understands*] You mean. . . .

LI We'll disguise ourselves,

CHENG Set out by starlight,

LI Launch a surprise attack,

LO Raid the execution ground, raise havoc in Sankuan,

ALL Strike panic into the diehards. [*Turn and strike a pose.*]

LI And the Communist. . . .

LEI KANG [*steps forward to grasp* LI's *arm*] You mean—rescue the Communist?

LI Right!

ALL [*elated*] Rescue the Communist?!

LI This way, at last, we'll get hold of a Party member!

[*A buzz of excitement.* LEI KANG *thinks it over.*]

WEN But Brother, we—
Have only a few dozen men,
A dozen guns.
An egg can't smash a stone.
Don't take such a risk!

LI Nothing venture, nothing win.

LO Let's get cracking.

CHENG That's the spirit.

LO Go ahead.

ALL Get cracking! [*They gather round* LEI KANG, *waiting for his decision.*]

LEI KANG [*resolutely*] Right. [*His head thrown back firmly he walks round the stage. Sings.*]

After frost plants long for the warmth of spring,
Now the spring breeze has reached Azalea Mountain.
Tomorrow we'll raid and make havoc of the execution ground.

GRANNY TU   Take this. [*Gives him the sword.*]

[*LEI KANG takes the sword and goes through dancing motions, in which the others join. Then they strike a pose.*]

LEI KANG [*sings*]

> We'll carry off a Communist to lead our way.

[*LEI KANG leaps onto the rock. All cluster round to strike a pose.*]

LEI KANG   May Heaven preserve us! [*Makes an obeisance.*]

[*All strike a pose. The lights are cut to show them in silhouette.*]

[*Curtain*]

SCENE TWO   Spring Makes Azaleas Blossom

The next morning.
Sankuan marketplace in front of the Sheh Family Ancestral Temple.

[*The curtain rises. The sky is overcast. The old temple looks forbidding, with cypress and bamboo visible over its walls. To one side of the gate stands a flagpole on a stone pedestal. The marketplace is half empty. LI and some other partisans disguised as vendors or customers, their backs to the audience, mingle with the marketgoers. LO is sitting on a cart. A beggar girl helps an old blind man to the flagpole and sits down. HSIAO-SHAN enters dressed as a hunter with a steel trident and some pheasants.*]

HSIAO-SHAN [*shouts*]   Wild geese, pheasants, foxes, wild goats . . . !

[*Enter CHENG dressed as a pedlar with a bamboo basket.*]

CHENG [*shouts*]   Dried lilies, fungus, mushrooms, ginger . . . !

[*LEI KANG strides in with a towel on his head, wearing a deerskin waistcoat. He is holding a trident from which hang a fox and some rabbits. He waves his hand and sets one foot on LO's cart. LI, CHENG, and Lo quickly surround him, watching in different directions. The other partisans also keep a sharp look-out.*]

LEI KANG   How are things going? ·
LI   Everything's ready.
LEI KANG   And the Communist?

CHENG Will be brought out any minute from the temple.

LO I hear it's a woman.

LEI KANG A woman? [*He is staggered.*]

LO Shall we still rescue her?

LEI KANG [*decidedly*] Yes, so long as she's a Communist.

[*Gongs sound.* LEI KANG *and his men make off in different directions. A guard enters sounding the gong.*]

GUARD Today is market day; a Communist is to be executed.
We must have quiet; rowdies will be arrested.

[*Several guards rush in to disperse the crowd. One of them knocks down the blind man with his rifle butt. The beggar girl, dropping her basket, kneels to support him, and the guard kicks the basket away. The girl glares at him. The partisans help her and the old man away while the crowd is dispersed. Four guards with rifles stand at attention. Their* CAPTAIN *comes on.*]

CAPTAIN Our commander orders: Bring—the—Communist!

FOUR GUARDS Bring—the—Communist!

[*The order is repeated by the guards in the temple. The* CAPTAIN *leaves.*]

KO HSIANG [*sings offstage*] A Communist stands firm through wind and storm.

[*The four guards withdraw.*]

[*The temple gate slowly opens. Six enemy guards with mounted bayonets rush out from the temple to stand on both sides of the entrance.*]

[KO HSIANG *in chains, her head high, strides out of the temple and turns to toss back her hair. Having crossed the threshold, she halts and strikes a proud pose.*]

[*The guards aim their bayonets at her.*]

KO HSIANG [*sings*]

> We shed our blood for the people's liberation,
> Fearlessly fighting to the last,
> Highhearted and undaunted.

SIX GUARDS Out!

[KO HSIANG *glares at them with flashing eyes and they fall back in fear. She smooths her hair, holds up her chain, and walks proudly down the steps. The enemy cower.*]

KO HSIANG [*advances swiftly holding her chain in her left hand and strikes a pose. Sings*]

> The Party sent me here to find Lei Kang.

GUARD   Get moving.

[KO HSIANG *whirls, raising her chain, to glare at him, then walks quickly to the center of the stage and strikes a pose. The six guards raise their rifles and surround her.*]

KO HSIANG [*sings*]

> Though trapped by devils, I keep my task in mind;
> Thrusting aside. . . .

[*She thrusts aside the bayonets, strikes one guard with her chain, then turns and strikes a pose.*]

> Thrusting aside their bayonets I gaze into the distance.

[*She moves left, turns back to look into the distance, revolves, feels a wound, advances on one leg, sweeps back her hair, swings the chain at the guards, then turns to strike a pose.*]

> I see gleaming spears in the forest, red-tasseled spears. . . .

[*She appears rapt.*]

> How I long. . . .

[*She turns, grasps at the bayonets, revolves on one leg and strikes a pose.*]

> How I long to leap up to the summit of the mountain!

[*Pushes aside the bayonets, turns and strikes a pose.*]

GUARDS   Get moving!

[KO HSIANG *suddenly turns to glare at the guards. Two of them quickly raise their bayonets. She seizes their rifles and walks halfway round the stage, the guards falling back before her. Some villagers surge forward.* KO HSIANG *sweeps aside the bayonets and raises her hands to greet them. The guards drive the villagers away. Glaring at the enemy,* KO HSIANG *walks round the stage among the bayonets, wheels round repeatedly, tosses back her hair, holds up the chain and strikes a pose.*]

KO HSIANG [*sings*]

> This execution ground is my battlefield
> To trumpet revolution and lash the enemy,
> Expose their lies, make clear the truth,
> Scatter the mist to welcome in the dawn,
> And fan the sparks of revolution
> In every mountain hamlet near and far.

[KO HSIANG *leads the guards round to the back of the stage, then whirls round and rushes forward. The guards hastily hem her in with their bayonets.* KO HSIANG *seizes two rifles and sweeps them aside, shakes the chain, and strikes a heroic pose.*]

[*Enter the* VIPER, *followed by the* CAPTAIN *and two guards.*]

VIPER [*blustering to hide his fear*]   You Communist bitch,
   We didn't wipe you all out in Shanghai and Changsha;
   Today I shall make an example of you to warn the country people.
KO HSIANG [*firmly and proudly*]   Where there's oppression
   There is bound to be struggle.
   I shall gladly shed my blood
   To awaken millions!
VIPER [*hastily to the crowd*]   Don't listen to this Red propaganda;
   Be law-abiding.
   Obey the rules of Generalissimo Chiang—
   That's the only way to save the Chinese nation.
KO HSIANG [*cuts in*]   Tell me: what year is this?
VIPER [*automatically*]   The seventeenth year of the Republic.
KO HSIANG [*lashes out*]   But your various levies, your taxes in money
       and grain,
   Have been collected for the thirty-seventh year of the Republic.
   Is this your generalissimo's rule,
   Your way to save the nation?
VIPER [*gapes*]   You. . . .
KO HSIANG   Fellow countrymen!

[*The villagers surge forward.* KO HSIANG *leaps onto the pedestal of the flagpole.*]

KO HSIANG   Chiang Kai-shek has betrayed the revolution,
He's the running dog of the imperialists;
His Nanking government slaughters workers and peasants;
His dark rule is dragging our country down to ruin.
Only Marxism-Leninism can save China;
The working people's saving star
Is the Chinese Communist Party!

[LEI KANG *shouts offstage:* "Well said!"]

VIPER   Who's that?
LEI KANG   Lei Kang! [*Leaps out from the crowd with his trident.*]

[*The* VIPER *cries out and the guards scatter in confusion.* LEI KANG *strikes at the* VIPER's *left arm with his trident. The* VIPER *draws his pistol and aims it at* KO HSIANG.]

LEI KANG   Look out! [*Leaps forward to shield* KO HSIANG *and is shot in the left arm.*]

[*Covered by* LEI KANG *and* LI, HSIAO-SHAN *and others help* KO HSIANG *away.* LEI KANG *hurls his trident at* THE VIPER *who rushes off, howling. As guards charge toward* LEI KANG, *who staggers in pain from the wound in his arm,* LI *whips out a spear from inside his carrying pole to fight them off. More guards try to get* LEI KANG *but* LO *blocks their way with his cart, grabs two swords from under its handles and chases the guards off.* LEI KANG *snatches a sword from a guard and uses the cart as a weapon too. He kills a guard, overturns the cart, and swings it at another guard.*]

[KO HSIANG *and* HSIAO-SHAN *rush in.* LEI KANG *catches a sword flung at him, puts one foot on the cart, and strikes a heroic pose with* KO HSIANG, LI, CHENG, HSIAO-SHAN, *and other partisans.*]

[*Partisans race past in pursuit of the enemy.*]

[KO HSIANG *tears a strip from her tunic to bandage* LEI KANG's *arm.*]

[LO *and* PARTISAN A *run in.*]

LO   The devils are on the run, shrieking and wailing.
PARTISAN A   The Viper, badly wounded, is making for the county town.
LEI KANG   Go on scouting, and post more sentries.
LO and PARTISAN A   Right. [*They leave.*]
KO HSIANG [*warmly*]   Are you Lei Kang?

LEI KANG [*nods*] And you?

KO HSIANG I'm Ko Hsiang.

LI Are you from the Chingkang Mountains?

KO HSIANG The Party sent us to find your chief, Lei Kang.

LEI KANG Sent two of you?

KO HSIANG [*sadly*] Comrade Chao Hsin. . . .

LEI KANG Chao Hsin!

[*Solemnly.*] Though I never saw this martyr,
I shall always remember his name.

[*All bow their heads in sorrow.*]

CHENG Spring has come early to our mountain.

LI This wasteland is turning green.

LEI KANG [*clasps* KO HSIANG's *hand*] You are the Party representative
We've been longing for day and night. [*Raises his fist to shout.*]
Welcome the Party representative!

ALL Welcome the Party representative!

[KO HSIANG *mounts the pedestal to wave to the crowd. Partisans and villagers flock eagerly toward her. Together they strike a collective pose.*]

[*Curtain*]

SCENE THREE Class Feeling Deep As the Ocean

The same afternoon.
The backyard of the temple.

[*The curtain rises. The sky is filled with clouds. In the middle of the stage is a grey stone wall, its top tiled. To the right is part of an annex. Through the moon-gate can be seen the eaves of the temple in the front court. On both sides of the wall grow bamboos and cypresses. Swords and spears are stacked on a stand. Two partisans cross the stage carrying posters: "Down with the landlords: share out the land!" "Support the Workers' and Peasants' Revolutionary Army!" "Long live the Chinese Communist Party!" Other partisans cross the stage with sacks of grain, weapons, firecrackers, and jars of wine. Some partisans seated round a table are drinking with* CHIU CHANG-KENG. *Enter* LO *and* HSIAO-SHAN *with a red-lacquered chest.*]

LO   Hey, Deputy Chief Wen's orders:
"According to the old rule,
All confiscated property belongs to us brothers." [*He opens the chest.*]

PARTISANS   Fine. Let's share the things out right away. [*They rush forward to take what they want.*]

[*Enter* LI *carrying a bushel of rice.*]

LI   Wait a bit, brothers. [*Puts down his load.*]

[*They look at him in surprise.*]

LI   We've new rules now for confiscated goods.
LO [*puzzled*]   What new rules?
LI   All silver dollars go to the organization;
Part of the grain is reserved for army use;
The rest of the grain, goods, and clothing
All goes to the local people.
PARTISANS   Who made this rule?
LI   The Party representative. [*Exit.*]
LO [*snorts*]   We shed our blood, risk our necks.
PARTISAN D   But she gives everything away to others.
PARTISAN C   An outsider, after all, is less close to us.
PARTISAN B   With book learning but no taste of hardships
How can she lead soldiers?

·   [*Disgruntled, they toss the things back into the chest and move it to a corner.*]

CHIU [*resentfully*]   Bah! If women can lead troops
Men will lose their authority.
No, we won't obey
Her orders.
LO   Just ignore them.
PARTISANS   Ignore them.
CHIU [*pounds the table and stands up*]   Come on. Let's go and have it
out with her.
What sort of rule is this?

[*They shout:* "Let's go." "What rule is this?" "Call this making revolution?" *They surge toward the moon gate.*]

PARTISAN A [*points off, tensely*]   Quiet! Here she comes.

[*The clamor stops abruptly.* KO HSIANG, *a smile on her face, appears at the moon gate carrying two baskets of rice on a shoulder pole.*]

[*In sullen silence the partisans turn away.*]

[KO HSIANG *looks thoughtful, then carries her load to the annex where she deftly stacks her baskets on the pile of baskets there. This done, she brushes the dust off her clothes.*]

[*Enter* LI, CHENG, *and* HSIAO-SHAN *carrying grain.*]

[*Silence.*]

KO HSIANG [*smiles*]   Well?
   Just now I heard the rumble of thunder;
   Why this sudden lull in the storm?

[LO *angrily snatches a bundle from a partisan, tosses it into the chest and bangs the lid shut. Then he walks over to* CHIU.]

LO   Stop drinking! [*Knocks the cup out of* CHIU's *hand.*]
CHIU [*tipsily*]   Ha!
   A woman . . . Communist
   Lording it over us. [*Draws his pistol.*]
   Know what's this?
   No needle for embroidery!
KO HSIANG   He's drunk.
   Take away his gun.
CHENG   Right. [*Reaches for* CHIU's *pistol.*]
CHIU   How dare you? [*Shoves* CHENG *away.*]
LI and CHENG [*warningly*]   Chiu Chang-keng!

[CHIU *rushes with his pistol at* KO HSIANG. *All are dismayed.* KO HSIANG *coolly steps forward and seizes* CHIU's *wrist. He stands motionless for a second, then starts to struggle; but she expertly wrenches the pistol from his grasp.* CHIU *staggers back, deflated, and drops on a bench.*]

KO HSIANG [*gives the pistol to* HSIAO-SHAN. *Unruffled*]   Take him away.
   Help him to sober up. [*Smooths* HSIAO-SHAN's *collar.*]
HSIAO-SHAN   Right. [*He leads* CHIU *off. Some partisans follow them.*]
CHENG [*admiringly*]   So in fighting and farming both
   You have what it takes.
KO HSIANG [*modestly*]   Roughing it all year long
   In wind and rain

Has given me nothing but
Iron shoulders and horny hands. . . . [*She appears lost in thought.*]
LO [*surprised*] Are you from a poor family too?
KO HSIANG [*sighs*] Hard to tell all the bitterness I knew,
   All the wrongs I suffered. . . . [*Sits down slowly. Sings.*]

> My home was in Anyuan close to the river Ping,
> Three generations of miners, like beasts of burden,
> My folk sweated out their guts but still went hungry
> In that hell on earth where all seasons are the same.
> Came a strike: [*stands up*] my dad and big brother fought the
>   bosses,
> Failed, were shot down, stained the wasteland with their blood.
> Then the blackhearted mine owners
> Fired our hut and burned alive
> My mother, younger brother and little sister—
> My whole family wiped out, a heap of bones.

CHENG [*fumes*] The bosses and their foremen—
LO Are vipers, wild beasts! [*Pounds the table.*]
LI We must take our revenge!
ALL We must pay them back!
KO HSIANG [*sings*]

> Like a sudden storm the Autumn Harvest Uprising,
> A bright lamp to show the way, lit up my heart.
> I saw we must take up arms to win liberation;
> I joined the army, the Party, to fight for the poor.
> Workers and peasants are brothers
> Taking the same revolutionary road;
> We must wipe out these wolves and jackals,
> Fight on until the enemy is destroyed!
> Until the enemy is destroyed.

CHENG We must advance together, united as one.
LI Carry the revolution through to the end.
ALL [*eagerly*] Right! That's the spirit.

   [WEN CHI-CHIU *slips in, followed by* CHIU.]

WEN What's the row about?

   [*All fall silent.*]

WEN The chief's wounded;
   He needs quiet. [*Tosses his gown to* CHIU. LO *and the others leave.*]
LI Deputy chief, what shall we do with the civil guards we captured?
WEN You know our old rules. [*Goes through the motion of chopping off a head.*]
CHENG And the merchant we detained?
WEN Confiscate his goods.
KO HSIANG [*mildly*] Deputy Chief Wen,
   We should educate prisoners and let them go;
   We must pay a fair price to merchants:
   This is our Party's policy,
   We have to carry it out.
CHENG [*worried*] Party representative,
   If you let them go
   Lei Kang will be out for your blood!
KO HSIANG [*smiles*] He'll see the reason for
   Our revolutionary policy.
   [*To* WEN.] What do you say, deputy chief?
WEN [*hides his dissatisfaction*] I'm nobody,
   What I say doesn't count. [*Goes sullenly into the annex followed by*
   CHIU.]
LI [*shouts*] Deputy Chief Wen!
   [*Turns to* KO HSIANG.] Don't mind him, Party representative.
   He used to be an army officer
   And still has some warlord ways.
KO HSIANG Oh? What's his family background?
LI He started off as one of the local gentry.
   In a squabble over a good burial plot
   He got on bad terms with the Viper;
   They went to law, Wen lost all his property,
   Joined the warlord Leopard Liu, then came to us,
   Became Lei Kang's sworn brother
   And joined our self-defense corps.
KO HSIANG So!

   [*A whistle blast. Wen calls offstage:* "All fall in!" *Partisans run in.*
   CHIU *hurries out from the annex.*]

CHIU [*provocatively*] The chief's in a foul temper.

   [LEI KANG, *his arm in a sling, storms out of the annex and stands on
   the steps.*]

[KO HSIANG *moves forward to greet him, but he ignores her. Tense silence.* WEN *slips in.*]

LEI KANG [*descends the steps. Puts one foot on a bench. Bellows*]
  Whoever wants to let go our prisoners and the merchant
  Is Lei Kang's enemy!

[LO *enters through the moon gate with a shoulder pole.*]

LO Report! We've caught a landlord.
LEI KANG Bring him in.
LO Right. [*Beckons to people outside.*]

[LEI KANG *stands angrily behind the table. Partisans with swords and spears range themselves on both sides. Wen sits arrogantly by the table.* KO HSIANG *stands on the steps watching the scene closely.*]

[*Two partisans offstage shout:* "Come on!" *They bring in* TIEN TA-CHIANG, *his hands tied.*]

TIEN Why have you nabbed me?
LO You were helping the landlord to ship rice out.
TIEN I'm a hired hand, I can't help it.
  I push barrows and carry loads to pay off my debt;
  If I stop work for a single day, my family goes hungry.
LEI KANG Better starve to death rather than be a slave.
TIEN [*angry*] What!
LEI KANG Just for this
  You deserve a good beating.
LO Right. [*Steps forward to push* TIEN *down.*]
TIEN [*struggles*] Call yourselves a self-defense corps?
  You're just like warlords! [*Stamps.*]
WEN How dare you insult us? Beat him!
CHIU Beat him.
KO HSIANG [*loudly*] Don't beat him.
WEN [*springs up*] Why not? Carry on.

[CHIU *snatches the shoulder pole from* LO *to beat* TIEN.]

KO HSIANG [*quickly intervenes*] Stop. [*Takes the shoulder pole.*]
  This is disgraceful.

[CHENG *takes the shoulder pole from her.*]

LEI KANG [*furious, pounds the table*] Ko Hsiang! [*Sings.*]

We risked our lives to save you,
That you might lead us to fight the enemy;
But instead of speaking up for the poor
You take the side of the landlord.
You will not let us beat the landlord's man
And want to free the merchant whom we captured.
Are you a true Communist or an impostor?
Before our brothers here you must give your answer.

[LEI KANG *stamps his foot on the bench and strikes it with his sword, glaring at* KO HSIANG. *Some of his men raise swords and spears to threaten her too.* LI, CHENG, *and* PARTISAN A *close in to shield her.* LO *watches anxiously.* WEN *stands behind the table, pleased by this clash. The atmosphere is tense.* KO HSIANG, *unruffled as ever, brushes past* LI *and the others to walk slowly toward* LEI KANG.]

KO HSIANG [*calmly*]   Comrade Lei Kang. [*Points at* TIEN.]
   Is he a landlord?
LEI KANG   He works for a landlord.
KO HSIANG   Is that any reason to beat him?
LEI KANG   A beating is letting him off too lightly!
KO HSIANG [*ponders, then turns to the crowd*]   Comrades!
   Which of you here
   Has ever worked for a landlord?
   Put up your hands. [*Raises her own hand.*]

[*The partisans are puzzled. They lower their weapons.*]

KO HSIANG   What?
   Has none of you worked for a landlord?
   None of you been fleeced by the rich?
LI [*suddenly breaks the silence, raising his hand*]   I have.
   I was a mason,
   I carved archways and made tombstones for the gentry.
LO [*raises his hand*]   I've done odd jobs for landlords,
   Hulling rice and turning the millstone.
CHENG [*raises his hand*]   Me too . . . how shall I say it?
   I've done jobs of all kinds for landlords.
   The year the ancestral temple was built
   Which of us didn't join in?
   In the old days
   You either worked or starved.

PARTISAN A   I've worked for the landlord. [*Raises his hand.*]
PARTISAN C   I've worked for the landlord. [*Raises his hand.*]
PARTISAN B   I've worked for the landlord. [*Raises his hand.*]
ALL   I've worked for the landlord. [*Raise their hands.*]
LI [*walks slowly over to* LEI KANG]   Brother!
> For more than ten years you carried the landlord's sedan chair;
> Have you forgotten all you went through then?

LEI KANG [*startled*]   Ah! [*Thinks.*] H'm. [*Slowly raises his hand.*]
KO HSIANG   Comrades,
> Does this make us all landlords?
> Should we all be beaten by revolutionaries?

[*They think this over and lower their hands.* WEN *sees the tide has turned against him and slinks off, followed by* CHIU.]

KO HSIANG   Comrade Mao Tse-tung has said:
> "Who are our enemies?
> Who are our friends?
> This is a question of the first importance for the revolution."
> And this means:
> Enemy captives should get lenient treatment,
> Ordinary merchants ought to be won over;
> The landlords and imperialists are our deadly enemies,
> The working people our revolution's main strength.
> Yet you would kill prisoners,
> Arrest merchants,
> And beat up a hired hand who pushes a cart—
> Why, he is our class brother.
> Who is your target in the revolution?
> Whom are you trying to down?
> Whose arrogance will you deflate?
> Whose morale will you boost?
> [*With deep feeling.*] Comrade Lei Kang! [*Sings.*]

> All the poor on earth hate the same enemy,

[*Goes to* TIEN *and unties him.*]

> Gall and bitterwort have the same taste;
> He pushes a cart, you carried a sedan chair,
> Both of you hate rough roads,
> Hate injustice among men.

See the welts showing through his rags?
How can you. . . .
How can you add new scars to his old scars?

LEI KANG [*sings*]

The sight of his wounds stirs painful memories;
All the poor are ground down by the landlords.

[*Remorsefully picks up the shoulder pole.*]

KO HSIANG [*grasps his hand*]   Comrade Ta-chiang, we welcome you.
ALL   Welcome!
LEI KANG   Party representative!
I didn't understand the Party rules.
From now on, all decisions are up to you.
KO HSIANG   Then . . . how about the prisoners?
LEI KANG   Release them.
KO HSIANG   And the merchant?
LEI KANG   Let him go.
KO HSIANG   The confiscated grain and goods?
LEI KANG   Share them out among the poor.
ALL [*eagerly*]   Fine!
KO HSIANG   Let's distribute the clothing and grain,
Rally the masses, expand our armed force;
Regroup and march back to the mountain.
LEI KANG [*cheerfully*]   Right. We'll do as the Party representative says.
KO HSIANG   Open the granary,
Share out the grain at once.

[*She takes a list of people who should receive grain and shows it to*
LEI KANG. *Villagers crowd in. The blind man enters supported by the*
girl. HSIAO-SHAN *enters with* GRANNY TU. KO HSIANG *presides over the*
distribution of grain. The villagers are wild with joy. The blind man as
he scoops grain from the basket is beside himself with excitement. KO
HSIANG *holds high the list and the others crowd round her to strike a*
pose.]

[*Curtain*]

SCENE FOUR   Bamboos Grow Apace

A fortnight later, in the morning.
A clearing on the mountainside.

[*The curtain rises slowly. White clouds drift through a blue sky. Sunlit mountains covered with terraced fields stretch off to the horizon. Bamboos are sprouting, azaleas are in bloom. In the distance are cottages with white walls and tiled roofs. A boulder stands at one side of the stage.* LI *is writing a slogan on the boulder:* "Step Up Vigilance, Beware of. . . ." *Villagers carrying grain and pumpkins cross the stage. Men and women partisans armed with red-tasseled spears, swords, clubs, shields, and chain missiles cross the stage, exuberantly brandishing these weapons.* LI, *brush in hand, watches them cheerfully.*]

LI [*sings*]

> Like bamboo growing apace on Azalea Mountain,
> Our self-defense corps trains hard and grows in strength.
> Down with the landlords, share out the grain, all are happy
> Amid red banners, battle songs and slogans.

[*Enter* GRANNY TU *with villagers carrying shoulder poles and bamboo baskets.*]

GRANNY TU [*jokes*]   Hello, young mason!
LI   Auntie, you're working hard for us again.
GRANNY   Just bringing a few sweet potatoes and some salt.
GIRL   And oil and paprika sauce.
GRANNY   You need feeding up.
VILLAGERS   Then you'll win more victories!
LI [*touched*]   Your loving kindness
   Warms our hearts.
GRANNY   Goodbye then. Look after yourself.
LI   We won't let you down.
GRANNY   Fine.
LI [*remembers something*]   Oh!
   The Viper may be fighting back;
   You must be on your guard.
GRANNY [*laughs, confidently*]   Just look:
   All these camellias on the slope
   Didn't shed their leaves even in the bitter winter,
   And now it's early spring. [*Laughs.*]

[*All laugh cheerfully.* LI *takes* GRANNY TU's *arm and sees her off.*]

LI [*turns and ponders. Sings*]

> The ice has melted, the spring thunder rumbled,
> But we must beware of frost in early spring,
> Watch for the smoke of war across the mountains
> And keep our guns well polished.

[LI *turns and completes his slogan by writing "Enemy Agents" on the rock.*]

[LEI KANG *enters reading from a copybook: "Overthrow the landlords, share out the land. . . ."*]

[HSIAO-SHAN *bounds in.*]

[*Enter* TIEN *with a bamboo crate on his back and a gourd containing medicinal herbs. With him is* CHENG.]

[HSIAO-SHAN, CHENG, *and* LI *tiptoe toward* LEI KANG. TIEN *sits down to sort out his herbs.*]

HSIAO-SHAN [*claps* LEI KANG *on the back*]   Hey!

[LEI KANG *gives a start and looks up. The others laugh.*]

LI   I say, Old Lei,
You are certainly going all out learning to write.
LEI KANG   H'm.
You can't learn politics and read textbooks
When you are illiterate.
Now that I've joined the Party,
I mustn't be like a blind man,
Muddling along. [*Laughs.*]
LI   Right.
LEI KANG   Come here, master mason.
Have a look at the characters I've written.
Are there any strokes missing?

[HSIAO-SHAN *snatches* LEI KANG's *copybook.*]

HSIAO-SHAN [*reads*]   "Overthrow the landlords, share out the land. . . ." All correct.
CHENG   Yes, all correct.

LI [*takes the copybook and studies it*]   Why has the character "land-
lord" one leg missing?
LEI KANG   Has it? [*Takes the book and looks at it. Laughs.*]
When we overthrew the landlord,
I must have broken one of his legs!

[*They laugh.* LEI KANG *adds a stroke with his pencil.*]

LEI KANG   H'm.
Seems to me it's not too hard
To learn to write.
Learn five words a day,
In ten days that's a platoon,
In a month it's a company,
In half a year a regiment,
In a year or two [*pauses*]
I'll be an army commander!

[*They all laugh.*]

[*A whistle.*]

HSIAO-SHAN [*mischievously*] Report, commander,
The new recruits want some sword drill.
LEI KANG   Oh, they're waiting for me to instruct them.
LI   Has your wound healed properly?
LEI KANG   Yes, thanks to Brother Ta-chiang's care
And the herbs he fetched from the mountains.
HSIAO-SHAN   Early this morning Uncle Tien went off for herbs again;
He swung on a creeper halfway down the cliff,
Tore his clothes and cut himself
To get this [*takes the gourd from* TIEN's *belt*] magic peach!

[*Blushing,* TIEN *takes back the gourd.*]

HSIAO-SHAN   If you don't believe me, look. [*He rolls up* TIEN's *sleeve.*]
LEI KANG   Ah! So many bruises. . . . [*Reflects.*]
TIEN [*quickly pulls down his sleeve. Smiles*]   Don't waste time talking.
The new recruits are waiting.
LEI KANG [*waves his hand*]   Right. Let's go. [*Turns to leave.*]

[*Offstage* KO HSIANG *calls:* "Old Lei!"]

ALL [*turn*]   The Party representative!

[*Enter* KO HSIANG *with a bundle of new straw sandals on her back, carrying tools.*]

KO HSIANG   Old Lei, take these sandals to the new recruits.

LEI KANG [*taking the sandals*]   Good. Just what we need. [*Turns to leave.*]

KO HSIANG   Wait.

[LEI KANG *halts.*]

KO HSIANG   Raise your foot.

[*In bewilderment* LEI KANG *raises his foot. The others see that the sole is worn out and laugh.*]

KO HSIANG   See, you need a new pair even more.

LEI KANG   No, these sandals are too small for me.

KO HSIANG   Here. [*She takes another pair from her belt.*] Here's a big pair for you. [*Tosses the sandals to him.*]

[LEI KANG *catches them and measures them against his feet.*]

HSIAO-SHAN   Ha, our commander is quite a chap,
The sandals he wears make a flap.

[*They all chuckle.*]

LEI KANG [*pushes him and puts on a stern face*]   Stop chortling. Off with you to drill!

HSIAO-SHAN [*springing to attention*]   Yes, sir. [*Marches off like a clown.*]

[LEI KANG *goes off with him, roaring with laughter. The others smile.*]

TIEN   Ever since he joined the Party,
Lei Kang has been training troops and studying hard.

LI   After the reorganization,
Our self-defense corps has changed completely;
It is so energetic and vigorous.

[KO HSIANG *takes some of* TIEN's *clothes from the bamboo crate and sits on a stone to mend them.*]

CHENG   Still, the ten fingers on a man's hands are of different lengths;
Some people are full of complaints and talking rubbish.

LI   What do they say?

[LI *and* TIEN *sit cross-legged by the stone, sorting through the herbs.*]

CHENG   They say: "We keep drilling all day
With nothing to eat but pumpkins and coarse rice,
Hiding in gullies so as not to fight—
What sort of life is this?
We should go places
And live on the fat of the land."

LI   What crap! Who talks that way?

CHENG   Who do you think? The deputy chief's man. [*Squats down.*]

TIEN   Just now Granny Tu said those two
Were in the wineshop this morning.

KO HSIANG [*breaks off the thread, puts the needle away, and hands the
mended clothes to* TIEN. *Significantly*]
When ants climb a tree it foretells a storm. [*Stands up.*]
When the mole-cricket burrows it can destroy a great dike.
We are all Communists,
All the more reason for us. . . . [*Points at the slogan.*]

LI *and* OTHERS [*catching on*]   To step up our vigilance.

[LO *and* PARTISAN A *hurry in.*]

LO   Report. In disguise we scouted round Sankuan:
The Viper's raised a levy, enlarged his forces.

PARTISAN A   Looks as if he'll soon be launching an offensive.

LO   Why not deal them a head-on blow?

KO HSIANG   Being so far outnumbered,
We'd come off worst in a head-on confrontation.

LO   How shall we fight then?

KO HSIANG [*her mind made up, decisively*]   When the enemy attacks,
we'll withdraw. [*Sings.*]

Our deep mountains and forests give us room to maneuver,
Guerrilla tactics will beat a strong enemy. [*To* LI]
Make haste to the Chingkang Mountains for instructions,
Every moment counts; don't delay.
We must also discuss this carefully with Lei Kang:
Our victory depends on unity.

Let's go!

[*They leave.* WEN *emerges from behind the boulder.*]

WEN   Go? Wherever you go,

You won't escape my clutches! [*He takes a few steps forward, craftily.*]

The Viper's just sent secret word through Leopard Liu:
He wants me to help him clean up Azalea Mountain;
Once that's done he'll return me my precious burial plot,
And make me the top man in his civil guards.
I shan't have to put up any more with the gall of these Reds,
Then, Ko Hsiang and Lei Kang,
You'll die—and nobody will bury your corpses!

[*Leering, he turns and catches sight of the slogan: Beware of Enemy Agents! He hisses in alarm. The light fades. A golden spotlight picks out the slogan; a blue light shines on* WEN.]

[*Curtain*]

SCENE FIVE   Firm As a Rock in Midstream

Several days later, in the evening.
Azalea Mountain.

[*The curtain rises on the forest with narrow paths, towering cliffs, flaming azalea flowers, and stately pines. In the distance mountains loom rugged and grey against the blood-red sunset. A gap at the back of the stage leads to the foot of the mountain. In front, on the left, are a cliff and a tree stump. Intermittent firing is heard.* LEI KANG *gazes anxiously toward the foot of the mountain.*]

LEI KANG [*turns and sings*]

> Our force just circles the mountains, never fighting,
> While the enemy runs amuck.
> Will we never sweep down to cut the Viper in two,
> Unsaddle the enemy and smash them up?

[*He whirls his sword and slashes hard at the tree stump to let off steam.*]

[*Enter* WEN.]

WEN [*provocatively*]   Too bad!
A fine sword to slash off heads only slashes a tree.

[*He sidles up to* LEI KANG.]

LEI KANG   An eye for an eye—
Our day of vengeance will come!
WEN   It hurts, brother, but you'd better take it;
Without her orders, who can go down and fight?

[LEI KANG *heaves a sigh of frustration and sits down on the stump.*]

WEN   Brother, have you heard
The talk that's going round?
LEI KANG   What talk?
WEN   Some of the men are saying. . . . [*He deliberately hesitates.*]
LEI KANG   Out with it! Don't hedge.
WEN   They say:
"A cloud's obstructing our chief's vision;
A giant of a man's come under the thumb of a woman."
LEI KANG   [*stung into action, springs to his feet and seizes* WEN's *wrist*]
What do you mean?
WEN   Brother! [*Makes him sit down. Sings.*]

The Party representative comes from the Anyuan coal mine.
Does she hate the Viper? Not she!
Though our folks are in torment at the foot of the mountain
She remains completely unmoved.
That she remains unmoved I can understand

[*He maliciously rounds on* LEI KANG.]

But how strange that a man
Born and bred here
Cares nothing now for our Azalea Mountain!

LEI KANG   [*stands up quivering with indignation*]   Who cares nothing
for Azalea Mountain?
WEN   This is setting adrift the boat once the river's crossed.
LEI KANG   It's a lie!
WEN   That's what everyone is saying.
LEI KANG   It's dirty slander!
WEN   No, the bitter truth.
LEI KANG   [*seizes* WEN *by the jacket*]   Get out!
WEN   Brother. . . .
LEI KANG   Get out! Get out! [*Shoves* WEN *away and turns his back on
him.*]
WEN   [*sighs*]   That it should come to this!

I've followed close at your side,
Risked my life to serve you,
But never a word of thanks did I get
And now—well, it's just too bad!
All right, I'll clear out.
Goodbye!

[*With a malevolent look at* LEI KANG *he goes off.*]

[*At the foot of the mountain smoke billows and flames gleam red.*]

LEI KANG [*turns, upset and bewildered*]   So I was born and bred here
But now I care nothing for Azalea Mountain?!

[*The fire below blazes more fiercely.* LEI KANG *walks up the slope to watch, burning with impatience.*]

LEI KANG [*sings*]

Smoke is billowing, flames are spreading,

[*Descends the slope.*]

Like tossing waves the tumult in my heart;
Yet the Party representative looks on
And will not let us fight.
Is she heartless and cold as ice,
Terrified by gunfire, a coward?

[*Ponders.*] No.

On the execution ground she never changed color
But lashed out at the enemy like a good Communist.
My head is swimming, my mind is in a whirl.

[*He frowns and goes up to the gap, then turns and rushes to the tree stump to pick up his sword. Thinking better of it, however, he whirls round. Sings.*]

Why is it so difficult to make revolution?

[*Strikes his fist on his palm.*]

[LI *hurries in.*]

LI   Lei Kang!

[WEN *sneaks back, followed by* CHIU.]

LEI KANG [*goes straight up to* LI]   What instructions have come down?
LI   "We're outnumbered; the situation is grave;
We're to withdraw at once from Azalea Mountain."
LEI KANG [*shocked*]   What! Abandon Azalea Mountain?
LI   Right. To preserve our strength, leave the mountain
And join the main force to smash the enemy offensive.
The Party representative says, "To save the situation
We must at all costs carry out these orders."

[*Offstage* LO *calls* "Lei Kang!" *and runs in from the gap.*]

LO   Bad news!
LEI KANG   What's happened?
LO   The Viper has arrested Granny Tu. [*Seizes* LEI KANG's *hands.*]
LEI KANG   No!?
LO   She's tied up at the entrance to town, being cruelly tortured.
[*Stamps his foot.*]
LEI KANG [*aghast*]   Ah! [*Shakes off* LO's *hands and dashes toward the gap.*]
WEN   You owe Granny Tu a great debt of gratitude, brother; You mustn't just look on with folded arms.
LEI KANG   Muster the troops. We'll set off at once. [*Rushes to the tree stump to retrieve his sword.*]
LI [*stops him*]   Don't be so rash—we're no match for the enemy.
WEN [*to* LEI KANG]   Resolute action's needed at this critical moment.
LI   We mustn't go against orders.

[LEI KANG *turns and rushes to the tree stump. Again* LI *stops him.*]

LEI KANG   No! [*Struggles. Sings.*]

> We must hurry—a life is at stake.
> I am burning to fly like an arrow from the bow.
> Even if the mountain falls, the earth gives way,
> I swear not to return [*seizes the sword from the stump*]
> Till I have killed the Viper!

[*Whirls his sword and prepares to dash off.*]

[KO HSIANG *runs in and stops him.* TIEN *and* CHENG *follow behind her.*]

KO HSIANG   Lei Kang!
LEI KANG   Granny Tu is in danger. . . .

KO HSIANG [*equally distressed, but calm*]   My heart is on fire.
[*To* LO] Where have they taken her?

LO   She's tied to that tree at the entrance to town.

KO HSIANG   At the entrance to town? [*Thinks.*]

LO   Those swine are beating gongs and cursing;
All hell is let loose.

KO HSIANG   Who are they cursing?

LO [*reluctantly*]   Just our chief, Lei Kang.

LEI KANG   Damn you, Viper!

KO HSIANG   Just cursing Lei Kang, eh? [*She thinks this over.*]

LEI KANG   What are they saying?

LO   "Lei Kang has no sense of gratitude, he's a coward
Afraid to come down from the mountain."

LEI KANG [*gnashes his teeth*]   Dirty snake! I'll have it out with him!
[*Brandishes his sword and turns to leave.*]

KO HSIANG [*stops him*]   Where are you going?

LEI KANG   Down to Sankuan.

KO HSIANG   Just what the enemy wants.

LEI KANG   What do you mean?

KO HSIANG   Why tie Granny Tu to that tree just in front of the town?

[LEI KANG *looks blank.*]

KO HSIANG   Why are they beating gongs, cursing, and raising hell?

[LEI KANG *looks blank.*]

KO HSIANG   The enemy's needling you.

LEI KANG   Because they think me a coward.

KO HSIANG   No, because you're hotheaded and easily taken in.
They're dangling a tempting bait
To hook you and destroy our force completely.

[LEI KANG *is still mystified.*]

CHENG   That's it.
To reach Sankuan from here. . . .

LI   You must go through the Passage to Heaven.

CHENG   They're bound to lay an ambush there.

LI   You'd be walking into a trap.

LI and CHENG   And you'd never come out alive. [*They hold* LEI KANG's
arms.]

LEI KANG Even if they try to trap me, [*throws off their hands*] I'll go
  down fighting and drag them to hell with me!
KO HSIANG One wrong move
  Can lose the whole game.
LEI KANG But her life is in danger;
  How can I just sit watching?
KO HSIANG First withdraw from the mountain,
  Then find some means to save her.
LEI KANG No, my mind is made up.
KO HSIANG You must think again.
LEI KANG You're too subjective.
KO HSIANG You are too impulsive.
LEI KANG I refuse to leave the mountain
  Till she's rescued. [*Starts dashing off again.*]
KO HSIANG [*stops him again*] Your rescue plan
  Can only make things worse.
LEI KANG [*astonished and puzzled*] Worse? In what way?
KO HSIANG [*patiently*] "If the fish doesn't rise to the bait,
  The bait stays untouched;
  If the fish is hooked
  That's the end of both fish and bait."
  Don't go down, and she can still be saved;
  Go down, and both of you may die together.
  [*With growing vehemence.*] You'll only
  Destroy yourself,
  Destroy our self-defense corps
  And destroy your old white-haired mother!
LEI KANG But. . . . [*He plumps down on the tree stump.*]
WEN [*not liking the way things are going, pretends to play ball*]
  What the Party representative says is right.
  You must act with prudence, brother. [*Takes* LEI KANG'S *sword.*]

  [KO HSIANG *is about to speak to* LEI KANG, *but* WEN *cuts in.*]

WEN Just take it easy.
  Cool off a bit.

  [LEI KANG *snorts.* WEN *leads him away, followed by* CHIU.]

TIEN [*suddenly*] Look, the fire below is spreading.

  [*All turn their heads.* KO HSIANG *walks up the slope to look, returning
presently.*]

KO HSIANG [*quietly to* LI]   Old Li,
  Call a meeting right away of our Party branch
  To analyze the enemy situation
  And decide on united action.

  [LI *nods.*]

  [*Offstage* PARTISAN A *calls:* "Party representative!" *and hurries
  through the gap. Other partisans enter.*]

PARTISAN A   That cruel, vicious Viper
  Has piled faggots in front of the tree
  And is threatening to burn Granny Tu alive.
  She is . . . in deadly danger!

  [KO HSIANG *burns with anxiety.*]

  [*Offstage* WEN *calls:* "Party representative!" *He runs in, followed by*
CHIU. HSIAO-SHAN *and others hurry in, hearing his shout.*]

WEN [*with a show of dismay*]   Bad news!
KO HSIANG   What is it?
WEN   When he heard that Granny Tu would be burned at the stake,
CHIU   Lei Kang charged down with some men to rescue her.
WEN   I did my best to stop him.
CHIU   He wouldn't listen.
WEN   He's headed straight for Sankuan.

  [*General dismay.*]

WEN   Our chief's plunged into danger,
  The situation is more serious.
  We must lead our men down like lightning;
  There is no time to be lost.
PARTISAN A   Give the order, quick.
PARTISAN B   We must go to the rescue.
SEVERAL OTHERS   Debts of blood must be paid with blood.
ALL   Wipe out the diehards!

  [*Gunfire is heard below.* KO HSIANG *wheels round and runs up the
slope.*]

WEN [*seizes this chance to incite the men*]   Come on!
PARTISANS   Let's go [*They surge toward the gap.*]
KO HSIANG [*turns abruptly and stops them*]   Wait!

[*They halt in surprise.* KO HSIANG *is about to speak.*]

WEN [*quickly*] Brothers!
Through thick and thin Lei Kang has shared our hardships;
He is our well-loved brother, flesh of our flesh;
Now to save that dear old soul
He has gone alone to fight the enemy.
If we make no move, afraid to risk our necks,
If we lift not a finger, just watch him go to his death,
We must be [*pretends to weep*] utterly heartless! [*Wipes his eyes.*]

[*The men are in a tumult. Some stamp their feet and sigh.* KO HSIANG
signs to LI *to keep cool.*]

WEN Brothers, as long as we have breath in our bodies,
We mustn't forget his goodness, mustn't be heartless.
CHIU [*incites them*] All those with guts, charge!
SOME PARTISANS Charge!

[WEN *and* CHIU *lead them toward the gap.* LI, TIEN, CHENG, *and* LO
leap to higher ground in front of KO HSIANG, *barring the way.*]

KO HSIANG, LI, TIEN, CHENG, and LO [*sharply*] Halt!

[*They stop.*]

KO HSIANG [*gravely*] Our chief has made a big mistake
By going down the mountain.
If we act blindly too
We shall all be wiped out.
WEN Hsiao-shan! [*Pulls* HSIAO-SHAN *over.*]
Your granny is going to be burned;
Our hearts are afire;
How can you take this so calmly?

[HSIAO-SHAN *beats his breast, unable to speak.*]

WEN Others may not care,
But how can you be so heartless?

[HSIAO-SHAN *squats down in anguish.*]

WEN Who brought you up?
Were you bred on Azalea Mountain?
HSIAO-SHAN [*springs up, overcome by grief and rage, and sobs*] Granny!

Even if I can't rescue you,
I'll turn to ashes with you!

[HSIAO-SHAN *stamps his foot, tears open his jacket, pulls out two daggers, and dashes off to the gap. The others rush after him.*]

KO HSIANG   Hsiao-shan! [*Stops him.*]

[HSIAO-SHAN *turns to charge forward again.*]

KO HSIANG   Hsiao-shan! [*Stops him again.*]

[HSIAO-SHAN *turns and charges a third time.* LI *quickly intercepts him.* HSIAO-SHAN *pushes* LI *aside and darts to the gap.*]

KO HSIANG [*with emotion*]   Hsiao-shan!
HSIAO-SHAN [*pulls up abruptly, turns away, and cries*]   Party representative!

[*He drops the daggers and rushes in distress to* KO HSIANG, *who clasps him to her, tears welling from her eyes. The others weep.*]

KO HSIANG [*earnestly*]   Hsiao-shan,
My heart, like yours,
Is torn with anxiety, with grief and anger;
If by going down the mountain we could save her,
I would charge through fire and gladly give my life.
But no, we cannot,
Cannot act so rashly.
WEN [*overbearingly*]   Brothers,
You can't believe her,
She's an outsider.
She has no place in her heart
For the folk of Azalea Mountain.
TIEN [*beside himself with rage, shakes his fist*]   You!

[KO HSIANG *motions to* TIEN *to keep quiet and looks angrily at* WEN.]

WEN [*avoids her eyes*]   Brothers!
She's not close, as we are close,
To Brother Lei Kang;
She doesn't grieve for him the way we grieve.

[KO HSIANG, LI, TIEN, *and* CHENG *all watch* WEN *closely.*]

WEN [*blusters*]   Brothers, let's get going!

CHIU and A FEW OTHERS   Let's get going.

[*A few partisans prepare to leave.*]

KO HSIANG [*sternly*]   Wen Chi-chiu!

[*Those about to leave halt.*]

KO HSIANG [*to* WEN]   You are the deputy chief
And you have been an army officer.
The enemy's stratagems
And the traps he lays
Are common tactics in war—
Can't you see through them?

[*The men think this over.*]

WEN [*flustered*]   Why. . . .
KO HSIANG   If we strike at random
Our force will be finished for good;
The serious consequences are all too clear—
Can't you foresee them?
WEN   Well. . . .
KO HSIANG [*raises her hand and cries*]   Comrades!
In a crisis we mustn't let ourselves be blinded,
We must distinguish between right and wrong.
The people's armed force must carry out Party instructions;
Go back to quarters now and wait for orders.

[*The partisans hesitate. They are about to leave when shots are heard at the foot of the mountain. They turn their heads, eager to fight.*]

[KO HSIANG's *mind is in a turmoil, but she resolutely signs to them to return to their quarters. Frowning thoughtfully, the partisans withdraw slowly on both sides.*]

[WEN *beckons to* CHIU *and they slip away.*]

[LI, CHENG, TIEN, *and* LO *step closer to* KO HSIANG.]

[*The twilight deepens.*]

KO HSIANG [*incisively*]   Sturdy grass withstands high wind,
True gold stands the test of fire.
Comrades,

Let's hold a Party branch meeting
And decide how to deal with the situation.

[*They look round vigilantly, then gather by the tree stump.*]

LI   I think we must obey orders and withdraw.
TIEN   But our dear ones are in danger, how can we desert them?
LO   Let's go down and rescue them.
CHENG   Impossible to get through the enemy cordon.
LO   You mean pull out at once?
KO HSIANG   If we don't rescue Lei Kang, morale will slump,
    And it will be hard to carry out our withdrawal.
LO [*worried*]   Then. . . .
ALL   What shall we do?
KO HSIANG [*decisively*]   In this new situation
    The crucial task is rescuing Lei Kang;
    Before daybreak we must set him free
    Then withdraw at once to safety.
ALL   Good!
KO HSIANG [*to* LO]   Go and find out from the villagers how the land
    lies.
    Is there any other way down but the Passage to Heaven? [*To* LI.]
    The rest of you quickly form a dagger squad;
    Get everything ready and wait for orders to start.
ALL   Good. [*Turn to leave.*]
KO HSIANG   Wait.

[*They turn back.*]

KO HSIANG [*calmly and firmly*]   Much depends
    On this night's action.
    Make all your preparations carefully
    And maintain strict secrecy.
ALL [*nod*]   Right. [*They leave.*]

[*The wind rises, clouds scud past. Gunfire breaks out again below, and the glare of the flames grows brighter.*]

[KO HSIANG *climbs the slope to listen and look into the distance, deeply disturbed.*]

KO HSIANG [*sings*]

Storm-racked clouds, soughing pines, surging mountains;

[*Goes down the slope.*]

> Bursts of gunfire—the battle is joined!
> Heavy the weight on my shoulders,
> My heart is burning.
> Granny Tu, cruelly tortured, is at death's door;
> Lei Kang may never return from the tiger's lair;
> Our men raring to rescue them are hard to restrain
> And Wen, out of character, is egging them on—
> What is he really up to?
> The Viper has laid a trap, crafty and sinister.
> We must watch out for hidden enemies in our own ranks
> Whose stab in the back may endanger our whole force.
> Victory hangs in the balance; my comrades' peril
> Weighs heavily on my heart.

[*Turns and paces round.*]

CHORUS OF WOMEN [*sing offstage*]

> With heavy heart
> I gaze into the distance,
> Gaze into the distance
> And think of the Chingkang Mountains.

KO HSIANG [*turns and sings*]

> I seem to see the red flags on those heights
> Where Mao Tse-tung charts our course,
> His brilliance illuminating our world!

CHORUS OF MEN and WOMEN [*sing offstage*]

> His brilliance illuminating our world!

KO HSIANG [*sings*]

> The thought of you
> Brings redoubled strength, resolution and confidence;
> Resolution and confidence;
> Relying on the Party and the masses
> We shall overcome obstacles, defeat all foes
> And turn back the powers of darkness,
> Our men fearless and highhearted.

[*Dark clouds lower, the night grows blacker.*]

[LI, TIEN, *and* CHENG *hurry on.*]

LI Party representative, we have organized our dagger squad.

CHENG When do we go into action?

[*Before* KO HSIANG *can answer,* LO *enters panting from the gap.*]

LO [*in a low voice*] Party representative!

KO HSIANG [*quickly goes to him and hands him a towel*] What's the situation?

LO I'll tell you. [*Mops his head.*]

KO HSIANG What of Granny Tu?

LO She's transferred to the temple lockup.

KO HSIANG And Lei Kang?

LO He fell into the trap and was captured.

KO HSIANG Where is he now?

LO All those captured have been taken to Sankuan.

KO HSIANG Sankuan . . . and the way down?

LO There's no way except the Passage to Heaven.

KO HSIANG No other way?

[*Lightning flashes, thunder rumbles.*]

[*All are wrought up.* KO HSIANG *racks her brains, tosses back her hair, and turns.*]

KO HSIANG Comrades!
Can we scale the heights and circle round to Sankuan?

CHENG Scale the heights? That's a tall order.

LI Why?

CHENG The cliffs are steep.

LO We have muscles of iron!

CHENG The undergrowth is dense.

LI We can cut through the brambles.

KO HSIANG The night is dark.

LO All the better for a surprise attack.

KO HSIANG And a storm is brewing. [*Whirls round and strikes a pose.*]

LI, TIEN and LO Good cover for our sortie. [*They whirl round and strike a pose.*]

CHENG Fine.
But I hear there's a chasm a thousand feet deep.

TIEN It's called Eagles' Sorrow.

CHENG Its sides are sheer precipices.

TIEN   And a torrent races through the valley below.

CHENG   An impassable barrier! What can we do?

TIEN [*confidently*]   I know a way.
   I've gathered herbs by Eagles' Sorrow;
   Both cliffs are overhung
   With long green creepers. [*Whirls round and strikes a pose.*]

KO HSIANG   Is it possible to swing across on those creepers?

TIEN   Yes, I've swung across and back again.

LI, CHENG, and LO   Right! We'll cross the chasm by the creepers.

TIEN   I'll lead the way. [*Lunges forward and strikes a pose.*]

KO HSIANG [*decisively*]   Fine. [*Leads them to the tree stump and uses
   it as a sand table.*]
   I shall lead the dagger squad
   To scale the heights, cross to the other side
   And swoop down on Sankuan,

LI and OTHERS   To rescue our dear ones from danger.

KO HSIANG [*to LI*]   Send out a scouting team
   To make a feint withdrawal from Back Mountain.

LI   Lure the tiger away from its lair, eh?

KO HSIANG [*nods*]   Our main force will keep under cover in the moun-
   tain;
   You'll take charge of Party work.
   And remember: [*leads them to the front of the stage*]
   Watch out not only for an open attack
   But for a stab in the back!

LI   A stab in the back!

[*They catch on and nod.*]

[*Thunder and lightning.*]

KO HSIANG   Comrades! [*Steps on to the stump. Sings.*]

Peals of thunder urge our heroes on.

LI and OTHERS [*sing*]

Bitter struggle strengthens our determination.

KO HSIANG [*sings*]

Swooping down on the enemy across Eagles' Sorrow

[*Leaps down.*]

At dead of night

LI and OTHERS [*sing*]

> Under cover of the storm

TOGETHER [*sing*]

> We shall drive fearlessly forward.

[*With* KO HSIANG *in the center they rush to the front and strike a heroic pose.*]

[*Lightning followed by a clap of thunder.*]

[*Curtain*]

SCENE SIX   A Lesson in the Lockup

The same night.
Sankuan, the lockup in the backyard of the Sheh Family Ancestral Temple.

[*The curtain rises. It is raining steadily. From the caves hangs a dim lantern. Outside are a rockery and bamboos. In the gloomy lockup is a prisoner's cage made of iron bars, with a massive stone lock in the center. In the cage* GRANNY TU, *haggard and disheveled, leans against the bars and looks out anxiously. She walks slowly to the stone lock.*]

GRANNY TU [*sings*]

> The savage white bandits have set a crafty trap;
> I only fear Lei Kang my headstrong son
> Will charge down from the mountain.

[*She leans limply against the stone.*]

[*Black clouds scud past overhead; rain pelts down.*]

[*Shout offstage: "Bring the prisoner!"*]

LEI KANG [*sings offstage*]

> After a bloody battle I fell into the enemy trap.

[*Shout offstage: "Come on!"* LEI KANG *in heavy shackles, his temples bleeding, is pushed on by four guards. He staggers forward then halts. A guard shoves him, shouting: "Get a move on!"* LEI KANG *leaps back and swings his chain at the man, kicks away another, draws himself up and strikes a pose.*]

[*Thunder and lightning.*]

LEI KANG [*sings*]

> Wounded, captured, and loaded with chains,
> Unable to take revenge, I burn with rage. . . . [*Staggers.*]

[*The guards open the cage, push* LEI KANG *in, lock the door, and leave.* LEI KANG *swings his chain against the bars. The sound wakes* GRANNY TU.]

GRANNY TU [*softly*]   Who's that? [*Struggles to her feet.*]
LEI KANG [*unable to see clearly*]   Mother?
GRANNY TU   Lei Kang?
LEI KANG [*with emotion*]   Mother!

[*They stumble into each other's arms. Thunder and lightning.*]

GRANNY TU [*sings*]

> I little thought to meet my son in prison.

[*She takes hold of his chain.*] My child, you. . . .

LEI KANG [*sighs*]   I came to rescue you
But fell into their trap.
GRANNY TU   Did you come alone?
LEI KANG   With a few other men.
GRANNY TU [*quickly*]   Did the Party representative send you?
LEI KANG   No, it was my own decision.
GRANNY TU   So you didn't listen to Ko Hsiang! [*Sits angrily down on the stone.*]
LEI KANG   My feud with the Viper
Is a fight to the death;
She has no private scores
To settle with him.
GRANNY TU   What? [*Stands up.*] No private scores?
Far from it.

[LEI KANG *helps* GRANNY TU *to sit down and kneels on one knee beside her.*]

GRANNY TU   Remember, two weeks ago,
How many were sent here from the Chingkang Mountains?
LEI KANG   Two comrades: one man and one woman.
GRANNY TU   The woman was Ko Hsiang.
LEI KANG   The man's name was Chao Hsin.

GRANNY TU   Ko Hsiang was wounded and captured.

LEI KANG   Chao Hsin died a hero's death.

GRANNY TU   But do you know
The relationship between them?

LEI KANG   The relationship between them?

GRANNY TU   They were husband and wife for three years. [*Weeps.*]

LEI KANG [*shocked, springs up*]   Ah, her husband?
How she must be longing for vengeance!
Yet she never breathed a word of this.

GRANNY TU [*with admiration*]   She takes the Party's instructions to
heart,
Swallows her own grief
And keeps the whole world in view. [*Stands up.*]
But what of you?
You act on impulse,
Ignoring larger issues;
You knew this was a trap
But you had to have your own way,
Involving others in danger
And putting your neck in a noose. . . .
How badly you've let down
Your old folk and brothers on Azalea Mountain. [*Sings.*]

Three times we raised the banner of revolt; three times we met
defeat;
The bright flames leapt a while and then died down.
Happy the day when from the Chingkang Mountains
They sent us a Party representative
Who led our forces back to the right road,
To grow from strength to strength.
Who could have thought that you
Would forget the lessons of the past, the lessons of the past,
Would lose your head and fall into this trap!
You have hurt our folk, broken my heart
And ruined the good work of the Party.

[*Sits down on the stone steps by the door.*]

LEI KANG [*sings*]

Mother's words like a flash of lightning
Make me see reason.

The Party representative suppressing her own hatred
Works hard, shouldering the heaviest load:
She is noblehearted.

[*Thunder.*]

LEI KANG [*sings*]

But I wrecked our plan by charging down so rashly;
If our force is wiped out through my fault,
A thousand deaths will not atone for my crime.

[*Stamps his foot and clashes his chains.*]

Remorse and sorrow cut me to the quick.

GRANNY TU [*stands up and sings*]

Leaning against the bars I think of our dear ones
And my tears fall like rain. [*Wipes her eyes.*]

LEI KANG [*sings*]

How I hope,
How I hope that our force
Will swiftly withdraw to win new victories.

GRANNY TU [*sings*]

Then the clouds will roll away from Azalea Mountain,

TOGETHER [*sing*]

And songs of triumph will echo to the sky.

[GRANNY TU *makes* LEI KANG *sit on the stone lock. A guard with a lantern leads in the* VIPER *to make an inspection. Another guard and the* CAPTAIN *follow.*]

[LEI KANG *starts to get up but* GRANNY TU *stops him.*]

VIPER [*to the* CAPTAIN] Are all your posts well manned?
CAPTAIN Inside and out, the town is closely guarded.
VIPER [*points to the cage*] Take special precautions here.
CAPTAIN Each bar has been checked several times.
VIPER Learn from your last lesson;
Don't let the tiger escape to the mountain again.
CAPTAIN Since we've gained our object, commander,
Why not kill him at once to avoid trouble later on?

VIPER   Use your head, you fool!
   To catch a big fish you have to pay out the line;
   Keeping this chair-bearer here
   Is bound to bring Ko Hsiang down from the mountain.
   So with one single cast
   We'll hook the whole lot!
LEI KANG [*springs up, bursting with anger*]   You poisonous snake!
   I'm itching to cut you to pieces!
VIPER   Ha, still talking so big, eh?
   Just wait.
   When Ko Hsiang comes down
   We'll send all three of you together to Heavcn.

[LEI KANG *batters the door with his chain. The* VIPER *recoils in alarm.*
GRANNY TU *makes* LEI KANG *sit down to examine his wounds.*]

[*Offstage* GUARD A *calls* "Report!" *and runs in. The* VIPER *signs to him
to keep quiet. They go to one side.*]

GUARD A [*in a low voice*]   Commander, there's a new development.
VIPER   Out with it, quick.
GUARD A   The self-defense corps is withdrawing toward the border;
   Our sentries spotted them.
VIPER   Withdrawing?

[*Offstage* GUARD B *calls* "Report!" *and hurries in.*]

GUARD B [*in a low voice*]   Commander, a confidential note! [*Hands a
   note to the* VIPER.]

[*The two guards go out.*]

VIPER [*opens the note*]   "The self-defense corps is leaving the moun-
   tain tonight. . . ."
   Confound it! This spoils my plan.
CAPTAIN   What shall we do?
VIPER   I'll take troops at once to Back Mountain.
CAPTAIN   How about Sankuan?
VIPER   We'll leave your company here.
   Don't let the prisoners escape.
   But most of your men
   Must guard the Passage to Heaven.
CAPTAIN   How many shall I leave here?

VIPER   One squad will do.

CAPTAIN   Just one squad?

VIPER   As long as we hold the pass,
Even if they had wings they couldn't reach this temple.

CAPTAIN [folds his hands in prayer]   May our ancestors protect us!
May all go well!

[LEI KANG and GRANNY TU are listening carefully.]

VIPER [waves the secret note and laughs raucously]
Aha, Ko Hsiang, Ko Hsiang!
Even if your withdrawal is a feint
And you try to raid our jail,
We're ready for you.
Come on!

[The VIPER and his men hurry off. LEI KANG and GRANNY TU are frantic.
The light fades.]

GRANNY TU [looks at the night sky]   Party representative!
On no account come down the mountain!

LEI KANG   On no account come down. . . .

[They gaze toward the distance, earnestly raising their hands. Lightning and thunder are followed by pelting rain. Blackout.]

[Curtain]

SCENE SEVEN   Flying over the Cloud-Wrapped Chasm

The same day, late at night. A storm is raging.
A rugged height between Azalea Mountain and Sankuan.

[With TIEN leading the way, in speed KO HSIANG, HSIAO-SHAN, and
two partisans, all wearing straw capes. They strike a pose. At a signal
from KO HSIANG, they race off. Enter six men and women partisans. Mim-
ing, they advance fearlessly, united as one, along muddy paths in the
teeth of the storm, then leave the stage.]

[The slope is steep, the path slippery. Six men partisans somersault
across the stage and off. Four women partisans bound in, do the splits,
spring up and run off. HSIAO-SHAN somersaults in, then staggers; KO
HSIANG bounds in after him and saves him from falling. Enter several

men partisans. They do the splits and KO HSIANG *helps them up one by one. They leave together. A group of women partisans bound in, whirling their straw capes. They are followed by men, leaping and dancing.*]

[*On a gauze curtain at the front clouds drift past, then mountains loom through the mist.* TIEN *springs in through the brambles, carrying a bamboo pole, and strikes a pose. He turns a somersault, leaps, shades his eyes against the wind, wipes rain from his face, then parts the grass to lead the way forward. The grass grows rank and the path is slippery.* TIEN *feels the ground with his pole, somersaults and does the splits, stumbles, struggles to his feet, then slips again. Finally he stands up and beckons to people behind him. Two men partisans leap in from the trees, hacking with their swords at the brambles.* TIEN *dances with his bamboo pole. All three turn somersaults, strike a pose, and lead the way off.*]

[*The wind blows stronger. The partisans battle against the storm and in succession whirl off. With* TIEN *in the lead, the partisans march briskly across the stage. They re-enter and go through the motions of climbing the mountain, clutching at the undergrowth and lending each other a hand. They do the splits and spring up again.* HSIAO-SHAN *and others somersault on. They reach the top of the cliff, gaze down into the chasm and strike a pose.*]

[*Clouds drift past on the gauze curtain. After the clouds have passed, Eagles' Sorrow appears. The precipices on either side are covered with green creepers.* TIEN *catches hold of a creeper and swings himself across the chasm. Other partisans follow suit. Partisans leap and somersault over the cliffs and off.*]

[*Clouds drift over the gauze curtain. After the clouds have passed, the Sheh Family Ancestral Temple appears.* TIEN *and* PARTISAN A *enter and drop to the ground. The enemy captain enters in a raincoat, followed by a guard with an umbrella, to inspect the sentry posts.* TIEN *overpowers the captain, takes off his raincoat and finds the key to the lockup on his belt.* PARTISAN A *kills the guard.* TIEN *puts on the captain's raincoat.* KO HSIANG *enters with other partisans. They slip into the temple.*]

[*Blackout.*]

[*The lights come on again, showing the backyard of the temple and one side of the cage in which* LEI KANG *and* GRANNY TU *are imprisoned.*

Guards with rifles in their arms are dozing on the steps outside the cage. Enter TIEN *and* PARTISAN A *in disguise. A guard stands up, approaches* TIEN *and salutes.* TIEN *turns toward the cage. The guard, growing suspicious, is killed by* PARTISAN A. *Other partisans run in. The guards wake up, but before they can resist* TIEN *trains his gun on them and shouts: "Don't move!" The partisans disarm them, tie them up, and gag them.* TIEN *unlocks the cage and opens the door.*]

[KO HSIANG *goes over to* LEI KANG. *He wants to speak, but she signs to him to keep quiet.* KO HSIANG *and* GRANNY TU *embrace.* KO HSIANG *signs to the partisans to lock the guards in the cage. A partisan shoulders the guns captured. Then they quickly withdraw.*]

[*Spotlight on the cage door. Inside, the guards huddle together disconsolately.*]

[*Blackout.*]

[*The lights come on again, showing a valley with steep cliffs by the chasm, a strategic pass.* KO HSIANG *directs the withdrawal of the rescued partisans and villagers.* LEI KANG *and* HSIAO-SHAN *enter, supporting* GRANNY TU. LO, CHENG, *and* TIEN *follow.* GRANNY TU *and* HSIAO-SHAN *go off. The sound of gunfire comes closer. They halt to listen.*]

TIEN Judging by the sound, the enemy's main force is after us.

KO HSIANG The Viper must know they've been foxed, so he's turned back.

CHENG Eagles' Sorrow's just ahead. The going's rough.

LO The enemy is close. We're in a tight spot!

KO HSIANG [*reflects*] Lei Kang, lead them over the chasm and back to the mountain, fast!

LEI KANG And you?

KO HSIANG I'll keep a few men on this height to cover you.

LEI KANG No, our brothers need you as their helmsman.

KO HSIANG They're longing to have you back.

LEI KANG It's my rashness that exposed you to this danger.
Leave the rearguard action to me. [*Comes over dizzy.* CHENG *and others support him.*]

KO HSIANG You've been wounded, lost blood,
And are half starved, too weak to fight.

LEI KANG We're outnumbered, short of guns;
I can't leave you in the lurch.

KO HSIANG [*exuberantly*] Just look! [*Whirls her cape and strikes a pose.*]

The trees will shelter us,
Stones serve as missiles.
With this gully as our defense works,
The cliffs as our fortress, [*flaunts her cape, climbs the slope, and strikes a pose*]
Even if the enemy [*walks down the slope*]
Surges forward like the tide [*circles swiftly round*]
I shall stand firm as a rock. [*Dances with her cape, turns, and strikes a pose.*]

[*The partisans join in the dance movements.*]

[*The sound of firing draws nearer.*]

KO HSIANG The situation is critical.
LEI KANG The enemy's closing in.
KO HSIANG You must leave at once. [*Tugs at* LEI KANG.]
LEI KANG I refuse to go back!
KO HSIANG This is the Party's decision;
You mustn't delay.
LEI KANG [*pleads*] Party representative! [*Staggers.*]
KO HSIANG Go quickly!
LEI KANG Party representative!
KO HSIANG Go quickly!

[*Two partisans help* LEI KANG *up the cliff. He wrenches free, turns and steps forward, meaning to rush down again. They hastily stop him.*]

LEI KANG [*leans down from the cliff. With emotion*] Party representative!
KO HSIANG [*waves her hand*] Hurry!
LEI KANG [*hoarsely*] Party representative, Party representative!
KO HSIANG [*firmly*] Quick! Hurry!

[LEI KANG *is dragged off, still protesting. Some partisans follow him. Intensive gunfire.* KO HSIANG, TIEN, CHENG, *and* LO *fire at the enemy and throw hand grenades.*]

KO HSIANG Comrades,
Save your ammunition;
Prepare for close combat.

[*Raising their weapons they strike a pose.*]

KO HSIANG [*sings*]

> The storm closes in, earth and sky turn dark,
> But a bright lamp lights up my heart.
> Our hot blood will turn into thunderbolts and lightning. . . .

[*Shouts go up offstage. The enemy chase in.* KO HSIANG *and her men put up a fierce resistance.* TIEN *parries and thrusts with his sword and kills an enemy guard, then picks up a rock and hurls it at the enemy. The enemy are forced back.*]

KO HSIANG [*beckons*] Withdraw!
TIEN, CHENG and LO Right. [*They rush up the cliff.*]

[*An enemy rifle cracks.* TIEN *is shot.*]

[KO HSIANG, CHENG, *and* LO *cry out and swiftly prop* TIEN *up. He presses his right hand to his chest and stubbornly raises his head to glare at the enemy. Blood seeps through his fingers.*]

CHORUS OF MEN AND WOMEN [*offstage vigorously*]

> Glory irradiates our land,
> Glory irradiates our land!

[KO HSIANG *and the others stand erect on the cliff, undaunted. They strike a pose. Lightning rends the sky; thunder shakes the earth. The light fades, showing them in silhouette.*]

[*Curtain*]

SCENE EIGHT The Sun Scatters the Mist

The next day before dawn.
Azalea Mountain, as in Scene Five.

[*The curtain rises, showing a scene after storm. Gray mountains stretch to the distance. Clouds drift over the moon: a few stars are visible. A red flag flutters in the wind on the hillside. Sporadic rifle fire crackles down below.* WEN *watches the scene below and listens uneasily.*]

WEN Sporadic bursts of rifle fire below—
Has Ko Hsiang gone to rescue the prisoners?

[CHIU *runs in, flustered.* WEN *hastily beckons him.*]

WEN Our intelligence?

CHIU I delivered it.

WEN Why the firing?

CHIU Ko Hsiang has raided the lockup.

WEN [*dismayed*] Damn!
Maybe she's seen through my plot,
And I've been trapped.

CHIU Let's join the Viper. Quick!

WEN Impossible!
Since our intelligence proved wrong,
The Viper is bound to mistrust us.

CHIU Then. . . .

WEN [*rolls his eyes*] That way is out,
But I have another plan. [*Produces paper and pen and scribbles a note.*]
Take this to Leopard Liu.

CHIU [*takes the note*] To Leopard Liu? What's the idea?

WEN On pretext of withdrawing
I'll take our force to his garrison area. . . . [*Gestures to indicate encirclement and mopping up.*]

CHIU [*catches on*] Ah!

WEN Off with you. Quick!

CHIU Right. [*Runs to the gap.*]

WEN [*hears someone coming, deliberately raises his voice*] Hey!
Go to that height
To check up on the enemy's movements.

CHIU Right. [*Runs off.*]

[LI *enters.*]

WEN Old Li, time's running out,
Why not start the withdrawal?

LI [*hedges*] Why all the hurry? [*Gazes in the direction taken by* CHIU.]

[*The firing becomes more intense.*]

WEN Come on! That gunfire makes it clear:
Ko Hsiang's small raiding party
Must have been routed.
As deputy chief
It's my duty to save the situation. [*Blows a whistle.*]

[*Partisans run on.*]

WEN   Listen, everyone!
No news has come since our chief went down the mountain;
Now the Party representative is trapped, in deadly danger.

[*The partisans exclaim in dismay.*]

WEN   We must carry out our orders,
Set off at once and withdraw to the border region.

[*The bewildered partisans start talking together:* "Yes, we should withdraw." "Withdraw?" "Of course, it'll soon be light." "But the Party representative's not back yet. . . ."]

LI [*in a loud voice*]   Comrades, don't listen to this nonsense!
Our Party representative has gone on a mission;
She told us to hold our ground here;
We're not going to pull out until she's back.
PARTISAN B   Right. Don't pull out.
ALL   We mustn't pull out.
WEN   But she won't be coming back;
Don't be so stubborn.
LI   You've made this up,
It's all a pack of lies.
WEN   As deputy chief I'm in charge;
I have the authority to make decisions.
LI   The army is commanded by the Party;
What right have you to order a withdrawal?
WEN   In this emergency
Who dares delay our plan of action?
LI   Even if the sky falls
We can prop it up. [*Points angrily at* WEN.] Wen Chi-chiu! [*Sings.*]

First you incite Lei Kang to charge down, disobeying orders,
Now you preach obedience to superiors;
You keep shifting like the clouds,
Are you trying to destroy us?

WEN [*sings*]

The situation's changed, we must be flexible to win.

LI [*sings*]

You are throwing dust in our eyes.

WEN [*sings*]

> Every second counts: how can we wait?

LI [*sings*]

> In this crisis we must stand firm and keep coolheaded.

WEN [*sings*]

> Let's take off our armbands, lower our flag, and pull out.
> [*Pulls off his armband and orders.*] Take off your armbands!

[*A few partisans hesitate, but the majority ignore him.*]

WEN Lower the red flag!

[*The partisans make no move.*]

WEN What insubordination! [*Rushes to the slope to take down the flag.*]

LI [*in a voice like thunder*] Don't you dare!

[*LI shoves WEN aside. Partisans spring forward to protect the flag. They strike a pose.*]

LI [*sings*]

> We'll hold our ground, guard our red flag;
> United, we're strong as a fortress.

WEN [*draws his pistol*] I'll shoot you!

LI [*draws his pistol*] Don't move!

[*They face each other tensely with leveled guns. The partisans intervene. Someone calls offstage: "Old Li!"*]

PARTISAN C The chief's back!

[*LI and WEN put away their pistols. Enter GRANNY TU, HSIAO-SHAN, and other partisans. They greet each other.*]

ALL [*happily*] Our chief!

[*LEI KANG hurries on.*]

LI [*grasps LEI KANG's arms*] Brother, where's the Party representative?

LEI KANG [*in distress*] To cover our withdrawal. . . .

LEI KANG and OTHERS She intercepted the enemy.

LEI KANG   But now the firing has ceased.
GRANNY TU   We are frantic with worry. [*Staggers.*]

[LEI KANG *supports her. A partisan helps* GRANNY TU *off and some others follow.*]

WEN [*to* LEI KANG]   Brother. . . .
LEI KANG [*eyes* WEN *suspiciously*]   H'm! [*Walks away.*]
WEN [*with a show of cordiality*]   Brother!
   I'm partly to blame
   For your leaving the mountain so rashly;
   Eagerness to save Granny Tu made me too impulsive;
   I should never have urged you on to act so wildly.
   It was very wrong of us to disobey orders;
   We must carry out all instructions to the letter.
   Let's pull out at once;
   We can't afford to wait.
LI [*strides quickly up to* LEI KANG]   The Party representative's not back
      yet;
   We mustn't do anything rash.
LEI KANG [*in profound agreement*]   True!
WEN   When the river bends, a boat must alter course!
LI   Who do you think you're fooling?
WEN [*to* LEI KANG]   Brother!
   If we wait till it's light
   We'll never get away;
   And when our force is wiped out
   Your remorse will be too late.
   You'll be unable to face Granny Tu,
   Unable to face our fellow countrymen,
   Unable to face the spirits of our martyrs;
   You'll have betrayed the trust of our Party representative.
LEI KANG [*with feeling*]   Our Party representative! [*Gazes into the
   distance.*]
A FEW PARTISANS   Brother, let's go.
THE MAJORITY   No, chief, we mustn't leave.
LEI KANG [*worried and confused, sighs. Sings*]

   The Party representative risked her own life to save me;
   She hasn't come back; my heart is bursting with grief.
   Our force must carry out the Party's orders

But I shall brave a thousand deaths to find her.
Let our main force withdraw at once
While I go back with a small rescue party.
We shall not return without her.

[*Staggers, recovers himself, and turns to go.*]

PARTISANS [*some urge him to go; some try to stop him*]   Chief, chief. . . .

[*Someone calls offstage:* "The Party representative's back!" *All rush eagerly up the slope.* WEN *hastily steps aside.* KO HSIANG *strides in swiftly in her cape.*]

LEI KANG and OTHERS [*with great emotion*]   Party representative!

[*Enter* CHENG *and* LO.]

KO HSIANG [*sings*]

Rejoining my comrades, I am too moved to speak.
[*Shakes hands with* LEI KANG, HSIAO-SHAN, LI, *and some women partisans, greeting them.*]

LEI KANG [*to* KO HSIANG]   At last you're back!
WEN [*steps forward*]   You had us all worried.

[*Silence.* KO HSIANG *turns slowly to look at* WEN.]

KO HSIANG [*meaningfully*]   Yes, deputy chief, you've been very worried.
WEN   Sure. The moon's sinking, the stars are fading. . . .
KO HSIANG   We should pull out right away?
WEN   Well, we can't stay here.
KO HSIANG   Tell me, where is it best to break through the enemy's cordon?
From Back Mountain?
WEN   The enemy have Back Mountain sewn up tight.
KO HSIANG   Must we make a detour then?
WEN [*promptly agrees*]   Right.
KO HSIANG [*raps out*]   Cut through Leopard Liu's garrison area?
WEN [*overjoyed because this fits in with his scheme*]   The very thing!
Great minds think alike—
This is my view exactly.
Leopard Liu's on bad terms with the Viper
But has no grudge against us:

On the strength of my old connection,
If I ask him to let us through he's bound to agree.
KO HSIANG   Deputy chief, you've worked the whole thing out;
You've really been racking your brains.
WEN [*struts round, elated*]   For the revolution
I have to do my best.
LI   H'm. For whom are you doing your best?
CHENG   For whom are you working?
PARTISAN B   Why did you want us to take off our armbands?
WOMEN PARTISANS   Why did you want to lower the red flag?
LO   What are you playing at?
THE MAJORITY   Just what is your game?
WEN [*approaches* KO HSIANG]   Party representative. . . .
KO HSIANG [*sternly*]   You've betrayed the revolution,
Sold out to the enemy!
WEN [*protests*]   This is slander,
Wild aspersions!
KO HSIANG [*forcefully*]   Our evidence
Is irrefutable.
Bring him in!

[*Offstage a partisan shouts:* "Come on!" CHIU *is led in.* WEN *draws his pistol and fires, wounding* CHIU *in the arm.* CHIU *falls down on his knees.* LI *snatches the gun from* WEN.]

CHIU [*nurses his wounded arm*]   Damn you, Wen Chi-chiu!
You're more vicious than a beast.
Captured the moment I left,
I've given them the dirt on you, I'd have you know.
Your letter's in her hands!

[KO HSIANG *signs to a partisan who takes* CHIU *off.*]

KO HSIANG   Comrades!
Wen Chi-chiu is in secret league with the enemy.
And they have had frequent contacts.
The Viper laid a trap to lure us down the mountain;
Wen, in our ranks, furthered the enemy scheme.
Now he's trying to use our dilemma
To entice us into Leopard Liu's garrison area,
To force our men to join Liu's bandits,
So that he can share their loot.

Wen Chi-chiu!
You want to sabotage the revolution,
To lead us to destruction;
You've sold your soul to the enemy,
Hoping to wade through blood to high position.
Here's the letter in your own hand to Liu.
Every word in it is evidence of your crime!

[KO HSIANG *produces* WEN's *secret message and glares at him with flashing eyes. The partisans, bursting with fury, brandish their weapons.* WEN *shrinks back, trembling.*]

KO HSIANG [*sings*]

His honeyed words hide daggers;
He has long schemed to seize control of our force
And stab us in the back;
This traitor is in league with the enemy;
Now we've exposed his true colors.

ALL [*sing*]

Death to the renegade!

[*They brandish their weapons.*]

WEN [*drops on his knees and crawls toward* LEI KANG] Brother!

[LEI KANG *trembling with rage seizes* WEN.]

LEI KANG Bah! [*Throws* WEN *down.*]

[WEN *scrambles to his feet. Thinking that* LEI KANG *means him to escape, he takes to his heels.* LEI KANG *takes a gun from* LI, *fires at* WEN, *and kills him.* WEN *topples over the cliff. The partisans throw stones at him.*]

[*Enter* GRANNY TU.]

LI Post more sentries.
KO HSIANG Prepare to pull out.

[*All assent and leave.*]

LEI KANG [*unable to express his remorse*] Party representative. . . .
[*Sways.*]

[KO HSIANG, CHENG, *and* GRANNY TU *help* LEI KANG *to the tree stump and make him sit down.*]

KO HSIANG [*to* CHENG]   Fetch some herb medicine,
Dress his wounds, quick!

[CHENG *fetches* TIEN'S *gourd of medicine and dresses* LEI KANG'S *wound.*]

LEI KANG [*recovering, sees the gourd*]   Where's Tien? [*Looks round.*]
Tien Ta-chiang?
[*Loudly.*] Where's Tien?

[CHENG *cannot speak for grief.* LO *rushes over to* LEI KANG, *sobbing.*]

KO HSIANG [*takes out* TIEN'S *armband. Sadly*]   He has shed his fresh blood on Azalea Mountain.

[*Thunderstruck,* LEI KANG *staggers forward and takes the armband.*]

LEI KANG [*sings*]

>   Rage sears my heart, tears scald my cheeks.

[*Wipes his eyes.*]

>   My crimes are past forgiving.
>   Not all the rivers' water
>   Can sweep away my anguish and remorse.
>   Grief is tearing my heart.
>   Ah, Ta-chiang!
>   After years of back-breaking toil
>   You had just won liberation, joined the Party
>   And dedicated your young life to the cause;
>   But because of me you fell on the battlefield.
>   Ah, Ta-chiang. . . .

[*Covers his face and sobs.*]

[*All stricken with grief shed tears.*]

CHENG [*sings*]

>   Wen Chi-chiu was a blackhearted landlord.

LI [*sings*]

>   How could we poor folk make him our sworn brother?

LEI KANG [*sings*]

> I nearly caused the death of my old mother.

GRANNY TU [*sings*]

>> It was the Party representative
>> Who turned the tables on the enemy,
>> Risking her life to brave the tiger's lair
>> And rescue us from danger.

LEI KANG [*sings*]

>> Azaleas bloom red as blood year after year,
>> What makes me repeat my mistakes,
>> Bringing loss after loss?

KO HSIANG [*sings*]

> Bear in mind all these lessons paid for with blood;

[*She and* GRANNY TU *help* LEI KANG *to sit down and dress his wound.*]

After this bitter lesson, think out the reason
Why having smashed your chains you were chained again,
Why the flag was raised three times but fell again
As those who had flocked to you scattered?
Why did you close your ears to the truth
And let blatant lies deceive you?
If you go to the heart of the matter,
It was narrow loyalty and longing for vengeance
That made you see nothing more
Than the blood and tears wrung from a single village,
Blinding you to the long, long road
We must take to make revolution.
For generations slaves have fought for freedom,
Year after year their battle drums have sounded;
But lacking a clear aim these rebels lost their bearings;
Countless heroes died in vain, cursing high heaven.
The peasants' armed forces must keep close to the Party,
Only then can they prevail and grow in strength
Like brooks flowing into the mighty, mighty river.
Never forget the first rule of revolution:
The Party commands the guns, commands the men in arms.

Braving the storm we shall advance and never drift off course,
We shall advance and never drift off course.

[*Elated, they strike a pose. Dawn breaks.*]

LEI KANG [*excited*]   Party representative!
The mists have scattered,
You have made me see clearly.
From now on, wherever we fight, I shall follow the Party,

KO HSIANG [*sings*]

> We must
> Fall on the enemy force

ALL [*sing*]

> And wipe it out!

[*They strike a heroic pose.*]

LEI KANG [*raises his hand*]   Quick, march!

[*The red flag flutters in the wind, their swords gleam. They advance swiftly and jubilantly.*]

[*Curtain*]

SCENE NINE   Keep the Red Flag Flying

The same morning.
Lion's Jaw.

[*The curtain rises on the same set as in Scene One but now azaleas are in full bloom. Several enemy guards scurry in with rifles and make a search. A partisan slips out from the trees, fires at a guard and kills him, then quickly takes cover. Another partisan slips out from the brambles, shoots and kills an enemy guard, and quickly hides himself. PARTISAN A kills an enemy guard with his rifle butt. Another partisan hiding in a cave stabs a guard with his trident. The guards panic. Suddenly a partisan leaps out with a spear, fights with an enemy guard, kills him, and conceals himself behind some rocks. Two enemy guards start searching for him, and he leaps out again, fights them with a chain missile, and kills one.*]

[HSIAO-SHAN *enters, snatches the other guard's rifle, and kills him with the bayonet. Then he and the partisan with the chain missile strike a pose. Many partisans emerge simultaneously from hiding and look round.* HSIAO-SHAN *fires the rifle to draw the enemy over. The partisans swiftly take cover.* HSIAO-SHAN *and the partisan with the chain missile leap back into the brambles. The* VIPER *enters with several guards. Two guards rush in, panic-stricken.*]

A GUARD   Commander, we've spotted the Communist main force. We've been surrounded!

VIPER [*gives a cry of dismay*]   Order our men to withdraw immediately.

[*The red flag is raised on high. Enter* KO HSIANG, LEI KANG, *and* LI *with other partisans. Standing on high ground* KO HSIANG *fires at the* VIPER, *who dodges and escapes. Shouts go up, bugles sound the charge, and shots ring out. The enemy is surrounded.*]

[*The morning sky turns a glorious red.* KO HSIANG, LEI KANG, LI, *and* LO *lead partisans armed with swords, spears, nets, and other weapons across the stage in pursuit of the enemy. Soldiers of the Workers' and Peasants' Revolutionary Army pursue the enemy. Several partisans carrying a red flag swing through the air clinging to creepers.* LI *enters pursuing enemy guards. With his shield and broadsword he fights fiercely, kills some of the enemy, and chases another away. Two more guards start after* LI, *but* PARTISAN A *stops them with his staff. They fight. Another partisan springs out of the cave, swings his sword and kills an enemy guard, then swiftly takes cover.*]

[LEI KANG *enters brandishing a sword and shouting battle cries. He fights with three enemy guards, who shrink back in fear from his sword. When they attack with bayonets,* LEI KANG *swings his sword, captures their rifles, and marches them off as captives.* HSIAO-SHAN *leaps out of the grass, a dagger in each hand, and fights several enemy guards. Thinking him a mere boy they charge at him together, but* HSIAO-SHAN *evades them and swings off on a creeper. The enemy guards give chase. The* VIPER *dashes in pursued by* KO HSIANG *with a mounted bayonet. She fights bravely, downs several guards, and knocks The* VIPER *over. He tries to escape.* LEI KANG, LI, *and others converge from all sides to surround the enemy. The* VIPER *and his men mill round in confusion.*

The partisans spread the net they have concealed and all the enemy are trapped.]

[*The crimson azaleas vie with the red flag.* KO HSIANG, LEI KANG, *and the partisans together strike a heroic pose.*]

[*Curtain. The end*]